the SEARCH

Adventures of a Restless Soul

George Biondic

ISBN: 978-1-7779039-0-9

1. Biondic, George
2. Cold War refugees
3. Children of gamblers-Canada-memoir
4. Mental health
5. Long distance runners Canada-autobiography/biography
6. Marathon running-United States, and Canada
I. Title

DEDICATION

For the three most important women in my life.

For the mentally ill—the wounded and the lost.

For the recently arrived immigrants—the dreamers.

TABLE OF CONTENTS

PREFACE

The events and conversations—some dialogue was used to re-create the essence of the situation—were written to the best of my memory. Although an honest rendering, my version of events may at times contradict other people's recollections.

In addition, I have used HASH—Heart, Action, Suspense and Humour—to entertain the reader, to comfort the immigrant and mentally ill, and to inspire the runner

Finally, and in all truthfulness, this book has not been completely altruistic: the writing process was an attempt to understand myself and those around me.

PROLOGUE

York University
Toronto, Ontario
December, 1976

Who would have guessed what a little backache could lead to?

I was sitting in a rapidly filling lecture hall awaiting the arrival of Professor Stack who was giving a computer science lecture about file management. If you've sat in a high school or university class impatiently waiting, daydreaming, you know what it's like. My mind was on streaking—as in naked, across that very auditorium—but my back just wouldn't leave me in peace.

Am I a rebel? Hardly. Conformist? Yes, so far. You see, streaking was the latest craze. Even the Oscars had a streaker on stage in 1974 during the live broadcast, but the director switched to a family-friendly camera. The exhibitionist brought a whole new meaning to "Grin and bear it." Having anticipated such shenanigans the co-host, David Niven, quipped that the guy was displaying his "shortcomings."

Over at the college coffee shop, Brian had goaded me in front of our friends. He claimed I was too chicken to streak. "Round up a hundred bucks and I'll do it," I had countered.

I shifted in the chair with the hope of finding relief, all the while studying how to pull off the dare. *I could give my clothes to Willy out in the hallway, put on a balaclava, enter through one door, dash across the room of unsuspecting students and a frowning Professor Stack, and exit through the opposite door to a waiting Willy* . . .

In truth, I prayed to God Brian wouldn't be able to round up the cash, because he was right. I *was* chicken. Even though our friends had seen me several times in the buff, albeit in a less public forum. As it turned out, without sufficient interest to see me embarrassed—my privates remained private.

The nagging pain was creating so much discomfort that I couldn't focus. I needed to see someone about it. The question was when? On my plate: regular classes, assignments and looming midterm exams. And on weekdays from 3 p.m. to 11 p.m., I worked at Simpson's downtown depot to pay for my university courses. By the time I got home to my parents' condo, everyone would be asleep. That's a long day.

Nevertheless, the situation was under control. Studying had to get done on weekends and while in transit on crowded buses and trains. It was critical to secure not just good grades, but excellent ones, for the all-too-important degree in Computer Science. I had been dreaming—of working at IBM—way too long to let this opportunity slip through my fingers at this stage.

I called the campus doctor's office for an appointment. "There's not much until next year," said the secretary.

"One quick visit is all I need," I pleaded.

"He's got a vacant slot on December 23rd at 1:30."

"I'll take it!" It conflicted with a lecture, but I decided to suck up my pride and ask somebody for a copy of their notes.

The doctor whirled into the examining room and barked.

"What's your problem?"

"My back's killing me."

After toe touching, resistance movements, twists and turns, he was done. All in under five minutes. He scribbled quickly as he explained, "One, sit up straight, you're slouching. Two, do these exercises." He passed me a sheet of hand-drawn stick figures.

"That sounds easy." I exhaled in relief.

"One more thing, here's a referral to a psychiatrist."

"You're kidding me?"

"Do I look like I have time to waste on humour?" was his reply as he ushered me out of his office.

Got to get going. I still had to run past a number of colleges and parking lots to the edge of the campus to catch the 2 p.m. bus down to the Jane subway station. Provided there were no delays, I'd make it just in time for my 3 p.m. shift, loading a conveyor belt. It was the peak Christmas season, packages had to be delivered on time. I couldn't afford to dawdle.

Months had flown by like the windswept calendar pages in an old black and white movie before the psychiatrist, Dr Rochman, had an opening. Over several sessions, I opened up and spoke about how I felt I was losing my mental acuity—my education and career days were numbered. He had sent me for bloodwork and neurological test including an EEG.

The day of my results appointment turned out to be the coldest of the winter and I regretted not wearing a thicker jacket. I stepped off the Red Rocket streetcar, watching out for ice and cars whizzing by. Dipsy-doodled through the intersection crowd, a din of honking horns.

The secretary had a congenial smile when I entered the reception room. "No need to rush, he just got off the phone." She was used to seeing me rushing in at the very last minute, but always on time. That's me.

Dr. Rochman and I exchanged pleasantries as I sank into a thick leather chair. He—the spitting image of Albert Einstein with the thick black mustache, wild gray hair, and sad puppy eyes—went straight to the point.

This is it. My heart thumped.

"In my opinion," he started as he took off his glasses, "you are experiencing anxiety, a consequence of an overloaded lifestyle." A pause for the words to sink in.

"It's possible you may hold latent resentment towards your father, originating from childhood events."

My left shoulder twitched. *Hope he didn't notice it.*

"It appears that you're convinced you are losing your mind."

Did I say that?

My attention drifted from the dark oak desk to the framed diplomas on the wall. *Graduated from a university in Zurich, Switzerland.*

He cleared his throat.

"Well? *Do* you think you are losing your mind?"

PART I

EARLY YEARS

Duka, his mother and the first Irena. 1955

Duka, his father and the bakery staff 1956.

Duka, his parents and second Irena. 1956

CHAPTER 1

FAMILY

Orahovica, Croatia, Yugoslavia
August, 1957

E nveloped by a lingering fog of apprehension, Duka had hardly slept the entire night. And now, the creak of a wooden step jerked him awake—alert with a feeling of dread. Covered only by a sheet, his tiny sweating body stiffened. An all-too-familiar sound of a pair of shoes crept down several creaking stairs, one tortured step after another. Just before the door on the right opened, he took a deep breath and held it.

The old landlady, who lived upstairs, crossed the bedroom—in her arm a sloshing enamel chamber pot—on the way to dispose of her *treasure*. The boy's father had said she kept it upstairs at the foot of the Virgin Mary statue as a crazy offering, until even Mary insisted the smelly pot be removed.

He exhaled.

Dawn was breaking. The early morning light filtered through the window revealing a clean, sparsely furnished room: another bed, a dresser, a wardrobe and a crib holding a slumbering baby.

From the kitchen came the comforting sounds of Duka's mother, Janja, preparing breakfast: slippers shuffling and tableware clinking.

Janja entered the bedroom, in a duster with a deep front pocket, to check on her beautiful sleeping baby. After meningitis cruelly stole her first much beloved daughter, Irena, God gave her another girl. Janja was determined to protect *this* precious child, this second Irena from all harm.

To freshen the air, she opened the main door slightly and then sat beside her son. How she adored his long, blond curls pulled up with a rubber band—like she had done for Irena—on top of his angelic oval face. Her own chestnut permed frizz surrounded a somewhat ordinary face, remarkable only for its dimpled smile.

Exchanging knowing looks, mother and child went speechless about their secret. Both parents trusted him, a six-year-old boy, with it. His father, Marijan, a shrewd and courageous man had left in the dead of night—the Party had informants—on a bold mission.

"Would you like cream-of-wheat?' Janja asked, wiping sweat from Duka's forehead.

"Da Mama," he replied. It always tasted wonderful with sugar and evaporated milk.

After breakfast, he received permission to go fishing with his friends, Marica and Ivanka. Once outside he wandered around the courtyard. It hadn't rained for days, so the ground was dusty and the rain barrel—fed by the runoff from the roof—nearly empty. Cautiously he approached the well. It had a protective cover and a pulley system with a roped bucket for drawing up water. Up on tiptoes, he just managed to peer over the stone wall into the cold, dark abyss.

"Anybody there?" A ghostly echo returned. There was a fairy tale about baby goats pushing the bad wolf into a well. Without a doubt, once someone fell in, there was no escape. The thought sent a shiver down his spine.

Moving around the compound, Duka came to a small, private cottage. Snooping through the window was wrong, that much he knew, but natural curiosity got the better of him. For a fleeting moment he witnessed something odd and undoubtedly personal between the man and woman.

Instantly, he turned and scampered next door to meet his friends. Marica was a year older; Ivanka, at the age of fourteen, an adult.

On this warm, sunny day the perfect place to be was down by the stream, more like a creek at this time of the year. Upon arriving they quickly set aside their flipflops. Ivanka sat on a boulder to dangle her feet in the clear, shallow water, while Duka and Marica waded in slowly, enjoying the tingling invigoration. Not seeing any fish, they moved over to a deeper section, full of really *big* fish: about seven cm long, perhaps more. Patiently they moved in, hands like hawk's claws ready to pounce.

Reacting to their sudden lunges, the schools of fish zigged and zagged out of harm's way. The result: a lot of splashing and joyful laughter. And so it went on for ten breathless minutes.

While waiting for the silt to settle and out of earshot of Ivanka, Duka whispered about what he had seen in the cottage. Marica listened keenly. After some plotting, they agreed to meet secretly next morning after breakfast at her house. In all the excitement, Duka stepped backwards onto a sharp stone.

"Ouch!" he yelled. Ivanka rushed to see what was the matter. Finding Duka's right heel with a superficial cut, she decided the only thing to do was to carry him home. Marica grabbed his slippers. For some reason the burning sensation evaporated the moment Ivanka's smooth, comforting arms picked him up and her braless breasts pressed against his ribs.

Next morning Duka sneaked off to meet Marica, following a rarely used path behind the houses. His mother, a pediatric nurse, had cleaned, disinfected and applied a Band-aid on the cut, so he was free to walk without concern. Marica stood beside the outhouse waiting. Before anyone could see them, she pushed him in. It was not exactly the ideal place for what they were about to do.

On the wall was a row of sharp protruding nails on which to pin precious sheets of newspapers in lieu of toilet paper. In desperate times, one could venture out for large leaves, but in winter your quest is hopeless. And if you're not versed in local flora you risk a nasty burning sensation to the delicate part of your posterior. The bottom line, don't leave these trips to the last minute.

Marica pulled up her dress and tucked it under her chin. Duka lowered his pants, keeping his legs wide apart to prevent the pants from falling to the ground. Now what?

They studied each other.

He took his *lili* as his mother referred to it, and tried to guess where it should go. Aha, the answer was obvious! The bellybutton.

However, this was not going to be easy so he went up on his tip-toes. They waited for something magical to happen.

His spindly little legs, before long, started to shake from weariness.

Suddenly, they heard someone approaching. To steady himself Duka reached for the wall but—to avoid the row of sharp nails—caught a sliver on his palm. Before he could yell out, Marica covered his mouth with her hands.

"Who's in there?" asked Ivanka.

"It's me," replied Marica.

"Are you all right?"

"Yes, I'm doing kaka." Unable to breathe, Duka's wrinkled face was turning beet red.

"You want me to come back later?"

"Yes."

As Ivanka's footsteps could be heard receding, Marica lowered her hands and Duka surfaced, gasping for air.

With the coast clear, Duka hightailed directly home, the palm sliver and heel cut forgotten. And as for the encounter, it was never mentioned again.

* * * * *

Zagreb, capital of Croatia

The mission held a high risk of being discovered since the authorities were particularly watchful for any suspicious behaviour in and around the train station. According to plan Marijan's collaborators should be in place, waiting, so his timing was critical.

At an outdoor café not far from the train station all the tables were full. Marijan sat at one table, well-dressed, sipping a strong American coffee and smoking a Marlboro. Having left home so early under the cover of darkness, he needed a clear head. An onlooker might have taken him for a business man relaxing in the afternoon sunshine. Friends said he resembled David Niven, down to the dark-hair and pencil-thin moustache.

He glanced at his watch, grabbed the suitcase and dropped a generous tip on the table before moving on.

Confidently, he marched through the heavy station doors toward the schedule board. One minute remained until the departure of the Maribor train on Platform 2. Perfect, he thought, anyone following would be hard-pressed keeping up. With a hiss and clatter the train started to pull out slowly gathering speed. Manoeuvring through the crowd like a mid-field soccer player, he reached the last car just in time to hop on.

All the seats were occupied, except the one across from a woman with a kicking and screaming child. Sitting beside them, Marijan introduced himself. Soon he was recounting the Aesop fable of the fox and the crow, to the great delight of the child and the relief of the mother.

Several seats ahead Branko, a Serb, had caught the attention of a vivacious blond. No surprise there, for he was a tall, handsome man with a deep baritone voice.

At the other end of the car, Dragan looked uneasy. Was it the obese, snoring man next to him or the stress of the mission? Short for a Bosnian, he had dark olive skin and midnight black hair.

By the time the conductor came Marijan's new friends were pleading for another tale. He greeted the agent and handed the ticket without incident. Branko passed his ticket, eyes glued to his flirtatious new acquaintance.

As the conductor approached, Dragan, heart pounding, nervously cast furtive glances. Sweat beaded on his forehead, and his hand trembled as he passed his ticket across the body of the sleeping bench-mate. The conductor watched him suspiciously, so Dragan eyed his neighbour, shrugged a shoulder and chuckled. A ticket poked outside the man's shirt pocket.

In Maribor, the departing blond gave her address to Branko, before the train proceeded a bit further to the end of the line—near the Austrian border.

Since it was dark and drizzling, Marijan assisted the woman and child with disembarkation, before returning for his own suitcase and raincoat. Eager for shelter, passengers rushed to the terminal leaving Marijan and the other two procrastinators last to disembark.

As the three men walked alongside of the train, careful to look casual—though who would suspect a Croat, Serb and Bosnian working together—they could see a field on their right and a thick forest beyond.

With a few deep breaths Marijan was ready. Suddenly they turned toward the forest and sprinted as best as they could through sticky mud. Legs and arms pumping. Hearts pounding. Only a hundred meters from safety.

To everyone's surprise, Dragan stepped into a gopher hole, tripped and fell hard. The other two looked if they had been noticed. Nobody. Quickly, each got under an arm and helped Dragan limp awkwardly onward.

Under the dense and dark forest canopy, they couldn't see very well. Searching through the suitcase, Marijan pulled out a flashlight to examine Dragan's leg. The ankle was already swollen and the pain severe enough that Dragan could barely stand. Obviously, their plan needed reconsideration. Dragan was supposed to be their guide, but in his condition, he would have a difficult time leading.

"Perhaps we could stay with your new friend in Maribor?" suggested Marijan, poking fun at Branko. They all burst into a hearty laugh, breaking the seriousness of the situation.

"There's only one woman for me and she's back home," said Branko. In fact, each man had a wife and children counting on their success. Motivated by thoughts of their loved ones, they decided to continue.

Without question the ankle needed to be stabilized immediately. Handkerchiefs were the only suitable items available under the circumstances.

And then, using the flashlight, they limped along as a unit, following a fast-flowing stream.

Exhausted by the slippery slopes and darkness, they finally stopped for the night.

Marijan quipped, "It's a good thing you're short. You didn't have far to fall." Once again, the other two laughed. Just as he slapped Dragan's shoulder an owl flew in so close they could feel the wind from its wings.

Silence fell upon them for a moment and Dragan shuddered. It was just a bird, so they laughed even louder, but an eerie echo hinted about the heinous secrets the brooding forest held.

* * * * *

World War II started in 1939 when Hitler's totalitarian government led Germany to invade neighbouring countries, including the kingdom of Yugoslavia.

The kingdom—comprised of the regions of Croats, Serbs and Slovenes—had its own internal conflicts, triggered in part by Croats seeking independence.

Germany and its partners, the Axis Powers, installed puppet states in Serbia and Croatia. The first ethnic cleansing in the area took place between the Croats and Serbs.

Tito's communist troops—with help from the U.S., England and Russian led USSR—formed a resistance that expelled the Axis Powers out of Yugoslavia.

In 1945, Croat and Slovene civilians living in Zagreb joined fleeing troops to escape to Austria. But Tito's army captured and marched them back, largely to Maribor for *processing*. Many were killed and buried in mass graves in the forests outside Maribor.

* * * *

During the night the rain continued, and other than a coyote howling, it was deathly quiet.

The next morning, their progress up and down exposed muddy slopes was excruciatingly slow. Although weary and out of food by late afternoon, their spirits picked up when Dragan, by now managing with a branch as a crutch, announced the border was only meters away.

He asked if they would go ahead a bit while he relieved himself.

Waiting an inordinate length of time, Branko and Marijan grew concerned and backtracked.

On the ground lay Dragan groggy from a head wound no doubt delivered by the two border guards pointing rifles at their chests.

"Lost, are you?" said the younger one with a smirk, but without lifting his gun. "Don't worry, we'll show you the way."

Arrested and returned for a trial conducted in a Zagreb courtroom that lasted about ten minutes sans family, friends or a lawyer present. Marijan, Branko and Dragan were found guilty of disloyalty to the Federation and imprisoned for three months. Just like that.

After being released from prison, Marijan decided that it was best to move on to a new town. Start with a clean slate.

Armed with a top of the class baking diploma, he got a job at the bakery.

Consistently arriving early to open the shop, he worked tirelessly; and still made time to enjoy cheerful conversations with coworkers and customers. His quick mathematical mind avoided mistakes at the cash register and at the bookkeeping. When his suggestions boosted sales, nobody objected to him having the managerial position.

* * * * *

Right after the war ended, Tito's communist party won the Yugoslav election. As premier he deposed the king and by constitution changed the country into a communist state. Through intimidation, Croatia and Slovenia returned to the Yugoslav Federation. All the power, however, was in the hands of the central government in Serbia.

Among the chaos and destruction of war, very little civil administration or courts existed. So, for the sake of expediency, Tito executed thousands accused of war crimes, suspected spies and many soldiers who fought against his troops during the war. In addition, he had Croat and Slovene separatists imprisoned, even shot to stop them from splitting up the country.

When elected as president it was for life; and elections always resulted in the same people voted in.

Large industries were nationalized, but the small businesses were permitted self-management, with communal ownership. However, the local party was in charge. Being a party member was a distinct advantage—but religious expression and government criticism were a distinct disadvantage—for advancement.

Neighbours spied and reported on neighbours.

* * * * *

Pozega, Croatia
July, 1959

Mr. Ambrozic, an elderly man with thick white hair, sat in a chair at the front of his house watching the young boys playing soccer in the middle of the unpaved road. Here on the outskirts of the town, a horse drawn cart, cyclist or even a pedestrian rarely went by to disrupt the game. Almost daily during the summer, he loaned the ball to the boys—generating wild excitement among the ever-improving group. A heavy metal door, the entrance to Duka's family compound, acted as the net. Although not an exceptional dribbler Duka never seemed to stop chasing the ball.

The oldest, Pepa faked a move to the left, shifted to the right and swung his leg with remarkable control; the ball struck the door with a loud boom. Nobody ever complained, after all, one of these youngsters could be a future star who would make the country proud.

When the game broke for lunch, Mr. Ambrozic crossed the road to give Duka a picture he had taken a few weeks earlier.

The boy took the photo with a soft "thank you" and scooted home to show it to his mother.

Janja was busy in the kitchen ironing, so he quietly leaned against the wall and watched. She started with transferring glowing embers from the stove to the iron. For a shirt she followed an unfaltering order: cuffs, around the buttons, sleeves and lastly the body.

Nearby, Irena played with a doll, the only toy in the house.

For Duka the ironing always turned into an exquisitely serene experience. The iron glided and Janja sang and his eyes closed. Then, like a raindrop on a leaf, he slid down the wall to the floor. "Que sera, sera" and "Marina" were such familiar songs, he was tempted to join in. But not wishing to break the spell, he simply hummed along, drifting away . . .

The photo dropped to the floor.

He picked it up and studied it. On one side stood two girls and on the other a well-dressed boy wearing a buttoned jacket and zippered pants. In the middle, Duka wore a faded sweat top and bottom held in place by an elastic that had apparently given up on life.

Duka
(with an apple)
and friends.

"Mama, are we poor?" Duka asked at the end of a song.

"No dear, we are—" She stopped and glanced to see what prompted such an unusual question.

Placing the iron on the stove, she came over for a closer look at the photo.

"Mr. Ambrozic gave it to me." Now she understood the question. Except for the Sunday best reserved for church and special occasions, he really didn't have much in the way of nice clothes.

"Your father has a good job and—" She paused to think. "You're going to need new clothes for school."

The matter was brought up at lunch, right after Marijan made the sign of the cross and everyone dug into the food.

After everyone—except Duka who was playing soccer again—had a siesta nap, Janja and Mrs. Ambrozic walked the two kilometers to the hospital for the afternoon shift.

To relax, Marijan played card games with the kids and read Mr. Ambrozic's newspaper. He and kids had to turn in early: the bakery needed to be opened daily at 3 a.m.

Saturday nights he gathered with friends at the Grabik tavern.

On the first day of grade 1, Marijan accompanied his seven-year-old son—who proudly wore a striped sailor T-shirt and pocketed shorts with a zipper. Excited by the prospect of learning, Duka hoped to be really smart one day, like his father. Although being the leader of a household was hard to imagine, because of all the responsibilities.

The two story, red brick school was one of the largest buildings in Pozega. The chain-link fence could barely contain all the rambunctious children. Only the first graders stood still and quiet, next to the parents. A bell rang and everyone followed signs to their designated classrooms. Guarding the grade 1 doorway was an attractive woman with short, curly hair.

"I'm Miss Radic," said the teacher. Marijan extended an arm in a handshake as he introduced himself and his son.

"This is his lucky day. Here we turn children into Tito's little Pioneers," she said, referring to the program of communist indoctrination.

Turning to his son, "You be sure to listen to Miss Radic," said Marijan. Duka was a good boy, so they both knew that this comment was for the teacher's benefit. Duka had already been taught to behave properly.

Nevertheless, it was evident Miss Radic was determined to force the communist consciousness into the minds of her students.

"Mama, may we go to the river?" asked Duka.

"Fine, but your sister must always be beside you and don't go far."

Outside, the enclosed courtyard was shared by another family living in an adjacent cottage. Each family owned a noisy chicken coop and a hovel covering logs ready for the stove. In between, hung a latched, wooden gate. Only meters away slept a lazy creek shaded by houses and trees, the perfect place for a hot Saturday.

An extensive search produced a reasonably flat, round stone. A sideways throw resulted in only two skips. Embarrassing. He hoped nobody was watching.

His sister picked one also, closed her eyes tight and flung it overhand. It bounced in front of her feet, far short of its intended target

Meandering along the embankment, they hunted for particularly colourful stones to bring home. Two houses down, the boundary of the search area, lay a discarded and yet intact wooden crate. It would be foolish to pass up this great find. How could he make use of it? While Duka thought about it, Irena crouched down beside him, head on palm, to do the same.

An idea struck him. With a solid hold, he slowly dragged it next to their property, his sister earnestly trying to help. Having watched his father build their hovel, he used a flat rock to rearrange two boards. Indoors, he found an old deck of cards and replaced the missing ace with a joker. Back outside again, he brushed the crate clean, quite satisfied with the result. Finally, he and Irena stepped in to play cards on the two boards now serving as a table top.

Throughout much of the project, Janja watched from the kitchen window with amusement: until the cards came out. Immediately, mirth changed to uncontrollable fury.

"Get inside, right now!" she shouted.

Startled by the sudden outburst, they ran in.

Shaking with anger, she ripped up the cards and threw them into the stove. A terrible loss of perfectly good cards, thought Duka, but the message was clear: NO PLAYING CARDS.

After an early supper the whole family looked forward going across to the Ambrozic house.

Waving and smiling, the old couple welcomed them in. The visitors were seated in a room with a china cabinet, a room specifically devoted to eating. To Duka that meant they were rich.

Ahead lay a candle-lit evening of relaxation, overflowing with interesting and candid conversation. Mrs. Ambrozic served chocolate cookies, milk and Slivovica. The adults talked about sports, life, politics, and far away places. In her father's lap, Irena fell asleep and, thankfully, Janja returned to her normal self— no longer upset.

As usual, at one end of the table waited for Duka comics cut out of a newspaper. A variety of comic strips to capture a young imagination: a man captured by scary giant aliens on a distant world (Flash Gordon), a cute dog getting into mischief (Scamp) and a detective solving crime (Rip Kirby) were of particular interest.

Bits of the adult chatter reached his ears. If he heard correctly, there was a country where people were cut up for some reason with a *real* saw. That country was called Russia. *What a terrifying place to live!*

* * * * *

A month later
October 1959

There wasn't much time, so Duka had to act quickly. After school he was supposed to go straight home. Instead, he stopped first at the variety store.

The three dinars clenched in his hand, received from the Ambrozics on his birthday, could be spent on anything. Just below the cash register in glass jars—sweets of various colours, shapes and flavours—shouted out to him, *buy me!* Afraid to stay and listen, he moved on to the back of the store where shelves abounded with knickknacks.

He desperately wanted to buy the right item, but which one? Aha, there it was right at eye level: a little rabbit with perky ears, round eyes and chubby cheeks. It wore a blue shirt and red pants. The price tag underneath showed 3 dinars.

Janja was cooking supper when Duka came into the kitchen.

"Mama, I have something for you." Today was her birthday and never before had he given her anything.

"What is it, dear?" she asked without looking up, stirring the goulash thoroughly.

"It's for your birthday."

A warm smile formed on her face like sunrise on a perfect morning. She put the spoon down and turned around.

21

He held out a small package wrapped in red paper, courtesy of the shopkeeper when he heard who the gift was for.

"Did your father give you the money?"

"No." And he explained.

She wiped her hands on the apron before removing the paper and opening the box: an adorable rabbit, arms folded in calm repose. This gift, I can tell you, she would go on to cherish for the rest of her life.

Gently, she swept curls from his forehead, looked deeply into his innocent, brown eyes and whispered, "Thank you." with such tenderness that can only exist between a mother and child.

He knew, there and then, he had chosen the right item. No candy could replace this feeling.

To celebrate the special occasion, they were all going out that evening. Leisurely, they strolled to the central square bordered by town offices, court house and police station. Pigeons dipped beaks in the ornate fountain. And the elderly sat on benches watching the young carry on, just like they had in days gone by.

Marijan held Irena's hand on one side and interlocked arms with Janja on the other, promenading past busy shops and restaurants. Never far behind, Duka scampered like a puppy from one spot to another, keeping an eye on his family. What a beautiful sight: his mother wore a shiny dress, pink and white magnolias on a black background; his father had on a tailored navy-blue suit and a grey fedora. His parents looked so in love and everyone was so happy.

At the ticket booth Marijan made a purchase. With great anticipation they entered the immense theatre. To sit in a wide, cushy chair with armrests and close to the front, was a real treat. Past movies included Ali Baba and several cowboys and Indians films. This evening's film transported them to the dense jungles of Africa: Tarzan, Jane and Boy lived high up above danger in an amazing treehouse. Duka felt a striking resemblance to Boy. Besides the entertaining chimp, Cheetah, many wild animals roamed on the giant screen: elephants, a lion, and man-eating crocodiles. The movie's climax involved Tarzan escaping a tower prison with the help of a herd of stampeding elephants. Right up to *The End,* Duka's eyes were glued to the screen.

On this particularly pleasant night, each gust of wind sent autumn leaves drifting to the ground. Some of the streets were deserted—the only sound that of their shoes on the pavement.

Just beyond the luminescence of the streetlight, a drunk lunged out of a dark ditch towards them, startling everyone.

Marijan instinctively dropped his son's hand and gently, but firmly, redirected the intruder aside. As calmly as that, trouble was averted and peace restored. They continued on their way home.

As long as his father was around, Duka knew they were safe.

Once a month the males in the household went to the barbershop. Having extra time today, they stopped off at the bakery, recognizable from a distance by the wonderful smell of the freshly baked goods.

Inside, trays of rye bread were pulled out of the hot stone ovens, then inserted into carts for wheeling off to the sales room.

"*Dobro jutro gazda*, good morning boss," shouted one baker after another, all wearing white hats, aprons and a dusting of flour.

"How's it going boys?" asked Marijan as he pulled out a pack of cigarettes to offer everyone.

"Who's this?" asked the new recruit.

"Duka."

"Would you like some *burek*, Duka?"

The boy shrugged his shoulders and looked up at his father who nodded. *Burek* is a phyllo pastry pie filled with feta cheese. It tastes absolutely delicious.

"Here, take a whole pie home."

"*Hvala*, thank you." While it was being wrapped up they all engaged in good-natured banter.

In the barbershop three doors down, the owner welcomed two of his regular customers. The chair was dusted before Duka jumped up, legs too short to reach the footstep. The barber, a friendly man sporting a handlebar moustache, covered him with a white cape and tucked it into the collar. The scissors snipped. So relaxing. Even more when the electric clippers vibrated on his nape. Ecstasy.

Gradually, a heated argument over politics developed between his father and the two men who had arrived shortly after them.

Never shy to express an opinion, Marijan however always did so in a diplomatic way. It was clear that the two strangers were ganging up on him. Concerned, Duka tried to think quickly. What should he do? What would his father want him to do? Got it!

Once the haircut was done, he asked if he could wait outside.

Casually he closed the door behind him and then burst out into a sprint. Through the square, down the dirt road and into their courtyard. His mother was washing Irena in a tub.

"What's going on?" Janja was surprised to see him like this.

"I can't talk. Tata is waiting for me." He could hear and feel the thud of his heart.

In the kitchen he found what he was looking for. Wrapping it in a white dish towel, he ran out without further explanation, retracing his steps as fast as his legs could carry him.

At the barbershop door, he stopped to take several deep breaths before entering.

Used to measured conversation at home, this debate had escalated to an intolerable level.

He nudged up to his father who was finishing his visit with a shave.

"Tata, when are we going?" he pleaded, tugging on his father's sleeve. That's when he surreptitiously passed the sheathed knife under the sheet into his father's hand.

Marijan was taken aback for a moment, but composed himself and slipped it into his pocket.

"We're almost done," he said and winked. Duka casually went over to his chair and picked up the *burek* box, ready to smash a face if necessary.

Final few strokes of the brush indicated Marijan was done. He got up, left the usual generous tip and with a tap on his fedora, wished everyone a good day.

On a bench near the fountain he sat Duka down; and bending on one knee, he studied his son's face.

With large, powerful hands he gently cupped his head.

"You're a smart boy," and kissed the forehead. And then without reservation, pulled Duka to his chest and said with a quiver in his throat, "You are my dear, dear son."

* * * * *

The front of the class was generally occupied by either ambitious or wealthy children. The back for the tall boys and few hiding gypsies. In the middle, Duka shared a desk with a talkative girl. She should have been at front on both accounts, if my generalization is to be correct. Being the quiet type, he was content just to listen to her, and yet today was going to be like no other.

You see, he had a crush on a girl at the front. At this very moment she was jostling and giggling with her desk partner, stirring something inside him. Miss Radic hadn't arrived.

Duka (4th row, 2nd) making a face.
Eva Gardner (2nd row, 3rd) of his affection giggling.
Miss Radic keeping an eye on her troublesome student, Duka.

All he saw and heard was her. He arose and walked down the aisle, possessed. Standing between the boyfriend and her, face to face, he was spellbound by her mischievous smile. It faded to puzzlement. Then, not fast, not slow, he gently placed his hands on her elbows and leaned in, eyes closed and lips pursed to—press a firm kiss on the middle of her soft, warm cheek.

He slowly pulled back watching her puzzlement reshape to a subtle smile. Somehow, she seemed to understand his motivation far better than he could.

The classmates—unnaturally silent in awe, like prehistoric man witnessing an eclipse for the first time—had their eyes upon him. As though his actions were somehow justifiable, he marched resolutely back to his desk.

The second he sat down good judgement returned: this sort of behaviour was forbidden! In all likelihood, her boyfriend was going to grab him after school and beat him up. And so he should. Duka would just stand there and take it.

The effect on his desk mate was also profound. She never spoke to him again.

Surely the word would get out to Miss Radic and eventually to his trusting father. How was he going to explain it? These desires had to be controlled!

When Miss Radic entered the room, everyone straightened up with hands folded on their desks.

In pursuit of conformity and strict discipline, she ordered a gypsy boy and his younger sister to the front and face the class. Rumour had it that they lived in a cave outside of town as the smudges on the faces and grimy clothes suggested.

With rubber ends of two pencils she parted their hair inspecting for lice. The girl squirmed in obvious discomfort.

Then, they were told to take the shirts off.

"Now!" yelled the teacher when they hesitated.

The girl started to cry, soon joined by two others.

"Fine," said Miss Radic annoyed, "we'll continue this tomorrow."

When Duka got home in the afternoon, his father asked, "How was school?" Could he already know about the misbehaviour? But Duka decide to mention the inspection instead.

Marijan grew angry.

"That's not right. One of these days I'm going over there." The day would arrive sooner than he expected.

In December, at the end of the first school term, Duka brought his report card home. To Marijan's disbelief, it showed straight *D*'s.

"That's it. I'm going with you tomorrow," he said without further discussion. His son was a far better student than the marks indicated, that's for sure.

Father and son—a queasy feeling in the pit of Duka's stomach—sat in the office across from the principal while Miss Radic stood by without even a hint of cordiality.

After Marijan's explanation for the visit, the principal thought it best to test the young Pioneer's progress.

The first part involved reading: Duka stumbled on every word. The principal raised an eyebrow as if to say "Well?" and Miss Radic couldn't suppress a smirk.

"Fine." Marijan conceded. "What's next?"

For writing Duka tentatively dipped the quill into the inkwell, careful not to splatter and formed a few letters. This time it was the principal's turn to say, "Fine, I've seen enough," and on the report card he entered a *C* next to Penmanship. Miss Radic was not pleased.

The last segment covered arithmetic. Duka answered instantly and decisively, to the principal's wide-eyed amazement. The *D* was replaced with an *A*. The teacher was seething.

On the way out of the office, Marijan turned around.

"By the way, it's not a teacher's place to have students undress in front of classmates for *any* reason whatsoever. Not all citizens have the luxury of easy access to water, like some well-established comrades." He did not wait for a reaction from Miss Radic.

That winter was a harsh one, so when Marijan was late coming home from work, Janja assumed there was a problem with supplies or the oven. Luckily it was her day off. Half way through supper he walked in looking upset.

"They've done it to me again," he lifted Irena and sat at the table. "The town council replaced me with someone who knows absolutely nothing about baking. The rep couldn't even manufacture an excuse for the change. Cold comfort in that I can stay on as a junior baker."

With a reassuring hug Janja said, "You'll have some income and with mine we'll manage." Still he didn't appear fully convinced.

That night, with everyone in bed snug under the duvet, he turned off the kerosene lamp and dashed back to escape the cold. When he landed on the bottom corner of the bed, a wobbly leg snapped underneath, whipped across the room and struck the metallic tub with a clang. In complete shock, Janja and Irena slid to the corner. From his bed Duka watched startled. Marijan braced himself so that when they reached him, they all held on to one another.

What could they do but laugh? Soon enough though, Marijan knew they couldn't stay shivering like this much longer, so he merely removed the other three bed legs. Problem solved, for now.

Once everyone was comfortably tucked in, he stopped to seriously ponder the current state of affairs: as long as he refused to join the Party, they could never get ahead. His family had no future in Yugoslavia!

* * * * *

Six months later
Misin Han, Bosnia, Yugoslavia
August, 1960

To distract the authorities from his true intentions, Marijan made it known to neighbours and co-workers that his family would be vacationing for a couple weeks with family in Bosnia. Only the Ambrozics knew of the audacious plan.

28

The stony road up the hill to Janja's parents' farm looked the same. Her mother had died giving birth and her father had passed on years later, leaving Niko, the oldest, in charge. As teenagers they all shared in the work until they left for higher education. Niko remained. Not having seen each other since her wedding, Janja was concerned how Marijan would be received. In the letter about the summer visit, she stressed there was no need to be met at the train station.

Niko, his wife Staza and young sons were watching from the front porch of the old, solid stone farmhouse. Having spotted their visitors as they were cresting the hill, they bolted down the stairs with wide open arms and smiling faces. The adults kissed, hugged and greeted one another with unbridled enthusiasm. When attention shifted to the children, they were lifted, jostled and stroked with joyous exuberance.

"Why are we standing out here in the heat?" said Niko finally. "Let's go inside." He grabbed two suitcases and Staza the third.

In the cool comfort of the kitchen, everyone gathered around the long oak table. With the sweet smell of Turkish coffee permeating the air, the adults stared at each other and declared nobody had changed one tiny bit. The family resemblance between Niko and Janja and his love and concern for his sister was most obvious.

"Now you need rest," he said. "We'll have dinner when you're ready."

The next day Mirko, the youngest and most educated sibling, arrived to great fanfare. He was sorry to say that Kaya, the younger sister, couldn't get time off from work, which Janja expected. Kaya never did like Marijan.

Having heard that Duka had difficulty reading, Mirko spent time helping him read a children's book he brought. "It's hard now," he said, "but one day you'll be able to read as well as anyone."

The visitors enjoyed pitching in with the farm chores, all the while speaking openly and from the heart. Soon the kids bonded with their newly discovered country cousins.

On the day before the vacation ended, Marijan took his son for a walk around the property. In their wandering, they came across a mature mulberry tree.

"Tata, can I climb up and have some?"

"Why not!"

So he eagerly climbed up; and with legs dangling, he gorged on the biggest, sweetest berries ever.

Once satiated and stomach bulging, he descended much more slowly, hands and face stained dark purple. His father burst into hearty laughter at the sight.

On the tree trunk, letters were freshly carved out. With the index finger, Duka followed the grooves and read, *Duka i Tata '60.*

"Maybe we'll come back one day," said Marijan.

That evening saw everyone commune over a delicious Easter-like feast. At one end of the table the men (Irena in her father's lap) discussed life and politics. At the other end, Staza read Janja's fortune. In the middle, the boys torn between who to follow.

After Janja finished her coffee, she was instructed to turn over the white china cup and leave it sitting in the saucer for a few minutes. When ready, Staza turned it right side up and proceeded with 'reading' the future based on the patterns and images formed by the now dry sediment. With abated breath, Janja and the boys waited. For a better view, Staza turned and twisted the cup.

"Your future looks bright," she started. "You will have a house of your own full of many wonderful things." Janja made a sign of the cross in gratitude to the merciful Lord.

"You and Marijan will have more children. A boy and a girl."

"Oh my!" said Janja. "How will we ever be able to provide for them?"

Staza brought the cup for a closer look, perhaps to read the small print. For the briefest of moments a strange expression flickered on her face. Her hand twitched, lost its grip and the cup fell with a crash startling everyone, even Staza.

"I'm sorry Janja, it's my arthritis."

"I'm the one who should be sorry. Your lovely cup is now broken."

"Let's not fret," Niko jumped in. As long as I have my sister, I don't care about any cup." He raised a glass of Slivovica, "A toast to Marijan, Janja, Duka and Irena. May your future overflow with health and happiness!"

They all knew the future was very uncertain.

The early morning train took them through Banja Luka and on to Novi Grad, Croatia. But instead of transferring for Pozega, they continued on to Zagreb.

As a former nurse at a hospital there, Janja had met Marijan, her patient. Everything she was looking for in a man he possessed: handsome, well-dressed and hardworking. When they married, she forgot about her siblings, except for the occasional letter.

Now, once again she was leaving her family with no idea when, or if, she would see them again. Back at the farm there had been a lot of melancholy faces saying goodbye, seemingly forever. "May God be with you," was their final farewell.

In the nick of time, they caught a third train to Sentilj, just beyond Maribor. The hope was that the authorities would not suspect such a difficult and daunting plan involving a woman and two young children.

In Sentilj they hung back behind other exiting passengers, careful not to draw any suspicion. At an opportune moment they veered into a cornfield, extremely mindful of the uneven ground. Marijan held Irena and a large suitcase, Janja two small ones and Duka had volunteered to carry a small bag—tucked inside was a carefully wrapped tiny rabbit.

Once safely hidden in the forest, Marijan decided they had gone far enough for one long day. The kids were tired. A grassy mound on the edge of a clear, gurgling stream was the perfect place to stop. As he replenished the water supply, Janja pulled out a thin sheet for all to sit on and enjoy Staza's smoked meat sandwiches.

Through the warm night, silence was broken occasionally by the sound of a shrill bird. The family slept clustered together, kids in the middle.

After breakfast the following morning, they continued their escape, Marijan at the front holding Irena's hand. Only four kilometers to the border, but progress was slow with the children.

By noon, they neared the fateful spot from two years before. The border path was in sight. As he crossed it, Marijan caught sight of someone to his left. Lifting up Irena, he rushed ahead; Janja, a little further behind, opted to stay back and hide in the bushes with Duka.

Long agonizing minutes passed, but she dared not move.

31

Finally, she heard a conversation as someone approached.

"Come on out," said Marijan. Was he at gunpoint, she wondered?

Trusting, she stepped out.

Beside Marijan and Irena stood two teenagers.

"These people live nearby." he said. "They are willing to help us."

At the farmhouse, the Austrian family kindly provided food, water and a bed for the night.

In the morning, having exchanged currency and received directions to a bus stop, the travellers felt re-energized.

For almost an hour no bus came. Through the entire trip the children hadn't complained, but now they started to fidget. Just as they were about to return to the farm the bus showed up.

The kids had been warned not to speak, out of fear of revealing their true nationality and intentions.

The bus driver watched with great interest as the children boarded the bus.

"Halt," he said. What now?

He motioned for his assistant to come to the front of the bus.

"These children look like they deserve some candy," he said with a fatherly smile. "Don't you think?"

And so that day and the following, they made their way through Austria and deep into Germany where they presented themselves to the local authorities in Munich.

* * * * *

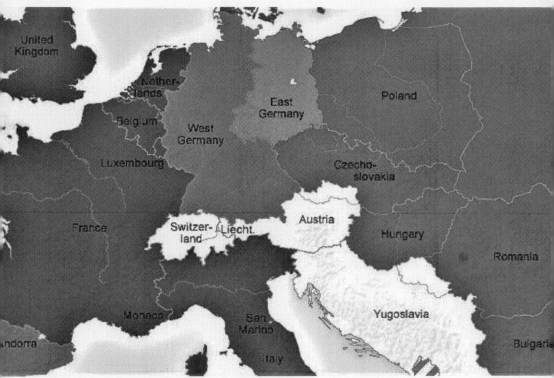

Cold War central Europe, 1945-1989 *Credit: San Jose de Benutzer, GNU Free Documentation License,* Zoomed

In Eastern Europe at the end of WWII, Nazi oppression was replaced with Communist oppression. The USSR (Soviets), led by Russia, installed puppet communist states, most occupied by the Soviet Red Army. Masses of people were terrorized by the Soviet political police. And elections turned into a sham.

Western Europe, USA and Canada joined in a defensive military alliance, NATO; they agreed to have US troops stationed throughout Western Europe.

As a counter, USSR and Eastern Europe formed the Warsaw pact, leading to the Cold War symbolized by the Berlin Wall. Germany was divided: East went under Soviet influence and West became a parliamentary democracy and emerged as a major industrial power.

The Eastern economies shrunk, most people suffering either shortages or complete lack of consumer goods. And rampant corruption.

Western Europe, on the other hand, with assistance of the US, underwent a reconstruction stage. An agreement to allow movement of goods and people between the nations triggered an economic boom—and a labour shortage. With social stability, welfare capitalism and democracy, consumer confidence was on the rise. So, by allowing asylum to those in distress from the Eastern Bloc, productivity increased and brought unprecedented growth!

* * * * *

Refugee complex
Zirndorf, West Germany
October, 1960

To the top of the hill, as in the legendary city of Eldorado, they came not in search of gold but a more valuable treasure: freedom. The refugees, whether oppression victims or economic migrants, hungered for opportunity and a better way of life.

The camp comprised of a massive three-story building, administration offices and a daycare centre. The main building contained about a hundred bedrooms, two bathrooms per floor, a cafeteria and a multipurpose room.

On a rotating basis, the cafeteria served spaghetti, rice or potatoes, spam or another meat, vegetables and an apple. No one complained.

The vast majority of the refugees—men, couples and occasionally families from Poland, Czechoslovakia, Hungary and Yugoslavia—were waiting for a western nation to accept them. Rumours circulated that the US, New Zealand and Australia were the best destinations. Due to long, cold winters, Canada appealed less.

All Duka heard, in America nobody spied on you and you could have anything, provided you studied, worked and saved. He yearned to be an American.

34

In a few days Marijan got a translator's job since he spoke several languages reasonably well and could type. Somewhere in the same building was a quiet Czechoslovak busy at his desk with paperwork. Their paths may have crossed, perhaps with a casual greeting. By coincidence, years later, in a distant country, their sons would become best friends.

For her part, Janja worked on an assembly line in a toy factory, very happy to be earning money. One time she brought home a toy motorcycle—Duka's first genuine toy since babyhood—with wheels that spun when he dragged it on the floor.

During the day the kids were kept occupied in the daycare centre with a variety of crafts. What they looked forward to most, if available, was sharing a sweet, incredibly delicious banana. After 'school' Duka found an abandoned chainless bicycle in the parking lot. He balanced on one pedal, pushed off with a few strokes and glided across the lot to his great delight. Presuming other kids used it also, he returned it to the original spot.

When possible after supper, Duka hurried downstairs to the packed multipurpose room. No chairs, everyone standing. On a shelf high up a wall sat a black and white TV. This was the first time he had seen something so wonderful since the movie theatre. Many of the viewers couldn't understand what was spoken, nevertheless, they watched with keen interest.

One weekend, when Duka was gliding on the bike, an older Yugo-slavian boy asked him to join a group of them to find a stash of WWII guns.

"I can't. My father doesn't want me leaving."

"Oh, but it's not far. Your father probably could see you from the window."

"I don't think—"

"We'll be back very soon, I promise."

On the way to the site, the boy told the group he had 'done it' with a girl from the first floor. Duka stayed silent, not wishing to reveal his lack of experience. Luckily, the girl had a younger sister his age. Perhaps she knew how to 'do it' and might be willing to teach him if he was really nice to her.

The search turned into a lengthy wild goose chase with no sign of military weapons. It was getting late and Duka worried about his father's reaction.

As he approached their building, Marijan was standing, fists on the hips and a stern look on the face. With a wave of the hand he ordered Duka to march upstairs.

During the unrelenting interrogation, all the questions were met with downcast eyes and silence. What was the point of explanations, Duka thought?

Not getting anywhere, Marijan retrieved a black leather belt from the closet.

Each stinging whack across the thighs left a red welt and filled the moist eyes. Duka raised his chin, squeezed his eyelids and forced the tears out. Was he likely to forget this? Not ever.

In the aftermath, and once his father had gone, Janja and Irena—completely still through the whole ordeal—drew close to him.

"We were all worried," said Janja, searching for any sense of awareness of the impact his actions had on everyone. He stood rigid, staring vacantly.

She continued, "Last week a child from this building wandered off. The police are still looking for her."

It was decided that as a good Catholic Duka should attend Cate-chism classes. A priest taught a dozen or so children once a week in the multipurpose room. Impressed with Duka's eagerness to learn, he recommended the polite student try out as an altar boy.

At the side of the makeshift chapel was a vestry, a cramped change room. Duka, another altar boy and the priest dressed sepa-rated by a privacy screen.

"Follow Johan and you'll be fine," said the priest.

Wearing a purple cope, he led the short procession into the full-to-capacity chapel. You couldn't tell who was prouder during the mass, the boys in the white surplices or the beaming parents.

In due time, Duka received the holy sacrament of Confirmation and a beautiful, brown rosary as a memento. Visions of being a priest floated in his mind.

As on many evenings in their room, the family sat at table doing one thing or another. Needing help with spelling a German word, Duka looked over at his preoccupied father working with an offi-cial looking document.

Marijan carefully placed a still-hot slice of egg white on the certificate.

"What does that do?" asked Duka.

"It removes ink from paper."

After a while he peeled it back looking satisfied with the result.

Had he removed some writing from the document? Was that forgery? A tight knot settled in the pit of Duka's stomach.

To make things worse, his father was riding a motorcycle around town. Without a legitimate license! If discovered they would be returned to Yugoslavia—as criminals!

Their future appeared to be in serious jeopardy.

CHAPTER 2

FREEDOM

Saint John, N.B., Canada
March 1961

M any of us in Canada are immigrants or their offspring, so there's a good chance the reader may have undergone similar aspects of the immigrant experience described below.

On the Canadian eastern seaboard on the Bay of Fundy lies Saint John, a major year-round port, pleased about its red brick and sandstone buildings. The two prominent industries, fishing refineries and pulp mills, needed a larger work force.

None of this apparent to us when we peered through the windows of the silver-grey Canadian Pacific DC-6. A lumpy white carpet of snow covered everything.

A platform was rolled out to butt up against the airplane.

The first to exit was Dad with Irene (the Anglicized version of Irena), followed by Mom and me, all huddled closely together for warmth and reassurance. Short on clothes, we felt the full shock of the bitter cold in our nose, lungs and exposed skin. Our breaths puffed out in white clouds as we cautiously climbed down step by step and onto the tarmac. Giant snow ploughs had created snowbanks above my head.

Grateful to be inside the terminal, our teeth still chattering, we were met by a very friendly immigration officer and a translator. A flash of bright light! Out of nowhere a reporter for *The Journal* snapped a photo just as Irene and I were handed gifts. First the cold and snow and now all this commotion. A bit overwhelming for Irene and me. Frankly, the America I envisioned looked more like a modern-day version of sunny Texas with cowboys and a desert. I kind of assumed this place was part of *that* America.

After a while we were led to a huge hall crammed with racks of clothes. The translator waved his arm, "Go. Pick whatever you want." This can't be true, I thought for a moment. Hesitantly, we started 'shopping.' Clothes—elegant, expensive, strange, summer, winter, sports, baby, work.

One treasure caught my eye: a colourful, striped sweater. I pounced on it before anyone else saw it, ignoring the fact we were the only family there. Responding to a wave of nausea, I stopped searching, afraid someone would take it away because of my ugly display of greed. Dad calmed me down and made sure I got some practical winter stuff. Mom found clothes for Irene.

Then, Mom was escorted to an adjoining room for discussions with officials. As best as I recall, we were diverted to choose toys sitting on shelves.

"When is Mom coming back?" I asked.

Dad hesitated. "She has to go to a hospital," he said, looking grim.

"But she's not sick."

"They say she has a sickness called TB." (People diagnosed with tuberculosis, were quarantined months in a sanatorium for bed rest and a rich diet.)

"We can take care of her," I said, trying to sound as sensible as an adult. "You and I can learn to cook," the words came flying out of my mouth. "We'll wash her face," I pleaded.

Dad choked up for a moment. "If we don't listen to them, we could be sent back." Already Irene was crying, so he picked her up and cradled her, but to no avail.

Outside in the dark, a car waited. The kind officer grabbed a doll and we followed— without Mom.

From the rocking of the car my exhausted sister eventually settled down and fell asleep.

At our destination the officer knocked on the door and after a brief exchange, motioned for us to come. Dad carried Irene and the doll inside and soon returned to shake hands and introduce himself to our hosts, a Croatian couple. Mrs. Sulic, a big heavy-set woman, had a hair growing from a black mole on her chin. Her thin husband stood directly behind her, like he needed shielding from the cold, cruel outside world.

"Take your shoes off," said Dad to me, "and listen to Mrs. Sulic." We knew who that instruction was intended for. "She will take good care of you, I'm sure." With a final hug, and "I'll see you in the morning," he was gone.

Two days later Dad was working in the Tydis bakery, sixty hours a week and boarding in the owner's house.

Based on my age they placed me in Grade 3 (not grade 2) where I languished quietly at the back of the class like a gypsy for three long, lonely months. No one spoke to me, neither teacher nor student. I was invisible, you see.

At lunch time I would come 'home' to eat with Irene and Mrs. Sulic's kids, a girl and boy matching our ages. Although the boy went to my school, we somehow never bumped into one another.

Lunch consisted of *two* slices of white toast, always browned to perfection and spread with salty, melted butter, (my mouth waters to this day at the thought) *and* a glass of milk. The alternative was steak, which was fine if you enjoy 99% bone, fat and gristle. On rare occasions a baked or boiled potato was available to complete the menu. Irene and I were served different cuts of meat than the Sulic kids. Theirs was actually chewable. Not wishing to offend Mrs. Sulic, I made a big production of cutting up my steak and, while supposedly enjoying it, I discreetly placed each piece on toilet paper in my lap. When the opportunity arose, I transferred it to my pocket for disposal in the bathroom.

One slice of toast was enough for Irene. Being a growing boy, I once requested another slice and received a mocking roll of the eyes, like I was asking for the world. After a few days, I got used to the Auschwitz Diet—guaranteed to lose 10 lbs. in thirty days or your money back. What do you know, it worked!

41

On Sundays, Dad would take all the household kids to church. After the service he took just Irene and me to King's Square, a centrally located park. He wore a grey suit, I the favourite sweater (even if it was too warm) and Irene the polka dotted shorts and a flowered shirt. We roamed around and eventually sat on a bench, just happy to be together.

One time, Dad showed us a photo of Irene and me at the airport on the day we arrived, and a newspaper article about our family as new immigrants. I couldn't understand why anyone would be interested in us—we didn't have anything or do anything special. We were boring.

In those days, a brush cut was a boy's hairstyle, so Mrs. Sulic took it upon herself to make me look "normal, not like some wild child." Under questionable lighting and with poor vision, she scalped me. The floor ended up covered with brown curls.

I didn't mind it at all because now I looked like Steve McQueen in the western series *Wanted: Dead or Alive*.

Unfortunately, Dad didn't have time for TV. When he saw the new me, he loaded his guns, aimed directly at Mrs. Sulic and fired.

"Nobody touches my children without speaking to me first."

By the time dust settled, he had corralled our things and we were gone. Before high noon.

Things turned out great because we moved into the one bedroom with him. The Sulics lost the government money for looking after us and that cost fell on Dad's shoulders. He didn't care. Bringing up his kids was his responsibility anyway, he said.

The landlords, pleasant French Canadians, spoke English with Dad. The lady offered to cook for us but Dad being proud declined.

Besides, we were eating well: Campbell's chicken noodle soup with *real* chicken. All I had to do was carefully open a can with several hand twists (a trick I learned after a few tries), toss the contents in a pan on the gas stove (convenient because there was no wood to deal with, like they do in some countries)—though I had to be super wary to turn it off—and presto, Irene and I were enjoying a complete meal.

For variety, we had Chef Boyardee spaghetti and meatballs using the same steps. No worries about leftovers as we had a fridge, a great place to duck your head on a rare, hot day.

This responsibility was short lived, not that I was complaining, Mom was finally coming home!

I don't know for sure how she did it, but she became bosom buddies with fellow patients—young or old, English or French. Language did not appear to be a barrier. I suppose sign language, real laughter and all that huggy-huggy stuff brought acceptance.

Mom in the middle.

Their chairs were lined up in the garden, the sun healing their bodies. She had gained a lot of weight but we spotted her instantly, like she was the only one there.

As we ran Irene cried out, "*Mama, Mama*."

Mom stood up and then dropped to her knees—arms reaching out—and with a smile bright enough to light up all of New York city in the middle of winter.

Among all our moaning and groaning, releasing the pain of her absence, she scooped us and hugged us so tight we could hardly breath. Then she stroked and kissed us with such passion that we knew *exactly* how much we were loved and missed.

Finally at arms length, she gave us the once over and said, "Look at you, you've lost so much weight."

Dad helped her get up and they also hugged and kissed.

"You too, Marijan, are skin and bones." And with absolute conviction said, "Well, I'll soon put a stop to that!"

While Dad worked long hours, Mom cooked and did laundry as well as every other chore. Often, she and the landlady took all the kids on outings. On Saturday evenings, the highlight of the week, we were invited downstairs to watch: *77 Sunset Strip*, *Dennis the Menace*, and *Bonanza,* to munch on finger licking chips and to sip 7-UP or Coke. The cold, sweet liquid lingered on the tongue and at the back of the mouth. The tingling fizz slid down the throat, the bubbles burst in the nose and a jolt refreshed the head. Wow!

Of course, the good life couldn't last forever—September and school were looming.

* * * * *

Much as we liked our new friends, a family of four in one bedroom was too crowded. We could afford better, so we moved to a small furnished house near a bus stop. Two bedrooms, kitchen, living room and bathroom all to ourselves! Life would never have been like this in Yugoslavia.

Dad gave me 25 cents for four bus tickets to go to school. After a few days I started running to and from, pocketing the money.

My English was woefully inadequate, so I was placed in Grade 2 for the mornings. And since my arithmetic was exceptional, I attended Grade 4 in the afternoons with Miss Tyner, my home room teacher. On the first day of school she seemed to be saying that it was very important to learn the language.

"I talk Canada," I said, switching at the last instant from saying America. Everyone in the class laughed; even Miss Tyner appeared amused but she must have corrected me to say 'English' for the kids laughed some more. Soon I discovered that if I said something improperly the class reacted. I was no longer a gypsy at the back of the class. I had become a somebody—the class clown.

* * * * *

With unlimited use of the kitchen, Mom cooked incredible meals: old country dishes of fish or meat, and all kinds of vegetables. I didn't like spinach though! My running to school continued until the weather worsened and I couldn't make it on time. When I came home at lunch, we gathered around our *own* TV for a matinee movie. The Bing Crosby and Bob Hope Road pictures, were irresistible. The problem: they ended a half hour after school restarted. Sometimes I would feign illness as soon as the movie started, just to get the afternoon off. Pulling this stunt too often would get my parents wise to that trick, so I had to pick my spots.

One fine spring day, walking past a bike shop, I stopped for a peek into the window. Propped up by a kick stand was a shiny, silver CCM bike with *three* speeds, a bell and, best of all, a chain. Oh, how I wanted it! Price tag showed $30. My piggy bank held about $7 so far. A long way to go. Weather permitting, I returned to running to school, and pocketed my ticket money.

At the end of the school year, a disappointed Miss Tyner handed me my report card—I had failed. There had been frowning signs of disapproval in regard to my behaviour and effort but I had ignored it. When Dad saw my marks, he chalked it up to simply a language barrier.

A few days later, Dad and I happened to be walking past the bike shop. I stopped to gaze at the great mechanical perfection.

"I'm going to buy that bike one day," I blurted out.

"Oh, how are you going to do that? We can't afford a bike."

I had opened my big mouth and the only thing to do now was to spill the beans.

"How much money are you short?" asked Dad.

"About $15."

"I'll take care of that," he said, "Let's go and buy it right now." Instead of being chastised, I was encouraged! He approved of working and saving enough to overlook the deviousness. Great! But for some reason I had a bad aftertaste in my mind. Not until years later did I understand the underlying discomfort: I didn't want to get used to, or even expect, handouts. It meant I was weak. No, I had to make it on my own efforts.

I road that bike the entire summer.

For years Mom had been dealing with Irene sucking her thumb. The doctor had warned that it would lead to dental issues and misalignment of the vertebrae in the neck. School would soon start and Mom was running out of time.

In a last desperate attempt, she told Irene that she would dip the thumb in poop while Irene slept. Of course Mom did not carry out this threat, but it worked. Irene never sucked the thumb again.

* * * * *

On the morning of the first day of school, a new notebook and a sharpened pencil at the ready, I sat upright with fingers intertwined on the desk, ready to listen to Miss Tyner.

Ready to repeat Grade 4.

Reading and spelling were easy at first through a series of simple books with large, colourful pictures, about Dick and Jane's happy family. "This is not so hard," I thought. In time the spelling morphed from appealing to appalling. Unlike Serbo-Croatian clear and consistent phonetic spelling, the endless English rules and exceptions led to extreme frustration. "Why don't they keep it simple?" was my recurring complaint over the years.

Nevertheless, my English improved enough for me to be understood and along the way I gradually formed friendships based on the real me.

Whenever a severe storm was forecast during winter, Irene and I would watch through the window as the snow fell doggedly, hoping that school would be shut down. On such celebratory days we bundled up and struggled joyfully through knee deep, crunching-beneath-the-boots snow, past a row of snow-burdened evergreens that guarded the back of the house from chilly northern winds to an abandoned property.

We would wave and call out to Shawn, my classmate and his younger brother who eagerly waited to join us.

After clearing an area, we built two opposing snow forts. Once satisfied they could withstand any strike, Irene and I shaped snowballs for an adequate (hopefully) supply of ammunition. Shawn was as good as anyone at this, even with only three fingers on his right hand.

Once both sides were armed and ready, a fierce battle broke out. Fling. Whish. Thump. Shout. Duck. Laughter. And so it went until we ran low on ammo, a dire situation.

"You cover me while I go," I would say. Irene threw—half decently for a girl—the remaining balls judiciously for their maximum effect. Of course the other team prepared to do the same. As Shawn and I passed each other the defensive partners would scream and shout and throw a snowball to slow us down from tackling their fort. Sometimes Shawn and I would fight it out in the middle and the other two joined in. The winners were those whose fort was still recognizable. But of course, having fun was the real objective.

Just before dark, at the front door Irene and I would shake and rub off the snow, laughing and giggling. We would hurry barefooted to the basement, leaving behind a pile of damp clothes on the floor and dripping galoshes on a tray. Mom never seemed to mind.

Beside the fiercely burning furnace, our cold red hands and numb feet would soon warm up. I'm sure Irene will say to this very day, those were some of the happiest days of our lives.

On Valentine's Day, every student had cards for their classmates. One envelope for me from Patsy George also contained a tiny gold heart. Twice after school I carried her books, walking her home. *Patsy George, hmm.* To remove the stain of being a foreigner, I had selected the name George. Interesting coincidence

As a consequence of the Cold War, our class performed periodic safety drills in the event the Russians dropped nuclear bombs on North America. We crouched under our desks with hands behind our necks until it was safe to come out—presumably not too long, now that I think about it, for after a while we might start to get hungry. During the Cuban missile crisis of '63, many people became extremely fearful over the threat of real war.

Miss Tyner asked me to do a presentation for the class about life in communist Yugoslavia and about our escape. I worried about being seen as 'The Enemy' if classmates knew I came from a communist country. Relying on Miss Tyner's judgement, I put aside my worry and took the leap.

On a limited vocabulary I recounted our journey, not shying away from the word "communist." Sincere, I ended with how lucky I felt to be in this great country of opportunity and freedom.

The response was overwhelmingly positive—I was not a misfit or foreigner, but rather a welcomed Canadian.

To my chagrin, just as I felt completely comfortable and accepted, Dad decided we would be better off in Toronto. Two weeks to pack. The bike had to be sold, too big and costly to transport on a train. I had to say good-bye to Patsy, Shawn and the rest of my new friends.

"You're going to like summer in Toronto. It's long. A whole two months," said Shawn. "Don't forget to write."

The 1963 school year would have to end in a huge and crowded city.

* * * * *

Meanwhile, precisely on the same day, on the opposite side of the globe, the hand of fate was at work.

Rose Memorial Hall
Central Philippines University (CPU)
Iloilo, Philippines
March 25, 1963

A delighted young woman named Erlinda sat on a wooden chair in the company of fellow classmates. On this pleasantly dry, warm day hundreds of Filipino and foreign dignitaries were in attendance for the graduation of not only College of Nursing students, but also other faculties—Engineering, Agriculture, Arts and Sciences, and Theology. At the back of the audience, Erlinda's stepfather was watching.

While waiting for the ceremony to begin, she reflected on the rocky road it had been for her to arrive here . . .

Chinese born Antonio and his Filipina wife Aurelia longed for a child. But having no luck, they adopted a baby boy. Two years later Aurelia was pregnant, but, unfortunately, her husband died of a heart attack just as WWII broke out. Shortly thereafter Erlinda was born.

At the end of the 19th century, the United States colonized the Philippines. To promote development, they built a vital infrastructure: roads, water systems and hospitals; and established an education system using English as the primary language. Midway through WWII, Japan bombed Pearl Harbour and invaded the Philippines.

Led by her grandfather, Erlinda's relatives and other families abandoned their homes carrying clothes, food and supplies into the mountains. As members of a small community they built huts of nipa, bamboo and rattan. For about two years they lived off the land.

At the end of the war the Japanese, in retreat, burned major buildings behind them. The Americans liberated the islands, granted independence in '45 and provided desperately needed aid to rebuild the country.

With better future prospects in Iloilo, Erlinda's family moved to one of the suburbs. After the grandfather died, Aurelia married a shoe store manager, to help with the two children. Fearful of her stepfather, Erlinda clung close to her mother. On the very rare occasion Erlinda misbehaved, Aurelia admonished her with gentle persuasion.

Known as an excellent seamstress, Aurelia was able to get her teenage daughter a summer job at her work. "Erlinda will do a good job if you don't scold her," she told the boss, who demanded perfection. The pay—a rate of fifty centavos (a nickel) for three hours—went towards school supplies.

They and two other families rented a four-bedroom house, a bamboo structure on stilts that allowed air flow and avoided floodwater. During the unrelenting rainy season, the galvanized iron roof drummed incessantly. Life centred in the kitchen thanks to the wood burning stove. Throughout the house lay rattan furniture, including the bedroom shared by Erlinda, another girl, and an old lady. Covering each bed was a tightly tucked in mosquito net. From outside drifted the sounds of exotic birds, cicadas and the occasional tuko (a giant lizard). Attached, but secluded at the back of the house, sat a toilet. Nothing was lacking.

After high school, any extra money went towards her half brother's education. Seasonally, Erlinda and Aurelia worked in the back-breaking rice fields. Paid with rice.

Erlinda was eventually accepted by the very competitive Central Philippines University nursing program, but her studies were interrupted, when Aurelia suffered a stroke. She had been silently skimping on her expensive heart medication so the children could get an education. The subsequent death of her mother left a massive void in Erlinda's life.

Reluctantly she accepted help from her stepfather, managing to avoid being alone with him in the house.

During her nursing program, the classmates got to know each other well and often gave each other nicknames. After a humorous Halloween skit, Erlinda earned the name Chut.

In Erlinda's second year, a water shortage meant each student was limited to one pail of washing water per day. To make things worse, a contagious disease, struck their patients. At the commencement exercise, the director commended the 'Unforgettable Class of '63' for the outstanding effort.

"Your turn, Chut," whispered Nori.

Looking solemn, Erlinda adjusted her black cap, smoothed her toga and with head held high marched up onto the stage to receive her diploma. The steady combination of hard work, perseverance and courage culminated in the happiest day of her young life. Her only regret: Aurelia wasn't there.

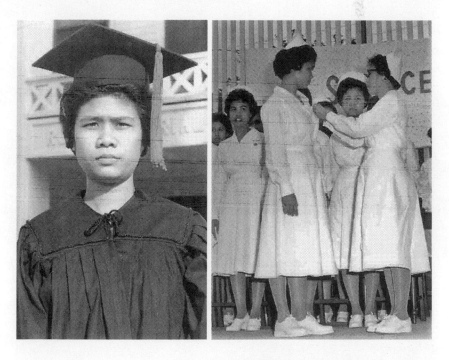

Beneath the respectful exterior, flourished a resilient and independent woman.

Her success at CPU led to acceptance as a RN at the prestigious Iloilo Mission Hospital.

What was she to do from here on out?

The safe option of getting married? Or the less predictable route— fulfill a desire to see the world?

For the latter, the best possibility lay in the Visitor Exchange Program conducted by the U.S. hospitals. Even then, two hurdles stood in the way: the unaffordable flight and a passport. Her birth certificate and other records had been burned during the war!

CHAPTER 3

AWAKENING

Toronto, Ontario
April, 1963

T oronto is centrally located in Canada, on the northern shore of Lake Ontario, a two-hour drive to the U.S. border. Although the second largest city in Canada, a population of about 800,000 (at the time), it was undergoing explosive growth: people from around the country and four corners of the globe.

Our family occupied space in a twenty-story concrete monolith where it seemed no one knew, talked to or cared about anyone else. Overpowering smells of mildew and strange food hung in the long dreary hallways.

As promised, I did write to my pen pals back in Saint John and their much-welcomed return letters kept my spirits up. A wave of nostalgia swept over me. I thought about Patsy and what could have been. Shawn came down on his own for a visit and Mom made sure he felt at home, comfortable and well fed. For two days it was happy times again.

As months passed, I wrote less and eventually stopped altogether. And so did they.

Once again a stranger, bored and boring, I slouched at the back of a class led by an elderly teacher counting her final months to retirement.

We moved again, but this time I didn't mind it, to an Italian neighbourhood in the west end. The widow landlady lived on the ground floor and we on the second. Her sons would often come for a visit and you would know it because you could hear them all talking at the same time, in Italian. *Mange,* eat, she encouraged them. Strong construction workers, they didn't need much of a push. Plus the food smelled *so* good, especially pasta in homemade spicy tomato sauce. We weren't envious as Mom could cook with the best of them.

On weekends, the sons sat on the edge of the plastic covered couch and chairs in front of a TV yelling and screaming, as did the old widow. Apparently, their wrestling hero, Bruno Samartino, needed a boost to bounce back from the eye-gouging bad guy, the Beast.

In contrast, our home was quiet, too quiet for Mom and Dad. Perhaps sensing that something was bothering us or they simply wanted us to be cultured, they sent us up the street for piano lessons from a retired opera singer.

Mrs. Horvat's house was full of fascinating objects like the aeriated aquarium replete with exotic fish. While waiting for our turns, we had permission to read any book at all in the small library. For my birthday, Mrs. Horvat gave me my favorite: *A History of Canada*, that occupies a prominent spot on my shelf even today.

However, lacking the discipline to practise, I came to dread the upcoming lessons.

One day Irene came home crying because she didn't like playing piano. Without any discussion, Dad let her drop it.

"Me too, me too!" I was shouting in my head but I had hesitated and thereby missed the glorious opportunity. Besides, I couldn't bring myself to cry and I knew that's what it would take. Reality came for a visit, however, at my recital at the Croatian Hall, where my fingers trembled in an embarrassing performance. Lucky for me, our family moved which meant Dad could let me off the hook.

On the positive side, I was treated like an adult. Take for example Dad sending me to buy his cigarettes. Perhaps he had already spoken to the shopkeeper, a Henry Kissinger looking and sounding man. Among a variety of interesting things, 'Mr. Kissinger' had a revolving stand of comic books. Superman sold for a pricey 12 cents. A white plastic tea set captured Irene's attention; we agreed to buy it before the end of summer.

It is true. Money does not grow on trees here in Canada, but in those days, you *could* find it lying around on streets and back lanes. Discarded pop bottles would fetch a nice refund of two cents per bottle. Anyone could tell I was striking it rich, just by the jingling in my pocket.

On one occasion I faced a dilemma: there were two got-to-have comics, I had enough cash for only one. Unable to decide, I sneaked one under the other, promising myself to take great care and return it in a few short days.

You don't need me to tell you, deep down I knew it was wrong. But I did it anyway.

As summer came to a close, Irene didn't have her full share of the money for the tea set. She was in no position to pull in the big dough like I was, so I covered the shortfall. When 'Mr. Kissinger' told us its true cost we must have looked rather glum. (We had read the wrong sign!) But his serious face soon melted into a smile. As his regular customers, he said, the money we had was good enough. On the way home, Irene bubbled with excitement about our purchase; my mind dwelled on the comic forgotten 'til now.

The following day I plucked up the courage to enter the store, to right my wrong. Once 'Mr. Kissinger' was distracted by the doorbell jingle of another shopper entering, I pulled out the perfectly preserved comic book from under my shirt, and returned it. If all this sounds easy, it wasn't.

By now both our parents were working, leaving minor chores for me to complete. Since St. Helen's Catholic School was a block away, Dad left it to me to run and pick up lunch at a nearby bakery: hot apple or blueberry pie or giant eclairs. Oh my, was it good!

In my class, amongst all the Italians, Poles and Ukrainians was an English kid, Mike. He lived next door. When I first saw him during the summer he looked odd, his ears were taped back. *Was that so they wouldn't stick out as he got older?* I tried not to stare. By the time school started, the tape was removed and, sure enough, his ears pointed in the desired direction.

When the teacher asked a question, Mike was first to raise a hand. Slightly overweight, he would stand, pull up his pants by the belt like a cowboy and adjust his glasses. We all thought he was smart; a big part of that image was the glasses. I wanted a pair.

In a year my wish came true, I required glasses. To be honest, it's been a lifelong curse.

One time in a conversation, Mike used a word I didn't know, "allowance." After an initial surprise at my lack of familiarity with the term, he explained it as spending money from his parents.

"What do you have to do to get it?" I asked.

"Nothing." He wasn't one to joke around so it made me wonder. *Is it possible to get money without doing a chore?* Not counting birthdays. I couldn't help feeling a stab of envy as I continued thinking about this strange concept.

Something was nagging at me . . . something missing.

Finally, an epiphany. It dawned that the satisfaction of having earned the money myself outweighed actual possession.

My envy vanished easily and completely.

Mike and I became great friends. Playing marbles in the schoolyard, we started with a bag of ten each—but after teaming up against others—soon amassed hundreds.

* * * * *

At the end of the school year, our family moved twice before settling down, at least for a while. Dad and Mom bought a house for the unthinkable sum of $10,000! Manageable because Dad worked at a hospital as an orderly and Mom on an assembly line at Roundtree making chocolates. "As a tenant you're helping the landlord get rich," said Dad. "Kiss your money good-bye."

The red brick Victorian rowhouse looked magnificent. Some might say the lot was narrow—but it was *all* ours. Including a kitchen, dining room and living room and upstairs two bedrooms with a bathroom. *Wow!* Appliances came with the house.

The only items left to buy were a few pieces of furniture and a phone, initially used by Dad.

After we settled in, Dad assisted a Croatian carpenter with a small renovation project and learned a few things. Having that experience under his belt, he worked on our recreation room with me now as his assistant, handing tools and supplies and holding things. Since Mom was often at work, I'd go upstairs frequently to check on Irene.

When the rec room was done, Dad assisted an electrician and a plumber on more difficult jobs picking up tricks of their trades. That meant I was free.

For days Irene had seen through the living room window, kids playing on the street.

"Let's see if they will let us play," she said.

A group, around our age, saw us coming and made room.

"We were wondering when you would come out," someone said. Instant acceptance and belonging.

The dead-end street was extremely safe, perfect for a popular hide-and-seek game. Very few people owned a car, so we ran with complete abandon. The day ended invariably when someone's mother shouted through a screen door, "It's getting dark."

A set of twin girls had a real, backyard treehouse accessible by a wooden ladder. Looking at it brought to mind the life of Tarzan and Jane. Club meetings were held weekly, but since there was room only for the four existing members, Irene and I couldn't join.

In our basement Mom had a washing machine with two rollers at the top of the washer that grumbled if the item was too thick. However, the clothes were hung outside, each piece clipped and pushed away on the circular line. A kind of calmness sweeps over you, seeing the clothes and sheets freely fluttering in the breeze, then smelling up close the marvelous freshness. To hang items, Mom stood on a small plywood platform supported by a couple of 2x4 posts. An idea hit me!

I gathered a few of Dad's tools and then scrounged plywood pieces and carpet remnants destined for the garbage. Mom and Irene watched me, wondering what I was up to.

"I'm building a clubhouse." I measured and cut plywood and carpet which I nailed to three sides of the structure for a soft, secure interior. A musty, muddy sheet of linoleum leaning against the back fence needed cleaning and cutting to be the flooring.

Overjoyed with the finished project, Irene and I barely managed to squeeze into the new establishment. To commence the club meeting, the first order of business necessitated a roll call, just to see who was in attendance.

* * * * *

My Grade 6 teacher was a wiry, little old lady plagued with advanced arthritis: hands, spine and legs warped and twisted like a bristlecone pine. You had to keep your distance, afraid to accidentally knock her over—in your pre-teen awkwardness—and send her to a premature meeting with St. Peter.

Many of the students were first generation Canadians from eastern and southern Europe. The girls were taller than the boys, with a couple of exceptions like myself who had grown four inches over the summer.

My wandering eyes stopped at a tall, slender blond, Margaret.

Although I was steadfast in my religious faith, Margaret, the perfect role model—surely to be canonized one day—soared in a school that vigorously promoted Catholic teachings. A chart hung prominently on the classroom wall, listing everyone's names. Any time you attended Mass a gold star was placed next to yours. If the objective was to promote competition, competition they got, however nobody admitted to it. On the surface it was about being virtuous. Masses were held often and daily, so there were no excuses. Even with a concerted effort I was in the middle of the chart, the leaders being Margaret and my rival Dennis.

Not only was Dennis favoured by God, but also by girls, although Margaret was my only concern. His popularity came because of his perfectly proportional face and angelic choir-boy voice. In complete contrast, my face and body looked like they belonged in a Picasso painting—a collage of geometric, asymmetric forms. And my voice had changed to a strange alien depth, cracking at the worst of times.

Because school was many blocks away and the traffic heavy, Dad told Irene and me to walk together. One day, she squealed to him that I didn't want to hold her hand along the way.

58

He asked why.

"Ah . . . it kinda looks funny. Um, in front of other guys."

"School is far and there's cars," as though I needed reminding. "You have only one sister." Of course he was right. Still, I didn't like it, which naturally was of no importance to Dad.

The next morning on the way to school, Margaret was in front of us. I dropped Irene's hand. Somehow she picked up on my embarrassment, grabbed my hand and wouldn't let go. A mischievous grin plastered her face.

"Who's this?" asked Margaret when she turned around.

"My sister," I said uncomfortably, my voice cracking.

"Nice of you to hold her hand."

The redness in my face faded.

On Sundays, rarely showing up on time for mass I sat more to the back of the church. In the front two pews, surrounded by older women, Margaret and Dennis knelt, bright halos floating above their heads. They were chanting what's known as ejaculations, which seemed like a poorly chosen word when I found an alternate definition in the dictionary much later.

I daydreamed often of gaining Margaret's favour: I would be Superboy flying over Toronto, employing super vision to find anyone in need of help. Margaret would be in grave danger, so I swooped down and carried her carefully in my arms to safety.

The ringing bells at the altar, snapped me back to reality. Our indispensable link to God, the venerable priest lifted and peered through the glass and gold monstrance, I suspected looking into our very minds and souls.

To conceal my jealousy, I scrunched down.

Each Friday our class went to church for confession. We entered God's house in a line of twos, talking not permitted. Every click of my shoe on the granite floor of the cavernous holy place announced my approach to the confessional. For readers not familiar, it consists of three adjacent small booths with the priest in the middle. He alternates side to side listening to us confess our sins.

In the dark cubicle, kneeling on the hardwood step, I am acutely sensitive to every sound. The other penitent is easily heard, so I quickly plug my ears—there's no point having someone's sordid confession occupying space in my already troubled mind. *Eavesdropping, even unintentionally, must be a sin.* The air is cool, but I'm sweating. The wooden window slides open startling me, confusing me, even though I have a well rehearsed confession. Thankfully, the priest leans sideways, never looking at me directly. On the off chance I meet him outside, I alter my voice, never thinking it too might be a sin. God, I'm sure, would recognize me even if I sounded like Daffy Duck and wore a Groucho Marx mask. He won't like what I've done, but hopefully accepts me as I am, warts and all.

Around that time in my life, I stumbled upon the act of, how do I say it delicately, self-pleasuring. My face and body became so contorted that I feared it might trigger a genuine heart attack or some other internal damage. *The body was not built for such stress.* However, I observed no signs of injury. In fact, if anything I felt better. *Surely nobody other than doctors knew about this form of self harassment.*

Before long I heard a couple of daring kids make indiscrete or joking references about it. Catholic teachings state (I thought), it to be a mortal sin. But, with completely frankness, I indulged in this gratification habitually. One glance at a shapely female forms, live or on paper, and I was out of control.

In the confessional, I spoke only of sinning against the 6th commandment (*Thou shalt not commit adultery*, the closest one to my offence) in thought and action, grateful I didn't need to be more explicit. Declaring the same sins every Friday, I must have sounded like a broken record. At least I didn't have impure thoughts about Saint Margaret. One time, I was pleased to confess to something different, something forgotten, but not admitted to: the theft of a comic book. Imagine! I could have missed out on eternity in heaven because of a 12-cent comic.

After being reminded about the sanctity of the human body and receiving absolution, I departed with the sincerest intentions to practice abstinence. Powerful forces, nevertheless, tormented me and won the battles despite my best efforts, so I resigned to a weekly quota.

To receive Holy Communion, I had a problem of timing. One has to be in a state of grace, meaning sin free. Sometimes between Friday's confession and receiving communion on Sunday, I succumbed to temptation. I hoped Margaret didn't notice that while everyone went up to receive the Holy Host, I stayed in my pew under a cloud of suspicion and guilt. I knew what everyone was thinking: He couldn't control himself even for *one* lousy day. Don't go near him, the disgusting pervert.

The reader has probably noticed that I am going on endlessly about the subject—the religious connection has never really left me alone.

That year I thought a lot about eventually joining the priesthood. As a missionary I could do a lot of good in far away places, like Tahiti. Upon deeper reflection, I realized celibacy would be impossible in the company of those beautiful Polynesian girls. Outstretched hands beckoning, perfect breasts cupped by coconut shells and shapely hips swaying in grass skirts. Oh my Lord! How in the world did male missionaries manage?

* * * * *

Life was good at home, at least for a while. After school, Irene and I conscientiously did our homework on the large, speckled Formica table. Our marks showed the effort. Beside us, Mom quietly practised basic arithmetic. I couldn't help being amused by her dedication. The answers checked out mostly correct, so I put an arm on her shoulder encouraging her to keep it up. How she got through nursing simply on addition and subtraction, who knows?

Saturday afternoons were reserved for watching wrestling on TV, like the Italians. There was no difficulty in figuring out who to cheer for. The good guys were Yukon Eric, Whipper Billy Watson and Sweet Daddy Seeky just to name a few.

It was of no help when fans shouted to the ref as the bad guy resorted to dirty tricks like pulling a "foreign" object from his trunks!

When the villain had the upper hand, he would strut arrogantly around the ring, chest puffed out. Jeered by booing and hissing spectators, he would jump up on the ropes and yell back in a fit.

The dropkick, a dazzling move, appeared easy enough to execute, so I asked Irene to stand still in the middle of our living room.

"No! You're going to hurt me," she said.

I promised I wouldn't be within even a foot of her.

My dropkick wasn't even remotely as flashy as the wrestler's, and to make things worse, I landed on my butt on the hard floor.

Oh, the pain! Irene laughed and laughed like it was the funniest thing ever. I tried to pretend, "It was nothing really."

* * * * *

Back in the old country people made *rakija* without a second thought. But here in Canada it's illegal. Nevertheless, Dad bought bags of grapes from a specialty store and dumped them in a large, shallow container. Glad to be of help, Irene and I washed our feet well, stepped in and stomped on the cool, mushy mixture. The process eventually led to a distilling apparatus where pure, clear *rakija* dribbled from the tap, drop by drop. Most of it was stored for Dad's and visiting friends' consumption and some proudly given away.

In slow, quiet times the three of us played cards. To hold Irene's interest Dad arranged she would win by switching cards. With a subtle wink he signalled to me to say nothing about it.

On one particular evening a heavy pounding on the front door alarmed everyone. Boom! Boom! Boom!

Dad hurried to see what was so urgent.

Burly men in dark uniforms carrying axes pushed past him heading straight to the rec room. Soon we heard smashing of the still, bottles of *rakija* and the barrel of red wine.

Frozen in our chairs, we said nothing.

As quickly as the police showed up, they vanished, taking Dad and leaving wine footprints on the grey linoleum.

Word spread throughout the neighbourhood like a virus in a retirement home as to what had happened. Although Mom, with some help from us, scrubbed away the blood-red stains, the social stigma stayed. Ashamed to play with friends we hid indoors; and lowered our heads to avoid eye contact when going to school.

During the summer, Dad took me along on a plumbing job in an old, dilapidated house. We were holed up for hours in the dark, dank basement. Once in awhile I would be called upon to find a tool or hold something. Mostly though I sat bored. My mind needed something to occupy itself, so taking a chance I posed a question, "Is there life on other worlds?" Dad would answer, "Please George, I'm trying to think."

Between his regular job and handyman projects, he was less and less at home. Mom got wind of him playing cards for money.

She was not pleased; an uneasy atmosphere settled over the household.

* * * * *

My principal had a problem: this year's crop of Grade 7 boys. But when Mr. Bona entered the office, the solution stared him in the face. An imposing figure and a strict teacher, Mr. Bona was assigned the unenviable task of keeping in line the toughest, meanest collection of boys that ever walked those hallowed halls:

Frudgy—The best fighter ever. For whatever he lacked in size, he more than made up for with speed and precision. When he leapt up like Bruce Lee and released the scissor kick, it always landed on the mark. Completely fearless.

Christoph—A muscular giant with a resemblance to Clint Walker in the *Cheyenne* western. Size alone ranked him second.

Kenival—A large, heavy-set guy. Not fast but definitely the most vicious. Notorious for the steel pointed boots.

John—An all-around good fighter with a nasty streak.

The tall thin twins were the bottom of the notable Dirty Dozen list.

The rest of the class consisted of boys (like myself) who had passed puberty but never looked for trouble. Mr. Bona was going to make sure of that. His high-speed gym classes were extremely gruelling, obviously designed to drain energy and any thoughts of misbehaviour.

Still, the well-advertised, after-school, in-the-back-lane fights were common and not short on spectators.

One Monday morning, Christoph—the gentle giant, usually friendly and talkative—slumped silently in his chair. A shiner stood out—no matter how he tried to hide it—on his dejected face. It was hard to watch someone I admired in such a state. Apparently, in an unscheduled main event, Kenival landed a sucker punch and a boot to the nuts—placing him automatically into second place in the toughness hierarchy.

There was no way Frudgy was going to let Kenival pull that stunt on him.

Shortly thereafter, the most shocking incident of the school year stunned all that witnessed it. I was there.

Classes were changing and the crowded hallway was quiet except for shuffling feet. From the end of the hall, a strained voice, like that of a dying animal, punctured the peace. It grew louder. Everyone stopped to see what was going on.

Jaws dropped.

Frudgy marched down the middle of the hallway, parting students like Moses did the Red Sea. Tears rolled down his face as he shouted, "He had no right to do that!"

At his side hung a red swollen hand. Obviously, it had been strapped by the principal for some misdeed. Frudgy must have tried to take it like a man, but he was just a thirteen-year-old boy.

The message from the principal was unmistakeable.

As unusual as the day had been, what happened next, I will surely never forget.

When Irene and I got home that day, she stayed outside to skip rope with the twins and I continued in. A commotion of chairs scraping the floor and raised voices in the kitchen. As I entered, here's what took place.

Dad and Mom, seated at the table, are in a heated argument. Never had my parents been in such an emotional clash. Neither notices me grab an apple out of the fridge and stay to listen.

With hands trembling, Mom is on the verge of shouting. She knows what Dad is up to with his expensive calls to Croatia. How could he think of sponsoring his nephews—while we don't have enough money for this month's mortgage?

"I work long hours to make the payments," he says.

"Then you go lose it on cards!" she bursts out.

Dad abruptly stands up nearly knocking the chair over, pulls back his right arm to strike Mom. By reflex she leans back, turns her head and bangs it accidentally against the wall. And begins to cry.

I dare not describe her face to you, the reader. My mind is about to explode from the unbearable pain like that of a razor blade slicing my heart.

Time and motion stand still.

So far I have remained quietly observant, but now I realize it's time to act. Immediately.

I run out, grab an item from under my bed, rush back and place it in the middle of the table. Mom's shaking hands are covering her face. Dad watches me, arm down at his side.

"There's almost $60 in there. That's all I got." I say confidently, knowing it's the right thing to do.

Then I hesitate . . . the words are going to sound rude.

"I'll need it back."

Dad slowly slides down into his chair, transfixed by the pink piggy bank.

Emotionally spent and uncomfortable by the silence, I politely turn around and join Irene outside.

About a week later I was in the school yard leaning against a wall waiting for the bell to ring. Grinning, John sauntered beside me and elbowed in the ribs. This sort of taunting I had avoided in the past by walking away, even if it made me look weak.

The Bible said to "turn and offer the other cheek," and yet Dad said to "never start a fight but never let anyone bully you either."

I was prepared to deliver a surprise right jab, a short left to the solar plexus and finish with a right uppercut. Having rehearsed this combination of punches hundreds of times—but never thinking about the consequences—my courage was firm. Today I was going to put an end to the aggression.

Tense muscles prepared to uncoil.

Unfortunately, neither he nor I were in the proper position for me to carry out the deft maneuver. I needed him to step in front, but he kept elbowing from the side.

Enough! My right leg darted behind him and swept the feet, landing him on his back.

Not wishing to be sent to the principal's office, I went indoors.

Before class started, I saw John at his desk still wincing in pain, so I went over.

"I told you not to mess with me," I said aloud, being sure everyone could hear. Then I leaned in and whispered, "Sorry."

He looked up puzzled, probably wondering if I was messing with his mind. In truth, I *was* sorry.

He appeared recovered the next day.

Word got around: under George's soft-spoken exterior hid an explosive fighter. I knew that guys who wanted to improve their standing might be tempted to challenge me. As a precaution, I made a point to be friends with all the members of the Dirty Dozen.

Late one dark stormy evening, the wind whistled through the trees and rattled my bedroom window. About to close it for the chill, I heard footsteps on the front porch. Two silhouettes halted at the door. A flash of lightening revealed unfamiliar male faces.

This was the day Mom and I had been dreading—my cousins had arrived!

She was the first to respond to the knock.

"You're not welcome here," she said breathlessly. "We have enough problems of our own."

Coming from behind Dad intervened, "Let me handle this."

She stepped back into the hallway but held her ground. After a brief verbal exchange—without further commotion—they left, never to be seen again.

Life calmed down after that. Unknown to me at first, Mom had an additional challenge: she was pregnant. As a testament to her strength, she worked almost to the last day before giving birth to a healthy baby boy. Davy was born on a brilliantly sunny day amid great rejoicing by *all* of us.

* * * * *

We were finally living the Canadian dream just five years after arriving. Dad bought a large, three-story brick house on a lot wide enough for a side driveway that went all the way to the back.

"There's room for three cars," Dad declared, even though we didn't own one. The location was within walking distance to many amenities, including a subway station. With potential for three flats upstairs, and still room for us on the first floor, this house would prove to be the best purchase he was ever going to make.

In addition to regular jobs, Mom and Dad worked almost night and day to prepare the units for renting.

My eyes bulged at all the cheques at the end of each month.

To complete the Canadian dream, we received our citizenship. No longer foreigners we could proudly say, "I am Canadian."

Like all babies, our new brother Davy needed care. Mom taught Irene to make formula, feed, burp and change a diaper, so that Mom would have time to take evening courses for sewing our clothes and English to become a nursing assistant.

I recall one afternoon when Davy was unusually quiet in the bedroom. A distinct stink indicated he was up to something. The three of us found him standing in the crib as if to say, "What are you guys looking at?" He had painted the crib an unflattering brown with you know what. While we cleaned up the crib and Davy, we couldn't stop laughing. I still smile thinking about it.

In mid mornings, Irene would put Davy in the stroller to meet Norma and her baby sister in front of our house. The girls pushed the carriages down the block—stopping to wipe drooling faces and adjust pacifiers—then turn around for home, chatting all the way.

Just as Irene looked after Davy, I had helped our parents with the work on the flats. Once finished I had free time on my hands, so I asked Mom if I could grow tomatoes in the back yard.

Provided with advice and money, the rest was left to me. I measured off the plot. The soil being of poor quality, I purchased peat moss, fertilizer, stakes and a dozen plants. Now came the fun part: tilling, planting, watering and watching them sprout perhaps too frequently. After all, how much could they grow in a day?

In time the tomatoes turned from green to pink to blushing red.

The first one I carried to the kitchen like the Hope Diamond.

"Should I eat it?" I asked.

"Yes, dear." Mom smiled.

I cut it carefully into four equal parts, dipped them in vinegar and sprinkled salt. Ready to enjoy.

"Aren't you giving some to Irene?" Mom asked. Not what I wanted to hear, after all *my* work. Besides, it was such a small tomato, not enough to feed two. My disgruntlement lay concealed.

I savoured this gift from Mother Nature, this miracle. Judging by the expression on Irene's face, she was enjoying it just as much.

On my got-to-have-it list was only one type of item: comic books about superheroes or Archie or Richie Rich. The new interest called for an injection of serious cash. So I offered my services to the tenants on the top level of the house—who were overjoyed to have their floors swept and mopped for 50 cents.

Encouraged by porn books lying invitingly on an end table, I worked feverishly to allow myself time to read. Soon I found out all the juicy parts at the end of a chapter.

When the tenants returned, the floor was clean and the books exactly as they left them.

I treasured my comic collection, reading each cover to cover, including "Letters to the editor." In the advertising section they displayed glasses that enabled you to see under clothes. Oh, who wouldn't covet that?

Sadly, the price was beyond the reach of my pay level. Besides, wouldn't girls get kinda suspicious about me wearing strange glasses with painted eyeballs that followed them no matter where they went? Without an explanation of the technology, it seemed gimmicky. But I had complete faith that—one day—science would come through for all of us woman worshippers.

Over at Towers department store, a table had on sale a pile of young teenager books. "The Mystery at Rustlers' Fort" by Troy Nesbit with a beautiful canyon (Grand Canyon) on the cover looked intriguing. I was hooked even though somewhat advanced reading for me.

On Sunday mornings, our family went to the Catholic church, Our Lady Queen of Croatia, run by the charismatic and outspoken Father Kamber. Parishioners filled the newly built church to capacity in appreciation of his local work and his views on a free and independent Croatia.

Periodically the father arranged for an afternoon picnic that featured suckling pig, mandolin music and a traditional folk dance called *kolo.*

In time, I joined the *kolo* troupe, enjoying the rehearsals and looked forward to performing across Ontario.

To my embarrassment in a very public dispute with the instructor, Dad pulled me out of the troupe in the middle of practice. Clearly, he showed no regard to how I felt about the whole matter. Was I ticked? Oh, yah!

Nevertheless, Dad did have diplomatic skills in dealing with people and because of his dedication to the Croatian cause, he became manager of the Croatian National Home (Hall.)

As his son, I got the job there working the coat check at the Saturday night dances. Great tips! Once the stragglers left, I and a partner cleaned up the tables and floor, working late into the night.

In the mean time Dad and the board of directors were in a conference room playing cards.

Drowsy and tired, I would wait for Dad in a corner.

My eyes closed. I would recall an unpleasant memory . . .

There's a thick early evening mist and a little boy emerges through the haze. Shapes take form and high above a doorway a sign reads Grabik Tavern. He enters the bar.

An acrid smell of beer permeates the air and clouds of cigarette smoke hover over the card table. All the players, cigarettes dangling from their lips, are concentrating.

Out of the shadow the boy approaches tentatively; and when the moment appears right, he opens his mouth and dares to utter, "Tata, Mama needs us home."

"In a moment." And . . .

The moment stretches without any sign of an end. His father can get irritated, so he is reluctant to speak again. "Is it time?"

At long last cards and money are put away.

I opened my eyes.

Dad and I have an unspoken understanding—Mom must never know about this part of the night.

With the hard-earned money, I bought and read the entire series of Troy Nesbit mysteries, craving more. An ad from Doubleday Book Club offered any four books from a lengthy list for only 99 cents. Wow! Could this be true? Pretending to be eighteen, I signed up.

A dictionary, two volumes encyclopedia, an atlas and two volumes *Classic Children Stories* arrived.

Soon after and in rapid succession they mailed offers for high-priced books I definitely couldn't pay for, and 'friendly' reminders I was required to buy at least one book per month for a year.

After days of worrying about it, I decided to confess in a letter. I was fourteen and therefore the contract did not apply to me; no point sending lawyers after a kid who had nothing.

Out of guilt I bought a couple of books and in time they gave up on me. The lesson learned here—read the small print, even if you need a magnifying glass.

My world was opening up with all kinds of wonderous experiences. I bought a pocket rocket radio, earbuds supplied, to study by or go to sleep with, a habit I still have. I loved having so much entertainment at my fingertips: catchy pop and rock songs that sometimes you couldn't help singing along with. Or call-in talk shows. The intelligent and open-minded Andy Barry dealt with a wide variety of current and thought-provoking subjects.

* * * * *

Once I became an adult—the older reader will understand the sensation—the years started to fly by. And yet, in my youth so much happened in a *single* year. Take Grade 8 for an example.

In English, we had the option to *write* a story—not exactly my strength then or even now but here I am before you, trying—or whatever format we wished.

A comedy skit, the germ of the concept came from a comic book, received the green light from Miss Williams. After planning it out on paper, I pitched the idea to the three smartest guys.

"Comedy? We're bookworms not comedians." They were the antithesis of the roles I asked them to play.

"*Exactly*. That's why you're perfect."

After a few rehearsals we were ready.

The scene opens with Batman and Robin in the kitchen washing dishes, aprons over improvised hero costumes, prompting a few smiles in the classroom. Hotline rings. "OK commissioner, we'll get on it right away." Our caped crusaders run through the streets of Gotham (up and down aisles) capes flying and tights stretching in all the wrong places. The classmates are laughing. At the Bank, the Joker and his goon are deep into their dastardly deeds. The four engage in hand-to-hand combat as seen in *professional* wrestling. Now the kids are laughing and cheering loudly. In the end, triumphant Batman and Robin stand over the prisoners on the floor.

"You know what this means, Robin?" asks Batman.

"That crime doesn't pay?" replies Robin. Batman raises a can of Ajax, the dish washing cleanser.

"No, that Ajax gets you out of the kitchen fast."

Lame yes, but the class and Three Wise Guys were satisfied so much that Miss Williams arranged performances for other classes as well.

An unforeseeable and unfortunate turn of events—all part of growing up—started with a public speaking contest. A two-minute speech on a topic of our choice. At first blush, it seemed like an *easy* way of getting extra marks. Right?

The most eloquent oration was delivered by the most talented student in the entire school, Meryl.

My strength and only sensible choice for a topic, 'Arithmetic: rote learning versus logic' sounded affected but I didn't care.

I attempted the tone and rhythm of the highly-respected newscaster Walter Cronkite. A reasonable fit for my voice and speaking pattern. The long pauses may have appeared deliberate for effect, but, in truth, I was having difficulty filling in two minutes.

To my utter dismay, Miss Williams declared me as the winner. Up to this day I say Meryl was robbed of the award.

Reluctantly I advanced to the next level of competition.

But that wasn't the last time Meryl and my path would cross.

I went to the regionals on my own, which suited me fine, the aim being to get in and out as fast as possible. The presentation went as before although it had started to feel stale.

Instead of announcing the results the organizers sequestered us in a room for part two?! Nobody had warned about part two.

We were required to write a speech on a *given* topic and deliver it *without* notes. Impossible! My brain was not capable of doing that on such short notice. While others wrote, I squirmed and schemed to escape.

A guard stood outside the door. I was trapped.

Five minutes remained. While my heart pounded I scribbled a couple sentences.

I vaguely recall standing in the middle of the stage, two girls in the front row smirking even before I got started. Unable to ignore the sweat beads, I wiped my forehead. The girls laughed.

Half way through the second sentence they were twisting and turning in laughter.

An adult did shush them but my mind went blank anyway.

Silence. Waiting.

I bowed mechanically to indicate I was done, walked off the stage and through the front doors. *This* time, even Zeus and all the other gods on Mount Olympus could not stop me.

Weeks later a package showed up in the mail. An astronomy book given for participation. I opened it gingerly and proceeded to read it cover to cover.

* * * * *

At the front of my class sat a little guy, Don. Girls saw him as cute, teachers found him polite and the guys thought him an entertaining prankster. He and I had been paired up for a science assignment, so we agreed to work at my house. The dining table provided ample space for all our books and papers.

Periodically, the silence was broken by a discussion about one point or another.

Deep in concentration, I sniffed a strange, unpleasant odor.

"You smell something?" I asked.

"Ahhh, nope."

Few minutes later it was worse.

"You *sure* you don't smell it?"

"Nope." He snickered trying to cover his face.

"Hey, you farted," I shouted. "In *my* house." He burst out into full blown laughter.

I reached over to punch his arm. He ducked and started running around the table, laughing hysterically, me in pursuit pretending to be angry.

Soon as he promised not to do it again, we settled back to work.

Every once in a while, he would start with that infectious chuckle and I would join in, until laughing so uncontrollably, we fell off the chairs and unto the floor. It was ridiculously funny.

One fine spring day, I was listening to the Three Wise Guys while nearby Don was joking with Annette and Dragica.

Ken, a cool-looking, tough guy came from behind and slapped Don over the head and told him to get lost.

Don stumbled over to me, eyes red.

I told him to stay there; walked over to Ken now having a grand time flirting with the girls.

"Could I talk to you?" I said. "Alone."

Surprised, he hesitated and then with a smirk, "OK, why not."

So nobody could hear, I leaned forward inches from his face.

"If you ever touch him again, I'll make you regret it."

For weeks a muscular Black bodybuilder from Guyana had been coaching me with weightlifting at the community centre. Let's say, I was confident.

"He's just a little twerp," he shot back.

"Just remember what I said," I replied. His shrug of the shoulder implied, "Whatever."

Having reached an understanding, I casually walked back to Don.

"What did you say to him?"

"Not much. I doubt he'll bother you again though."

1967, and Canada was celebrating its Centennial; the enthusiasm for making the track team was high. I lined up at the first 800-yard trial race. Watching and giggling at the side were Annette and Dragica.

Right from the get-go Tony, a tall slender Italian, and I were leading.

A hundred yards remaining, I took off for the finish line.

To my joy, Annette and Dragica were jumping up and down cheering for me and then gushing with compliments.

"We never knew you could run like that!" said Annette.

A week later the same participants were eager to start the final and most important trial race. The girls already in high gear cheering for me.

Same as before, in the last hundred yards I picked up the tempo. *This* time Tony not only kept up with me but won convincingly. I had been duped.

The girls disappeared.

The next day, Annette, for whom I had a secret crush, was flirting with Ken.

Dragica, I suspected had a secret crush on *me*, went out of her way to tell me I did my best and looked strong. I smiled in thanks. We remained good friends for the rest of the school term.

When summer break started, Don introduced me to his next-door friend, Nick, a stamp collector. His impressive album held stamps from around the world dating back to the 1850's, many in mint condition.

Quite earnest to get started, I asked him for suggestions. Among other basics, he explained how to make a purchase at a shop. If the dealer claims it's a mint, examine it carefully anyway.

In addition to a standard album I bought several packages of stamps. Invariably, some were duplicates which I offered to Nick as trade material.

Next time I met him he was furious.

"You cheated me," he shouted. "You gave me a ripped stamp."

He was correct—I knowingly traded a ripped stamp.

"It's . . . it's up to you to check," I stuttered.

"Yes, against dealers. *Not* against friends!"

"OK, you can have yours back." That's all I could think of.

"No, I don't want it." And he stomped away.

The reader should not even for moment consider accepting my feeble excuse. No two ways about it: It was pure greed.

I can't tell you how much I regretted my deceit. To date this was my greatest sin. Of course there will be more. Other than Saint Margaret and the priests, I was the most virtuous person I knew. And yet Nick, an ordinary *agnostic,* was the better human being. Which one of us deserves heaven more? I ask you.

When Nick comes to the Pearly Gates, I'd like to be around to defend him. And if he's *not* allowed entry, then there's no such thing as justice in this universe.

There were things I could learn from him but would he ever forgive me? Keep me as a friend?

While I struggled with this issue, Erlinda was doing just fine . . .

University of Texas, Medical Branch
Galveston, Texas
May 17, 1967

In an affidavit, a CPU professor had vouched for Erlinda's birth in the Philippines and a lawyer notarized it, so she got a passport. One problem down and one to go.

After she searched around, her stepfather's employer lent the funds for the flight to Galveston.

Even though the U.S. hospital welcomed her, she still felt compelled to prove her worthiness. The training and experience back home had prepared her for many challenges, including assimilation into the new working environment.

Navigating through western culture was not always clear cut.

On buses, she didn't know at first where to sit—Blacks at the back and Whites the front—luckily both accepted her.

The washrooms were segregated also but the decision was easy: the whites' washrooms were better maintained.

As for parties and special occasions hosted by the White staff she was always cordially invited.

One line she refused to cross: foul language, unheard of at school.

Overall, life had been pretty good: delicious food, great pay and a well-appointed dorm, walkable from the hospital.

Now at the end of the two-year contract, Erlinda followed a classmate to Toronto where a furnished apartment awaited. As did a job at Wellesley General Hospital.

And the next chapter of her life.

CHAPTER 4

FRIENDS, FUN AND FEMALES

Toronto, Ontario
July, 1967

F inally we could afford a few family outings, like picnics at
Centre Island, although half the time Dad was on another
handyman job. He brought me along once, but seeing me bored he
gave up on that idea.

When Don moved away, I was at a loss until Nick invited me to
meet his friends. At a nearby park we played an unfamiliar game
called touch football with an oddly shaped ball, not round like in
nogomet, but pointed at two ends like a cat's eye. Unlike soccer,
you were *required* to carry the ball. I didn't catch well, but if I
managed to avoid fumbling it, my leg speed assured a touchdown.
Nick could do everything: throw, catch and deke—quite remarkable considering he was born premature, ill and weak. Apparently
his first six months had been a period of great worry for his mother,
who focussed exclusively on his health. In time, he was playing
physical games with other kids even though he was thin and undersized.

A smaller group of us played canasta on Nick's front porch. He
didn't care for going to someone else's house, which nobody
minded because he was a great organizer and host. More often than
not he won which Ed attributed to luck, even though everyone
knew full well his marvelous mind created that luck. In Diplomacy

you could make side agreements with opponents, but if you double crossed him, he made you think twice about it next time.

Nobody liked losing, especially Ed, so it got quite competitive between the two of them. A prolific reader, Ed had a broad range of knowledge which I truly admired. According to family lore, he was a descendant of a Belorussian count. After that I thought of him as the Baron.

Nick's neighbour, Doris, came over to watch the card games perhaps hoping to join in but beyond a "Hi" she was pretty much ignored. No point letting a girl disrupt the relaxed and natural chemistry of the group. Foul language wasn't the issue; rather, it was about feeling self-conscious. With everyone absorbed in trying to win, you could burp, hiccup, sneeze or cough and it would go unnoticed. If you farted, the strong western winds would take care of your problem. Even on a still day, everyone almost subconsciously held their breath, until the air quality index read *low risk.* You could even scratch your butt or adjust your balls, without anyone so much as blinking.

When not engrossed by cards, we turned to analysis of last night's hockey games. My introduction to the sport took place a few months earlier. In the middle of turning channels, I stopped to watch Toronto's captain George Armstrong score the winning goal to clinch the Stanley Cup. Over fifty years have passed and the diehard fans have not seen the Leaf heroes hoist another cup.

As passionate '*experts*' we knew all the players by appearance, style of play and statistics. The Baron would make fun of the Toronto goalie's trademark move: slide down like a seal even before the puck was shot. Inevitably this led to visual gags, hilarious jokes and silly puns.

Nick's mom, Mrs. Navralatova, a super nice lady, welcomed everyone into their home and kitchen. Heaping bowls of munchies and ice-cold pop were there for the taking. One guy, Stan the Hungry Man, showed no inhibition going to the kitchen eating anything he could get his sticky fingers on. To charge up the mood, the Baron teased how Stan's parents never fed him; How someone should accompany him to the kitchen to keep an eye out; Or just put a lock on the fridge. This always led to uproarious laughter and more jokes. Stan was a good sport about it all, clearly enjoying the notoriety.

When I first met Mrs. Navralatova, her pleasant Serbo-Croatian voice, just like Mom's, was music to my ears. At some point I gathered she was Serbian and Mr. Navralatova Russian. But I placed no negative consequence on that matter, as this family was very much like mine, always warm and welcoming.

She often invited Irene over, and the two thoroughly enjoyed each other's company. Perhaps she was hoping to match up Nick and Irene who eventually did become close confidants.

One conversation that still sticks in my mind was with Nick's older sister Svetlana (a couple years later). I had been sitting on their porch step waiting for Nick when she came out and sat next to me.

"Can I get your opinion about something?" she asked.

What?! A mature and confident woman, in fact a beauty pageant winner, seeking *my* advice!

Lifting my shoulders, "Sure," I said enthusiastically.

She proceeded to describe two suitors pursuing her for a serious relationship, possibly marriage. Which should she pick?

Knowing this was a life altering decision, I thought long and hard before speaking. Essentially, one guy was exciting and extremely handsome; the other a nice, caring guy who shared many of her interests.

"Go for the nice, caring one."

"Why?"

"Looks will not last. A caring guy could make you happy for the rest of your life," I said.

"Interesting," she replied.

* * * * *

At the time my high school was built in the '20s, an auditorium and gymnasium were considered a *frill*. How times have change. The very first principal, a veteran major of WWII, enforced a military style of behaviour: when he entered a room all students were to stand up straight, chins high. At a doorway, a student was expected to hold the door open for the teacher to go first.

The current principal, cut from the same cloth, imposed the following rules:

1) No jeans. For 'ladies' (girls) no pants or miniskirts. Bras were required.
2) 'Gentlemen' (boys) were not permitted facial or long hair.
3) No discussion of religion and politics.
4) No holding hands.
5) Only chairs could be sat on.
6) No skipping classes, including spares.
7) Nearby poolhall and restaurant were off limits during lunch. (Staff watched for violators.)

Breaking any of these rules lead to a detention or even a suspension. Over four decades not much had changed. By the end of my high school years, not only were these rules broken on a consistent basis, but also, incredible as it sounds, in a few cases actually encouraged. So revolutionary were the '60s.

I entered the school through a side door, use of main entrance being forbidden. Not that long ago, gentlemen and ladies left by separate exits; for what reason, your guess is as good as mine.

The main foyer, ghostly quiet an hour before, was bustling with whispered excitement. Pictures on the walls trumpeted proudly the many successful teams, especially the numerous football champions. What would be the contributions of the current student body to that legacy?

Occupying the vast territory of my mind was not sports however, but rather, girls! Each one had something of interest: a face full of exciting personality, breasts that popped out at you, shapely hips that protected the sacred zone and, my favourite, legs with curved calves in fishnet stockings exposed beautifully by miniskirts. Oh, so sexy! This is why I had been aching to go to high school.

These girls, although physically nubile, were not yet emotional adults and the boys even less so, we just didn't know it.

Along the hallway lockers stood like sentries guarding our valuable *stuff*. I searched past the science lab set up with beakers and Bunsen burners and the geography room with a world map and giant globe—each promising many wonderful things to learn—to finally find my home room.

After 'teaching' math for decades, Mr. Jackson wasn't particularly interested in what you were doing or how you were doing it. To him, a lesson entailed him directing us to read a chapter, us doing the exercises, and then a review. Jerry Wong the genius dispensed the answers. Since Mr. Jackson was perpetually busy at his desk, questions were discouraged, disregarded or passed to Jerry for the very 'obvious' answer, with some of us still staring blankly. Have you ever had one of those teachers?

I didn't need Mr. Jackson or Jerry, for me solving a mathematical problem was pure joy, like unravelling an intriguing mystery. The mathematical process, always clean and logical, resulted in an unequivocal answer; unlike the essay writing process which seemed always open to interpretation.

I grew fond of music, playing the flute and practised frequently.

Weekends were largely reserved for getting together with Nick and the gang or a family outing

To help Mom, Irene continued looking after Davy. In his bottle she combined milk and crushed Arrow cookies; warmed the mixture to just right temperature in a sink of hot water. And when a diaper was soiled, she put on a fresh, reusable-cloth diaper. For a change of scenery, she took him to the park and eventually let him enjoy the slide and swing.

"He's *my* responsibility," I recall her saying.

After school I rushed through homework so Irene and I could watch TV. We liked: comedy, *Get Smart;* adventure, *Lost in Space;* western, *Bonanza;* family, *Leave it to Beaver* and on and on. The problem was that after the excitement I found it difficult to sleep, so I resorted to my sedative, listening to radio talk shows. To make things worse, I woke up the next morning groggy and uninspired.

And yet, the allure of TV was simply impossible to resist.

Late one night after everyone was asleep, I sneaked back to watch a movie. To hear the reduced audio—I got up very close to the screen. Then, unable to sleep, I tossed and turned even with the reliable sedative. The entire next day I felt nauseous and unsettled—my brain drifted in fog.

Dad had said that too much television, the boob tube as it was called, wasn't good for you. You're vegetating, he meant. It sure seemed that way, so to keep mentally sharp I took to reading even more. With the help of a librarian I discovered the small science fiction section. In two months I'd gone through the best books. I wasn't a fast reader, but I couldn't get enough of the genre. And the best part: the books were free!

One day while waiting for music class to start, I was hiding behind a music stand. Mr. Kruger who didn't tolerate nonsense, called me out in front of everyone.

"George, what *are* you doing?"

Raising my head and a book, I felt uncomfortable as the centre of attention.

"Reading sir."

"What?"

"Science fiction," I said, glad it wasn't porn.

The baton tap, tap, tapped the lectern. He was thinking. It seemed like an unusually long time to wait for punishment.

"See me Monday after school," he said finally.

Concerned about what punishment would be administered, I made sure to show up just as the last class emptied.

He looked up from a score sheet with amusement and reached for the bulging plastic bag at his feet.

"Here."

Confused, I took it with both hands and peeked inside: over a dozen paperbacks. I couldn't believe it.

"They're yours. You obviously like sci-fi," he said.

"Yes sir. Thank you, sir," I said enthusiastically.

"Enjoy them, like I did."

Nick and the Baron still attended primary school, so even though I was friendly, I was friendless except for an Italian girl, Filomena.

Her desk was directly in front so we talked easily and pleasantly every day before class. I took for granted her friendliness, having a secret crush on another girl. Sometimes Filomena's voice faltered and face flushed, I speculated, either from a period or an unmentioned illness.

On the last day of school, I got home eager to read classmates' entries in the school yearbook. On the final page, in the middle of a giant red heart it read:

I hope I never say "Good bye"
To this nice, handsome guy
For he is tall and he is cute
But most of all he plays flute
Best of luck in future years.
    Love Filomena
(Don't forget me — please. Whenever you get sad and lonely read this. It will make you feel better. OK?)

How could I have been blind to the emotions of someone who was literally in front of my nose and played flute beside me in the band? Next September I looked for her, but she had disappeared without a trace.

* * * * *

The decade ended on some sad notes: the Beatles were splitting; Martin Luther King Jr. and Robert F. Kennedy were assassinated. On the happier side, people lined up for blocks at movie theatres to catch the epic sci-fi *2001: A Space Odyssey*. When fiction turned to reality with the 1969 landing on the moon, I dreamt about one day being an astronaut at NASA.

During the 'Summer of Love' in San Francisco, hippies decided to 'drop out' of society to enjoy rock 'n' roll, drugs and sex. They represented, for the better or the worse, an idealistic generation that rejected established middle-class values and a needless Vietnam war. The free expression of love and the altered state of consciousness—through the use of psychedelic drugs—was already spreading across Toronto's Yorkville area and Rochdale College to the doorsteps of many high schools.

The day after school ended, Dad came home excitedly waving papers in his hand: an "Offer to Purchase." He needed Mom to sign immediately. Other than telling us it was a butcher shop in a great location, he was short on details. There wasn't much time. I couldn't imagine any reason to uproot—from a profitable rental house— to an unfamiliar and unproven business.

Chaos prevailed for three weeks while we lived at an apartment. The sale and purchase dates didn't match, a bad omen of our future.

Once we did take occupancy, the truth became painfully evident. Granted, the high traffic arterial street next to a subway station spelled an excellent location for a business. Not a home. Presumably Dad picked it up for a good price, however, we couldn't ignore all the work the place needed.

Decades of forgotten junk had to be collected for curbside pickup, enough to make a garbageman curse. Mom scrubbed from top to bottom, Dad and I painted rooms a neutral beige and Irene cared for Davy. All hands on deck for this ordeal!

Luckily the top floor was rented to ideal tenants, two quiet girls. The second floor was ours and crowded, with Irene sleeping in the living room. On the ground floor Dad created a bachelor apartment, renting it to a guy of questionable character.

The centrepiece and main reason for the purchase of the semi-attached building was the delicatessen, a depressing place. If you're getting the impression I disliked it, you're not too far off the mark. Nothing could change the fact the freezer, counter and peripheral equipment were on their last legs. The showcase's fluorescent lights flickered an unflattering greenish tinge over the meat. Apparently, the cost of new equipment had been overlooked.

What deli meats we were to sell was unclear. The limited supply of beef, pork and poultry was Grade B, delivered unreliably by an underground supplier. Except for the few smoked-sausage customers, one look at the product line and they never returned.

The shop was manned four hours per day by Dad, Mom filling in on occasion. Don't forget, they still held regular jobs. When my suggestions on how to improve the business were ignored, I lost all interest in helping and made myself unavailable. Dad complained often that I wasn't around, then his complaints shifted to anger and finally he gave up—I had abandoned him.

It was going to take *two* years before he faced the fact the business was a dismal failure.

The bachelor on the ground floor, at first late with rent and then not paying at all, was salt in the wound.

Late one evening I heard a clanging downstairs. Concealed by darkness, Dad and a stranger were carrying a metal drum to the basement. A queasy feeling dropped to the pit of my stomach when I saw the coil of copper tubing. *Surely this is not happening again. Why?!*

A few days later he called me to that dirty, musty basement to reveal his latest creation, another fully operating still. I could hear in my mind the police insistently pounding on the door.

With a glass in hand, he closed one eye, took a sample sip and said, "Ahh, that's good."

"You want to try a little?" he said. I was going to say no, but I noticed he was trying to cover an amused smirk.

Is this some kind of test? Well, if he's offering then I am permitted to say yes.

"Sure." Without further thought I knocked it down. For a couple minutes, I coughed like an old coalminer. While Dad gleefully laughed clearly enjoying the show, I suffered burning agony.

"I'll have some more," I said as soon as I could spit the words out. He raised an eyebrow, hesitated, but gave in.

After the third shot, my head spinning beyond control, I dragged myself wordlessly upstairs to puke, lie down and die.

After that nonsense, I wanted nothing to do with Slivovitz anymore.

"Hey George, we're going to shoot pool. Wanna come along?" asked Tony, a classmate.

"Nah, school rules say we can't."

"Relax man, they can't touch us after four."

The billiard hall across the street from the school was surprisingly cheerful and smoke free. With the place being empty, the Italian owner offered a discounted rate of a quarter per game. Very reasonable when split.

Swearing punctuated the lively banter. I refrained, it wasn't me. But I threw in prepared lines like "That's a bunch of Bolshevik" and they laughed. I was accepted.

To my surprise, as the loser I had to pay the full quarter, not half. *This is gambling.* That queasy feeling returned to my stomach. Sensing I was uncomfortable, Tony asked me what song I wanted from the jukebox, his treat.

"Delilah," I said without thought.

"You're shitting me. That's your parent's crap."

To redeem myself, "Kidding. Anything by the Stones or Dylan." Their kind of music.

I can tell you, we played a heck of a lot of billiards after school in that hall.

Then after supper I would rush through homework, looking forward to the new season of fall TV shows. Irene and I would sit like bumps on the proverbial log the whole evening.

A pattern of half-hearted efforts and even late submissions crept into my essays and assignments. For midterm exams, I crammed late into the night. The next morning I would wake up early for a quick review.

During the first exam, most of the words on my palm were fading from nervous sweat of getting caught cheating. I looked around. Almost everybody in the exam room was busy writing.

At the next table Caesar, totally relaxed, looked over and opened his jacket to reveal on the inside a full summary sheet. *Gutsy.*

Another exam, an essay, was easier: we were given the question days in advance to prepare. My forearm did not sweat, but I still struggled just to get started. I was distracted by the fact Caesar was sitting there, not *really* writing. Halfway through, he exchanged the exam's blank booklet with his, the essay already written on it. *What audacity!*

Dad sat in the living room reading a Croatian newspaper, another strong supporter of Croatian independence. *I might as well get it over with.* Showing no emotion, I handed him my report card. The usual average of 70% had dropped significantly. If not for the solid math and music mark, it would have been worse.

"What happened?" he asked.

"I don't know," my head hanging in shame.

Of course I knew. Watching TV and playing billiards happened.

"Want to shoot some pool?" asked Tony.

"Can't. Got an assignment to finish,"

"Up to you man." He shrugged as to say, "Whatever."

In search of friends with values and goals similar to mine, I mixed in with a bunch of jocks and mostly straight-A students. We went to Friday night dances, house parties and church organized weekends.

Along the way I became best of friends with Willy, a gymnast. I enjoyed watching gymnastic competition during Olympic TV coverage. Thanks to Willy, I was now trying out gym equipment.

* * * * *

On the basis of Mom's outstanding reputation as a nursing assistant, Toronto General, the second largest hospital in Canada, gave me a summer job. After a week-long student training, we replaced the vacationing orderlies on various wards: Emergency to Urology to Psychiatry. At the age of 17 (I claimed to be a year older) I was exposed to situations meant for adults. We had been warned to avoid hooking up emotionally with patients. "Be courteous and professional," they said. But it's impossible not to feel empathy for some people. One small act of kindness could have a huge impact on an ill person and their family.

To cope, I had to adapt to staff, patients, relatives and circumstances with a boatload of positive energy. *That's* why they hired summer students.

Among all the many people and situations at TGH the following still stands out. In the intensive care unit a woman, let's call her Mrs. Wilson was struggling, change that to, *not* struggling for her life. According to her chart, she had attempted to end it by consuming a significant quantity of mercury. The next 48 hours were critical to her survival.

My role was to assist the nurse in turning her bony, comatose body every two hours to prevent bed sores. The poison had turned her skin dark and wrinkled.

I emptied the urine bag at the side of the bed, waiting for the nurse to leave before I spoke, on the off-chance Mrs. Wilson could hear. Someone once had said, coma victims could still hear.

"Ah . . . whatever pushed you to do this," I paused, "must have been very difficult to bear." *What should I say next?*

I looked at her lifeless face. The nurse had mentioned she had three children under the age of six.

"You *can* overcome this burden for one very good reason." *Is this a waste of time? Maybe not.* "Your children do and will need you to grow up."

The following night as we turned her, right there in front of the startled nurse, Mrs. Wilson opened her blue eyes and slowly, very slowly slipped an arm around my neck. And whispered, "Thank you."

Two days later, she was sitting up and eating, while we chatted like best of friends about her family. The next day the bed was empty.

I spent five summers at TGH before someone realized I no longer qualified as a student. Along the way, I gained valuable experiences and put the hard-earned money directly into a TD savings account for my future.

I assure you the following did take place, although the dialogue is not necessarily verbatim. I was scared sh . . . spitless. Nevertheless, it is faithful to the general sentiment.

Dad came home excited after working the graveyard shift at Riverdale hospital.

"Guess what you're going to do today?" he said, dangling a set of keys in front of my face and pointing to the neighbour's jalopy parked outside.

"Drive a car?!"

"If you're old enough to work, you're old enough to drive." I was about to remind him I was 17.

"It's an automatic. On Sunday morning, a piece of cake, right?" He assured me.

"I've never driven a car," I said, still leery.

"You did at the Exhibition."

"That was a bumper car. I was *trying* to hit other cars."

"I'll teach you. My nerves are bad, otherwise I would drive it myself."

"Ah, aren't you suppose to have a licence?"

"I got one for a motorcycle in Germany."

"But—"

"If police ask for it, we can drive back and I'll find it somewhere."

After he showed me the brake and gas pedal and said, "That's all there's to it," I shifted to drive, white fingers choking the wheel. The car didn't budge.

"Give it more gas, George." Reluctantly it eased out groaning, uncomfortable as I was.

"We'll go around the block. Right turns."

At the first intersection, while turning, I watched extra closely for vehicles, "Did we just go through a stop sign?" I asked.

"It's not really against the law if police don't see you."

I was relieved to be back on a side street. "It's good to look in your mirror." He pointed at the rear-view. A pale face with wide open eyes stared at me. "I just see myself."

"I'll fix it." He grabbed the mirror but it disconnected and fell into his lap. "That's OK, we don't need it. It's only if you don't have a side mirror. We got two of those." When I looked up, a car was coming straight at us, scaring the bejesus out of me. Reflexively I pulled us back into our lane. The other driver honked loudly, so Dad glared and yelled back, "*ajde krvagu,* go to hell." I feared we would get there first.

Now that we were safely pulling into our parking spot, I detected a burning odour. "What's this stick for?" I asked looking around.

"Oh, *that*. It's the emergency brake." He paused. "I guess we should have released it."

* * * * *

For the last year of high school, I was determined not to waste any more time, having dawdled the previous years sitting on the sidelines.

"Who is this guy?" said someone jokingly as I entered the homeroom class. Over the summer my appearance had changed: German helmet shape afro, goatee, granny glasses, tight multicoloured flared pants, tie-dyed T-shirt and a golden-brown tan. Influenced by the prevailing fashions of the day, I had shed the conservative image for good.

At first opportunity I swung by the guidance office to review career options. My strengths were well suited for computer programming; with annual salaries starting at $6,000, what was there not to like? I decided to register for an evening computer course at another school, none offered at mine.

I did try a few new sports but with little or no success. In the first football practice, a human tank tackled me, sending me to the showers. Game over.

Tough early morning swim practices proved to be more productive. Even though Willy and I finished last in a meet, we received a few points just for participating, enough to bring the school into first place by a nose.

A friendly rivalry grew between us, like who could do more push ups in a minute. He annihilated my sixty by completing a staggering one hundred! Competition brought out the best in me. If I came in second that was fine, there would be another time.

Mr. Stewart, our history and philosophy teacher, left an indelible impression on many students. Every morning, wearing a black leather jacket, he rode in on a motorcycle, kicked down the side stand and removed the white helmet, the wind blowing his long hair and beard. Rumour had it that he clashed with the principal for his liberal views on education.

But the students came to his classes—taught from the top of a five-foot filing cabinet. His spirited and rational debates involved listening to all sides of an issue, and questioning traditional conventions and authorities with healthy skepticism.

I extended Mr. Stewart's approach to my views on the church and its teachings which over the last few years had seemed less infallible. Should I muddle along and let life happen to me with the understanding God or fate was directing the course of events? No. Gifted with free will, I had the right or rather, the *obligation* to control and create my future. I knew I wouldn't be happy simply existing, filling in time until the inevitable end.

My locker was next to Earl who sold grass, hash and who knows what else. Tony and Gary, glassy eyed and tip of their noses red, were making a familiar exchange when I arrived.

"Hey man, you want something for your brain?" asked Earl.

"Nah, I'm too much into chess now," I said.

"I know you're straight, but if you ever need anything, I'm here for you."

One class in the afternoon was a 'spare' held in the cafeteria, so to free up my evening I did homework. Nearby, sadly, were my former friends Tony and Gary sprawled on their desks sleeping the whole time.

My introduction to chess had been when Dad had brought me along on weekends to High Park to watch him play. With my interest piqued, we played at home, me losing until I joined the school chess club and read chess books. Once I started winning *his* interest waned.

Immediately after regular classes, I hustled upstairs to the crowded chess club, Mr. Stewart presiding. Nick, now six feet tall and the president, was forming an official team of four to represent our school in a Toronto league.

At Board One, reserved for the best player, he placed Dion, the 'flower child' who often brought a flower for any girl he happened to see. Caesar, as the next best player was Board Two. Nick and myself made Boards Three and Four.

"Let's do it differently this year," said Caesar. "We should move Biondic to top board to be the sacrificial pawn, so the rest of us play weaker opponents.

"Hey, why am I a pawn?" I said jokingly. "Why not a bishop or even a rook (stronger pieces.)"

"You want to be a queen?"

"No, but…"

"Trust me, you're no rook." We all laughed.

"I can dig it. Count me in," said Dion, holding a carnation and looking around for the nearest girl.

"Right on! What do you say, Biondic?" asked Caesar. I was undecided.

Over Nick's objection the scheme was adopted.

In league competition, I lost all my games, Nick won all his and the other two won most of the time. By Christmas we were in first place. Although the league eventually folded, chess took root and flourished in Mr. Stewart's room. In the background Cat Stevens sang on the record player so much that we knew all the words to *Tea for the Tillerman.*

There's nothing of interest to relate about my chess experiences for I was a very average player. However, I do recall one day tournament in a cavernous hall, with perhaps a hundred high schoolers participating. Nick, Dion, Caesar and I were checking a large board to see who were we matched up against.

"You are gonna get your ass kicked, Biondic," said Caesar over my shoulder. The name Steven Hunter, intimidated many players. *Calm down,* I told myself. *You're the underdog, so do what you can.*

Previously, Steven had beaten me soundly in league play when his powerful team came to our school. Products of blue-collar versus products of white collar. You could tell what socioeconomic status they enjoyed by how they dressed and behaved. In post game analysis among themselves they had commented loudly about our play. "That was a redic (for ridiculous) move," with emphasis on the last syllable. Their exchange was peppered with redic. Obviously, it was their way of psyching us out, as we were battling them for league's first place.

In the washroom, I splashed cold water on my face and armpits.

When I sat down, Steven showed no recognition or concern of me, after all, *he* was Toronto's Junior Champion. His fine flaxen hair lay almost invisible on a giant head barely supported by an undersized body, as though all its energy went to creating his genius brain.

He advanced a pawn to K4 with a loud *bang*; and noticed the wet underarms. My hand trembled with a responding move.

By our 10th moves, he had commanding control of a congested centre, my forces very much hemmed in a defensive posture.

To win I had only one prayer, a 'Hail Mary pass' into the end zone. I slid a bishop and hopped a knight down the left flank toward a supposedly well guarded king. With absolute confidence Steven captured two central pawns, leaving my defense looking like a smile missing two upper front teeth.

At this juncture, a checkmate via four less-than-obvious moves seemed unstoppable. In my favour. He didn't appear concerned. Perhaps he assumed I didn't have the smarts for it.

Did I miss something?

By the time Steven realized what was about to happen, his pale face reddened; with a forearm he swiped the board clean, shattering the hall's sacred silence. And stomped away.

The director came over, "What happened?"

"I guess he didn't like my last move," I said, signing the move sheet.

In ten games Steven lost only in the final game against the overall winner and against myself.

The guys came over to pat me on the back and congratulate me. "You fixed his wagon good," Nick used one of his favourite expressions.

"I was wrong," said Caesar. "You're not a pawn, you're a bishop."

That day I felt like a king.

One afternoon at the Chess Club, my mind preoccupied by a hopeless struggle in a game against Nick, I looked up.

There she stood, a tropical island princess: shiny, black hair, perfect brown skin and a shapely body in a pink dress.

"What's your name?" I couldn't resist.

"Angel," she said amused. *Is she pulling my leg?* "Really," she added.

We ended up necking in front of her locker and completely ignoring the whistlers.

My status skyrocketed to a category reserved for football stars. This came as a genuine surprise to me, but I'm not going to pretend here that I didn't feel like something of a big shot.

When I invited her over, both my parents were cordial enough.

I took her to my room to show her the book collection, and closed the door. We sat on the bed to make out, but the sound of bedsprings must have triggered alarm bells.

Mom walked down the hallway, past the bedroom. Then it was Dad's turn.

Not exactly coitus interruptus, but it did put a damper on the situation.

Disappointed, I walked her home, prematurely.

A single sentence was what I got from Dad in the aftermath: "Where there are two, there can be three."

One day, Willy alerted me to Angel flirting with the guys operating the sound and lighting system above the auditorium.

She denied it was anything serious and pleaded I not get upset. But I was gone.

From the time I woke up, I was rehearsing my lines as I had been for days. Fifteen minutes remained until showtime when I left home. I entered the auditorium's back stage, just as the 'five minutes' call was announced.

"Phew, we were worried you wouldn't show up," said the play's director. I put on a navy-blue cloak, closed my eyes and focussed on slow, deep breaths.

On queue, I stepped onto the well-lit stage as Shakespeare's Macbeth.

At one point in the performance I sat next to Lady Macbeth—played by Meryl, still the smartest female student in the school. She had represented us on *Reach for the Top,* TV quiz show hosted by Alex Trebek. The list of her commanding stage performances were as long as my arm.

My mind went blank.

Meryl and the audience waited in silent anticipation. No one laughed. No one moved.

I stood up, locked my hands behind me and walked leaning forward as in deep thought.

Then turned around to continue speaking.

* * * * *

The whole family was waiting at the supper table for the wiener schnitzel sizzling in the frying pan, to complete a meal with steaming roasted potatoes and glazed carrots.

Dad brought up the subjects of Prime Minister Trudeau's excessive spending and how the country was drug filled and decadent. He inhaled a couple of short breaths before two loud sneezes exploded. *No attempt to muffle the sound. At least he turned his face to the side.*

"In Russia everyone obeys the law or else," he said sending spittle in my face. I leaned away. "The people sing with joy." *Hardly a new story and I had enough of it.*

"That's because they're drunk on vodka," I said, sounding like Meathead talking to Archie in *All in the Family,* but I couldn't help it. "You don't hear people rushing to live over there."

Never had I contradicted him before.

He ignored me.

"As soon as we have the money, I'm going back to Croatia."

Don't include me. Canada is my home.

"Let's be thankful to Canada for what we have," said Mom, bringing a bowl of chicken noodle soup.

Oh oh! Here come the slurps. Normally, I cringed and bore it, but today my head was going to explode.

On the verge of screaming, "Stop it! You're driving me crazy," I dashed to the silent sanity of the bathroom.

After supper he sat in the living room reading the *Hrvatski Glas* (Croatan Voice) newspaper. I sat directly across, interested in continuing the conversation. It shifted to Tito.

"He's the one holding Yugoslavia together. Once he dies, all hell will break loose." I wasn't interested in Tito or Yugoslavia. So he switched to Hitler.

"He built Germany into a military power and restored the country's pride."

"By killing Jews and invading other countries," I was nearly shouting, in defiance. "Is that good? Where would we all be if he hadn't been stopped?" I persisted, in no mood to accept that garbage.

He squinted at me, trying to figure me out.

"Ooh, you think you're so smart with your education." He snorted. "Trust me, it's no substitute for experience."

With that said, I calmed down and eased back in my chair. I suppose now, I finally felt recognized and, on some level, an equal.

* * * * *

I hid behind the concrete wall, at the edge of the stadium where the girls track club was running 100-yard sprints. I was curious.

The girls were tall and slender; my sister Irene was short and curvaceous, rightfully proud of her hourglass figure. Her long, blond curls danced with abandon, as Irene dashed down the track, obviously feeling full of power and confidence.

Gone were the days of the bouffant, when she teased the hair at the top, puffing it up.

I returned to playing chess, knowing she would never ask me to protectively hold her hand ever again. Immense pride swelled in my chest for who she had become.

Later at home, striding up the stairs two at a time, I heard Irene say, "He was watching me. Can you believe it?" *Oh oh. I'm in trouble now.*

Around the kitchen table, Mom listening to Irene and Davy colouring a book.

"He was following me," Irene repeated angrily.

"He shouldn't do that," said Mom consolingly.

96

"Who are you talking about?" I asked.

"Dad, who else?" She described how a boy had walked her home after school. "He doesn't trust me."

"Maybe it was by accident," I suggested.

"Doubt it." Dad was unfair she believed, because sunset was her curfew and none existed for me. "Anyway, I can take care of myself."

Davy was tugging my arm, "Look at this George." He pointed to the bold colouring.

"Way to go, man," I said. He beamed.

This seemed like a good time to bring up the subject of a trip for Irene and me to Man and His World expo in Montreal. She had enough money saved to cover her share.

"Why not?" said Mom. Irene pursed her lips, scratched her head supposedly in thought and then shouted with delight, "Yes, yes, yes!" Pulling Davy by the hands off the chair, they danced and sang "Ring Around A Rosy" until they fell down. Mom and I clapped along the whole time.

As so often happened, Davy wanted to wrestle in the living room.

Down on my knees I raised my arms, flexed the biceps and bellowed. "I'm the Mighty Moses." And then switched to a Mickey Mouse voice, saying "and you're Little Igor," and tickled his tummy.

He giggled and panted loudly.

"No, no, no. You're Little Igor and *I'm* the Mighty Moses."

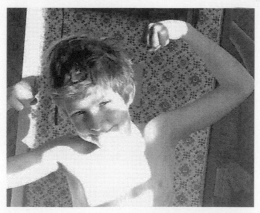

Little Igor displaying massive muscles.

We went back and forth until we started to wrestle. Rolling around on the floor, I put up a valiant effort, but of course he won every time.

On the occasional Friday evening, Irene and I would take the time to dress carefully and stylishly for the school dance. She wore a miniskirt or hot pants, a halter top and a choker; I put on a mesh T-shirt and tight bell-bottoms. Both of us had platform shoes. Ever so cool.

A natural dancer, she displayed freestyle moves for me to imitate in front of a full-length mirror. Tom Jones and I belted out his megahit "It's Not Unusual."

Finally I felt primed for the school dance.

I hung out with my friends and she with hers, enjoying our teenage vitality and innocence.

Irene shining.

That summer there was a charity walkathon Miles for Millions that Irene, Norma, Willy and I entered. The distance of 31 miles (50 km) sounded daunting, but we promised the girls we would quit anytime they had enough.

Amongst all the fun and talk on that sunny day the miles went by unnoticed until mile 29. At that point the girls were tired.

So I challenged Willy to race to the finish.

"Great, and leave us behind, why don't you!" said Irene.

"No way. Hop on," I said, turning and offering my back.

With the girls on our backs, we ran nonstop down the middle of University Avenue, around the Parliament buildings to city hall screaming with joy like four inmates escaping from a mental asylum.

* * * * *

Seared in my memory is the tragic event that crashed upon us about a month after our great trip to Montreal. The crime altered irrevocably the course of every member of our family.

As I recall, Dad and I were late getting home after an unexpected stop at the hardware store. Even from the bottom of the stairs we could hear the sobbing. Alarmed, we rushed up and into the living room.

Irene lay on her bed in a fetal position crying uncontrollably.

Dad motioned for me to go to my room.

Once behind the closed door, I paced back and forth.

Then, prostrate on the linoleum floor and ear pressed to the gap under the door—wanting to hear and not wanting to hear—I picked up bits of the conversation.

Apparently, Pavlovic (I refuse to use *Mr.*), a family friend, had knocked on the front door looking for Dad. Irene told him we were not home, yet he asked if he could wait upstairs. Since we knew his wife and young son, she said fine. Initially they were seated on the opposite sides of the living room, but then he came closer and started grabbing her.

Irene was wailing now, so Dad came down the hall to get something from the fridge. I stood up and stepped back.

When I dared to return to the floor, the conversation was muffled.

Agonizing minutes passed.

I heard a whimpering, and realizing it was mine. I had wept so heavily my face was sliding in a puddle of tears. Eventually my snivelling and slobbering stopped.

Catholic teaching asks us to forgive. Let me clear: *No way!*

My rage turned to fear. Having witnessed Dad's explosive side, I worried he would seek vengeance and we would lose him to prison.

No, I am better suited to exact revenge. Right away? No, let the bloody bastard stew looking over his shoulder. One day out of the dark, with a bat in my hands . . .

Dad and Mom spoke over the phone to the wife who admitted Irene was the second girl he had assaulted; She was leaving him. It ended with Mom shouting at the woman for not warning us. On that note, ties were completely severed between our two families.

But Irene wanted the attack reported.

A neighbour, a policeman, advised Dad against it as she would be forced to relive the entire nightmare and in public.

The police never came for Dad.

One day when I wasn't home, an ambulance rushed Irene to an Emergency Department to have her stomach pumped. She had overdosed. I was told only what I write here.

At my graduation, smiling facades hid the depths of our despair and sorrow. We were like islands in the middle of the ocean after a class 5 hurricane, completely devastated. Rebuilding was going to take time and great effort.

There was nothing else to do, except to go on.

* * * * *

What am I to do with the rest of my life?

The burning question ricocheted within the walls of my skull, searching for a reasonable answer.

It came late one evening on the way to work. I peeked into the red newspaper box stationed in front of TGH. The headline announced American Bobby Fischer had defeated Boris Spassky and the Russian Machine in the much anticipated, multi-game chess tournament for the world title.

I found a quiet room to sit back and read the great news. Bobby's win was proof that anything is possible if you set your mind to it.

Working forty years at a company and then having a heart attack was not the road I wanted to travel. I was going to make my fortune and come back home like the second son in the prodigal son parable. But young enough to enjoy it.

I stood up and walked over to a panoramic window. From the top floor of the hospital I gazed dreamily at the serenity of a thousand city lights.

While the world sleeps, I am awake, alert and actively planning my future. The thought sent exhilarating shivers through my body.

Fortunately, the plan had received a strong start when Nick explained in convincing fashion and detail the tax benefits of placing earned income into a RRSP. I had already saved enough for my education.

That night and right there, I formed a three-point action plan: obtain a university degree, work as a computer programmer at IBM and retire by the age of thirty-five. *Fifteen years is not a lot of time.*

The clock started ticking at that very moment.

CHAPTER 5

LOST

Erindale College
Mississauga, Ontario
September, 1972

O rientation week at the Erindale campus of the University of
Toronto was generally sedate. "University," the word had a
wonderful ring to it. One of the goals my parents had was for their
children to receive the proper education—not too uncommon for
most immigrants—unavailable to them. As the oldest I was to lead
the way. I had left home to spend the better part of the next four
years in these buildings and to come out with an Honours BA.

A foregone conclusion.

I found, easily enough, a guy to share a two-bedroom apartment
in a high-rise, bus ride away. Any issues that would crop up, we
promised to resolve like adults. But we got along fabulously. Hearing I was into chess he called me Boris, so naturally I called him
Fish, after Boris Spassky and Bobby Fischer.

At the Thrift Store, we bought everything we needed except a
TV. A distraction to avoid anyway.

I had the distinct pleasure of discovering a treasure in a kitchen
drawer: a huge stack of Playboy magazines. So I graciously volunteered to plaster the *entire* kitchen with the lovely centrefolds. Everyone, including the three girls down the hall, wanted to see the
one-of-a-kind kitchen because of the exquisite artwork. Of course,
it had to go down briefly when Mom came for inspection.

Fish and I were consistent about cleaning, as in never, unless a VIP was visiting which fortunately was rare. Dishes were washed strictly as a last resort. If you needed a dish or plate, lots were lying around just for the taking, all over the apartment. As long as the old sauce vaguely resembled the freshly cooked one, you were good to go.

Grilled cheese sandwich was a breakfast favourite; and for variety, we altered between cheddar and cream. Should it ever get burned a little, the smoke detector and the open door would announce to the neighbours what fine food we were enjoying. There was no misunderstanding between us about drinks. I glugged milk straight out of the three-quart jug; and Fish emptied beer and pop. Bottles conveniently landed behind the couch until shopping day.

The courses I registered for were varied and challenging. A big step up from high school. Nobody cared if you were present or not.

Hay fever was particularly bad that year and in the region. Itchy eyes, runny nose and frequent sneezing made it difficult to focus. Of course taking antihistamines never occurred to me.

On top of that, every morning I blow-dried my shoulder length hair—for some reason the dryer made my thinking muddled— going from frizzy hair to fuzzy head. I *had* to look good. I sprayed it to hold shape and used a net at bedtime, but the elastic left an embarrassing telltale ring on the forehead.

The whole country was excited about the long-awaited hockey showdown between Canada and Russia for world supremacy. Our team of NHL all-stars was the overwhelming favourite to win. What a stunning blow when the Russians defeated us 7-3 in the first of eight games here in Canada. Fish and I watched some games on the girls' TV down the hall. We kept losing.

To win the series we had to take the last three games, all in Russia. Games six and seven we won.

Classes were cancelled for the final game. The entire country shut down. Sixteen million screaming Canadians watched Paul Henderson score the winning goal, in the last minute!

Never has this nation been prouder or more united. Phew!

104

The family had moved to a bungalow in a remote part of Toronto, for *two* unconnected and unspoken reasons: firstly, Dad had finally accepted his dream business wasn't going to fly. He had recently opened a small Croatian 'social club' somewhere in a strip plaza where members played cards on weekends.

Secondly and more importantly, the *new* place was available for Irene to call home.

After the attempted OD, she had seen a social worker weekly at Sick Kids Hospital. Irene told her she couldn't take the arguing between Mom and Dad about the gambling, and that Dad ruled over the household heavy-handedly with no room for discussion. For sanity, she needed a stable place and a safe one where Pavlovic couldn't find her. Apparently, after meeting Mom and defensive Dad, the social worker found a room at McVail House for teenage girls where she had lived for several months.

On many weekends I used to come home.

"Mom, I'm home!" I yelled as I opened the front door.

"Over here in the kitchen," she shouted.

I tossed my giant bag of dirty clothes in the laundry room before pursuing the sweet smell of *palacinke* pancakes.

Mom's hands were full, but I gave her a loud kiss on the cheek and a huge squeeze. She shooed me away with the elbow, smiling with dimpled cheeks the whole time.

Just as I sat at the table, Davy came in looking mildly upset, so I noisily smothered his face with kisses.

"What's up kiddo?"

"Johnny wants to fight with me," he said, wiping his cheek.

"For real?"

"Uh-huh."

"Tell him you just want to be his friend."

Still in pajamas Irene, lethargic from her medication, eased out of her bedroom. One by one, we hugged her before she quietly took a seat beside me. I pretended not to notice her hands trembling.

Mom served the golden *palacinke*, hot from the frying pan to be topped with marmalade and sour cream. Delicious.

Food and love.

That evening Irene and I went to the theatre to see the sci-fi movie *Soylent Green.*

Near the end I heard her sniffling, so I looked over. She tried to smile but her lower lip only quivered. I stroked her shoulder.

Somehow she managed a sigh.

On the way home we talked about E. G. Robinson's death scene. *I should be more careful what movies I take her to.*

Irene glassy eyed from medication.

Six months later
Mississauga, Ontario
April, 1973

I was in a bedroom with three girls, a situation I tried to avoid. Honestly. Let me explain.

Fish had already gone home for the weekend to see his family and girlfriend. The girls down the hall were being picked up by boyfriends the next morning, so they came to check up on me. And I was staying behind to study. They brought up the subject of smoking pot in their place; Before I could say "snowball's chance in hades," they were dragging me.

"Come on Boris."

In the bedroom farthest from the hall (on my urging), they stuffed a towel under the door and closed the window. We formed a sitting circle on the floor, legs crossed.

Someone lit a joint, puffed and passed it around to me. I put it in my mouth, faked a drag—no way I was going to get addicted—and passed it on. Don't laugh, it was serious stuff as far as I was concerned.

They eased back to mellow out; I did also, glad it was over.

The next morning, I was grappling with an assignment when a song popped into my head. I put on Gilbert O'Sullivan's "Alone Again, Naturally."

Ugh. Yes, I wanted something to resonate with my mood, but this was too much.

Richard Harris's "MacArthur Park" was mournfully perfect. His powerful voice and dramatic orchestral background spurred me to action.

After reading a chapter, two tape recorders caught my eye.

So I recorded Tom Jones singing and me, his backup, throwing in quips. Speeded up for special effect we sounded like Alvin and the Chipmunks. On the second recorder, I added a track where I introduced the performance like a hyperenergetic, overcaffeinated DJ.

If all else fails, I may have a future as a comedian.

* * * * *

107

Toronto
Summer, 1973

By the end of the school year, the family had moved again to an upscale condominium building well-located near High Park. I moved in with them to save money, and to be away from ragweed and closer to York University.

To increase the opportunities of finding a girlfriend, I needed a car and *real* driving lessons.

Soon everyone was checking out my straight-from-factory Pinto: sleek, sporty exterior and fresh smelling interior. Dad liked the hatchback feature for convenient transporting of his tools to the next handyman project.

On Friday evenings I picked up Willy and Kingston, a friend I had met at Erindale. Kingston and his family lived, by sheer coincidence, across the street from us. Through the summer, the three of us hopped around discos and taverns in search of the elusive *right* girl.

In September Kingston went back to Erindale, and I joined Willy at York where I focussed on Computer Science.

York was going to be more fun than Erindale. On the very first day Willy introduced me to all his friends in the coffee shop. A great bunch!

* * * * *

8 months later

TGH hired me for one last summer. Working the day shift meant being in constant motion but I was used to whatever came my way. Most visitors are probably not aware of all that goes on behind the scenes, so please try to be more understanding of the staff looking after your loved ones. My comments are meant in the kindest way.

Here's some unpleasant parts of the job. *Warning*: description will get ugly! Consider skipping next three paragraphs.

When you as the orderly enter a room, be prepared to encounter nauseating *smells* (sweat, urine, vomit, feces and death); pain's haunting *sounds* (from moaning to screaming, sometimes even incessant); and horrific *sights* (too much for the reader's innocent imagination, I suspect.)

Be prepared in the middle of the night to get an order from the nurse to take the body in room 666 down to the morgue in the sub-subbasement. Be prepared for a long search for another orderly to join you in this little escapade, hopefully not the guy who thinks it's fun doing Dracula impressions while hovering over a dead body. Be prepared for the creaky service elevator to descend too slowly to the underworld and jolt when it hits bottom; struggling with a rusty, manual door; a dark hallway that hasn't seen natural light in sixty years; the gurney pleading with you through its screeching, metal wheels not to leave it behind in that God for-saken place; the pungent smell of disinfectant; the numbing cold seeking a warm body behind the grey double thick freezer door; and other occupied gurneys and shelves of glass jars filled with formaldehyde preserved *brains*(?).

Your reaction will be visceral—shove the reluctant gurney, close the door firmly to keep ghosts from escaping; and get the hell out!

On the afternoon that I had promised to visit Irene at Women's College Hospital, I was working in the Emergency Department at TGH. It had been a particularly busy day, so I was eyeing the clock for the shift to end. The charge nurse assigned me to clean up the homeless alcoholic (let's call him Otis) a familiar patron of our department. She knew full well there wasn't enough time, but everyone was swamped and I was the best choice. Besides, nobody else wanted to touch him.

I entered the room prepared: mask, gloves, gown and tweezers. Otis was lying naked except for a white sheet, snoring.

If you're squeamish, I *strongly* recommend skipping the next two paragraphs!

Below the beer belly, in the creases of the swollen scrotum, maggots had found a comfortable refuge, with easy access to nutrients. The stench and sight were turning my stomach. With the tweezers I removed, one by one, the wiggling grub unhappy to be so rudely disturbed. As for Otis, he didn't feel a thing. By the time I pinched the last one, the scrotum seemed to have shrunk in half. My clothes and forehead damp with perspiration and I desperate to leave, but no one came to replace me. I pulled back the foreskin, to reveal a ring of maggots squirming at the base of the penis head. *Yuk*!

Once done, the groin was raw red but free of infestation. Working as quickly as possible, I finished him with a good sponge bed-bath, twenty minutes into the next shift. When I left, the replacement orderly was in hiding behind a semi closed door.

In the locker room, I peeled off the soaked uniform, cleaned up absolutely as much as possible, put on fresh dry clothes and grabbed the gift—before dodging traffic to get to Women's College Hospital.

Over an extended period, the psychiatrist had put Irene on several powerful drugs and still nothing helped. It was discovered much later, that Irene's illness was misdiagnosed, so the medication was inappropriate anyway. In fact, it may have harmed her. As a last resort she received Electro Convulsive Therapy (ECT)—also known as Shock Treatment. Simply stated, in this procedure electrical stimulus causes a brain seizure. I was relieved to read that it's extremely successful in treating depression although initially there may be signs of memory loss.

Before entering, I paused to take a few breaths.

The room is quiet and airless, like King Tut's chamber upon first opening. From the doorway I can see her face, porcelain white, and lungs perfectly still.

Just as I am about to shout for a nurse, her eyes partially open. She must have been aware of my presence.

Looking frail, she bravely puts on a smile just for me.

"How are you?" My voice is gentle.

She licks her dry lips.

"Fine," the word comes out slowly and softly, but I am in no rush—just as long as she can speak.

After all these agonizing months, she may have turned a corner. I am inhaling hope.

* * * * *

That summer my dating life exploded at TGH: candy striper, ward aid, RN and a girl visiting her father. The change of fortune I attribute to gaining thirty pounds of muscle from body building and doing my job as well as anyone.

Two bubbly Norwegian student nurses, Delilah and Agnes, and I got along especially well. I recall one occasion when they were having trouble using a broken hoist to place a patient into a tub, so I carefully picked him up mindful of using the quads and very gently placed him into the warm water. Not difficult since I was bench pressing almost double his weight. The girls were whispering and giggling, so when I turned around it became clear they were ogling my butt.

Shortly after the three of us went out to the Exhibition, Delilah told me privately that Agnes had an illness and about five years to live. Naturally, I felt sorry for Agnes but from then on I dated exclusively Delilah, a fun-loving buxom blond. Her sister, mother and grandmother approved of me, she said. In time our relationship became, for me, the most serious to date.

Much later, Agnes told me there was no truth to her being seriously ill.

Four months later
Toronto
April 25, 1975

Physical love life between Delilah and me advanced to the next level, almost always ending with us wanting more. When she felt ready, she said. To my pleasant surprise she became ready when I announced Nick and I were going on a three-month summer trip through Europe.

I reserved a room at York University half expecting a last-minute change of mind. It was the right time of the month she assured. We sat at each side of the bed, back to back.

"I'm ready," she said. Although we were both virgins, I assumed it should be easy if we simply let instinct take over. No thinking required.

The next morning we exited the building into glorious sunshine. I was a new man. *Finally,* I had discovered how to satisfy a woman. I knew, also, this immense power could be used either to manipulate their emotions or to show understanding and restraint. Such supreme confidence was exuding from my pores.

Truthfully, my prowess barely impressed Delilah (I suspect), never mind any other discriminating woman. But you couldn't have changed my mind on *that* day.

Nick and I were seated at the front of the bus, itching to see the world, the Old World—the whole family outside waving good-bye, knowing they would meet me in Zagreb. The bus carried us to Boston where we boarded the *Leonardo de Vinci* for a cruise across the Atlantic to Genoa, Italy.

We shared a crammed bunkbed cabin in which previously un-noticed habits turned to nagging irritants. Too often, I called out from the upper bunk—as he tried to sleep—asking how to spell a word for the diary. On the other hand, he had dry skin from psori-asis, so it was difficult to write with all the noisy scratching.

Among the people we met was Helen of New York who was being hustled by a self-described ladies' man. She came to Nick and myself for protection. I asked Nick if he was interested in Helen beyond friendship. Simply said, "No."

Our land route took us from Scandinavia in the north down to the Mediterranean countries, utilizing a three-month, unlimited-travel Euro Rail pass. To save money on accommodation, we chose riding night trains—sitting up was not the best way of getting good sleep! —and sightseeing cities by day.

Lonely Planet's *Europe on* $5 *a Day* was my bible. But, un-known to me, it had been *replaced* by the $10 version some time back! Due to lack of sleep and food, plus walking everywhere, I was losing weight and gaining petulance. Nick ate well.

In Germany we split up impulsively, promising to reunite in Barcelona, Spain.

The familiar old refugee camp in Zirndorf was fenced in and silent, awaiting demolition I suspected.

Like it or not, I was still considered a Yugoslav citizen and could be conscripted into the army. *Going there is very risky!*

My family and I connected in Zagreb.

Before heading to Niko's farm, a stop at the car rental office. They had only standards, no automatics. Operating a clutch and gearshift was going to be confusing, but Dad kept insisting I would pick it up in no time.

Once on the road, I struggled with the car and worried about getting into an accident. He kept badgering about it.

"What's wrong with you?" he said, inhaling a cigarette and trying to figure me out. For as long as I could, I took it.

Once I had enough, I pulled over to the shoulder of the road. Still holding the steering wheel, I stared straight ahead . . .

"Marijan, let him drive," Mom said. "Take your time, dear."

Eventually we made it without further incident.

We put on a happy front when we got out of the car to be received by Niko's family and Uncle Mirko. Ebullient greetings! Then they herded us indoors carrying on the conversation nonstop.

While Turkish coffee was served in copper cups along with *cevapcici* (small minced meat rolls) and *kolace* (cookies), they wanted to hear how we were and what life was like in Canada.

Mom and Dad said we had everything we wanted—but had to work *really* hard for it. Nevertheless, people and attitude about life were not as good as in Croatia.

Staza hugged Davy and admitted she got it wrong about the number of children Mom would have. By now, Mom was at menopause.

Uncle Mirko wondered about my reading skills. I smiled and said I had no problems, thanks to him.

The following days we immersed ourselves in farm chores.

Before we left, Dad asked if I wanted to go for a walk. Knowing he was thinking of the tree with the fifteen-year-old carving, I made an excuse that all the kids were helping with laundry down at the well. During the entire visit, I had avoided him.

We promised to write, but must have known that wasn't likely to happen—we were much too busy embracing capitalism.

"Don't wait another fifteen years to visit," said Niko, his age showing. "You're always welcome here."

I continued my adventure through the Mediterranean countries, journaling a lifetime of experiences. Like-minded travellers were easy to hook up with in hostels and trains.

One day at a flea market stall in Barcelona, a young girl (perhaps sixteen) and I struck up a conversation; she invited me to her family's farm.

After a spirited supper discussion with the girl's hippy parents about Richard Nixon and the Vietnam war, I was shown to my bedroom. To be shared with their daughter, no less! There was a bed for her also, and yet it felt like a scene from the farmer's daughter and the travelling salesman story.

"Go over there," I could hear the Baron say, "that's what you came for."

Put yourself in my shoes and consider what you, the reader would have done at that age in that situation. The parents approved. Maybe she only *sounded* under eighteen. Call me an idiot if you choose, but my better judgement intervened.

In the morning at the bus stop, she said she loved me and cried. I understood infatuations having felt that way for a teacher once, so I listened, but not too long, I was to meet Nick at the hostel.

It was a great reunion, sharing stories about sites, people and misadventures. What friction had existed between us was gone—we were lifelong friends.

In Brussels, Belgium, on the day of our return flight, I got up early.

"Where you going?" asked Nick.

"I'm walking to the airport," I said.

"It's like ten miles away."

Five dollars a day was still my target.

* * * * *

Life for Irene took a turn for the better after the shock therapy. Colour returned to her face and energy returned to her movement. She sounded extremely pleased to announce that she had found a Human Resources job with the Toronto Police.

When I stopped by at her work, I couldn't believe the change. She described the job with such confidence and knowledge. Evidently, her boss appreciated dedication and attention to detail.

On weekends she was home with Davy, allowing Mom to have a second job cleaning houses. Christmas was coming.

As always, we enjoyed Mom's big feast, even though Dad was busy somewhere. Everyone went to great lengths to get the 'right' presents, piled up under the Christmas tree. Irene put on the record player, Jose Feliciano's "Feliz Navidad." Surrounded by opened gifts and wrapping paper, and with Mom clapping, we danced just like in the old days.

Davy found this the perfect situation to make fun of us.

* * * * *

Adjacent to TGH was the nurses' residence where I used to pick up Delilah. As a visitor, I was permitted to use the handball court. On one memorable day the whole gang came along: Nick, the Baron, Willy and Kingston. The rivalry was fierce. Guys were running, bodies were flying and sometimes diving for the ball like our lives depended on it. If you came out without a bruised knee or elbow, you weren't trying and you certainly weren't having fun.

After showering, we congregated in the lounge.

"I was robbed," said Kingston, referring to a shot he felt was inbound.

"You was *robbed*," the Baron repeated in a high-pitched mocking voice. Sometimes he pounced on Kingston's height insecurity also. The two barely tolerated each other, but I decided to go ahead with the proposal I had been cooking up. I waved my arms for attention.

"Guys, guys. There's something I want to say."

One by one they turned my way.

"Ah, here's a wacky idea. It's gonna be hard to believe but—"

"You mean the loafers (Leafs) winning the Stanley Cup?" the Baron cut in and everyone laughed.

Moving on, I proposed we create a real estate empire, with each of us having an equal stake in it.

Everyone waiting for the punchline. Crickets could be heard.

"I'm serious." I suggested we start with one house, a prototype. Down payments should be no problem split five ways and we could easily renovate with our fathers' help. (I was confident Dad would jump at the opportunity). Then sell at a profit. The next building could be an old mansion or a multiplex. And so on, on the road to unimaginable prosperity.

I was losing them. "You could retire early," I quickly added.

"I'm not thinking about retirement. I've got women on my mind," said the Baron. Willy nodded in agreement. Kingston showed barely minimal interest. Nick, as the most respected, got the last word, "It's very risky mixing money and friendship."

Nick was wrong, I thought, but it didn't matter: they weren't ready anyway. I had no clue how right he would prove to be.

Fine. I'll do it on my own.

* * * * *

North York, Toronto

I convinced Willy to share an apartment about ten minutes off campus. The shorter commuting time would give more time for studying. I wasn't doing that well with my courses.

The coffeeshop group, along with Willy and I, formed a co-ed water polo team, a welcome break from the demanding classes. After each game we ended up in the sauna nude, girls and guys. The first time, I felt self-conscious and definitely avoided a cold shower before going in but soon enough became comfortable. I desperately wished for normal vision as my glasses fogged up instantly from the humidity and the hot chicks.

There's not much I recall about that school year except that I enjoyed the comradery of the group and the high intensity workouts in the gym with Willy.

Months later
York campus
April, 1976

Final exams behind us, the only thing to do now before graduation was go wild and party, but I was in no mood to meet the gang. We were all to gather at the coffee shop where Willy was working the counter. I made sure to be first.

"Where you going?" asked Willy, since I was putting on a jacket, gloves and toque.

"I gotta get home," I said without further explanation.

"Nobody's getting out of here today. There's already eight inches of snow." He watched to see if I was kidding. "The roads are *impossible*." After all these years, Willy knew me well enough not to say that.

"I'll be fine. Have fun." But I wasn't so sure. No longer could the truth be denied—I lacked discipline; and consequently, for the last four years I had been floundering. Faking it.

My last chance of receiving a degree hung by a thread. So poor were my marks, I had to return for another year.

"We'll miss you," said Willy, trying to sound cheerful.

It was a freak April storm. The wind-swept snow stung mercilessly my face on the way to the Pinto, hard to find in the whiteout conditions. A driver was about to throw his shovel back in the trunk, giving up on getting out.

While he kindly waited in his car, I furiously shovelled a starting path.

"Good luck buddy," he shouted as he rushed indoors.

I snaked around an abandoned vehicle and then picked up speed to plow through a snow drift.

The roads were hazardously slippery. On the hills, it got especially tense: the Pinto's all-season tires slid sometimes backwards and sometimes forwards. The heater was on *just enough* to keep the windshield clear because the gas was running low.

The drive time home: four times the usual.

* * * * *

117

On a picture-perfect spring day, the family was seeing Irene to the airport for a trip to visit Niko, Staza and our cousins. More than any of us, she had kept in touch with our Croatian relatives.

The weight she had gained during the prolonged illness was gone, leaving behind the high school figure.

During her visit she met a guy, Nebo, with whom she kept in touch upon returning home.

Weeks grew into months.

She flew back again to visit and this time returned with an announcement—they were getting married.

The day was looking very busy, so I made sure not to be late to take Delilah shopping for porcelain figurines at the mall. I wouldn't have spent a dime on one, but she couldn't resist even though they were outrageously pricey.

"Can we stop to get jelly beans?" she said, at one point. I couldn't comprehend the appeal of them, either.

"I don't have time," I said. Out of the blue, she looked ticked.

"In that case, you can leave," she said like a queen dismissing a servant. It went against my grain to leave her stranded, yet I wasn't about to take that from any girlfriend, so with a mixture of guilt and anger, I did leave.

Once home, Mom said Delilah was on the phone.

"I'd like to talk to you, in person," said Delilah.

"Fine. After the game."

"I'll be there at eight."

I had promised Davy to take him to the afternoon football game at Varsity Stadium.

As I whipped up and down streets frantically looking for a parking spot, it happened.

An oncoming car was barrelling towards us because I had carelessly pulled into his lane to grab the vacant parking spot. Helpless, I watched the accident unfold in s-l-o-w motion.

A sickening thud.

I looked over at Davy, "Are you OK?"

"Yes," he said, like nothing happened. To make sure I checked him over head to toe.

The other driver came at me shouting, "That was your fault!"

"Right," I said.

Dave and I took the subway home.

"Most important, nobody was hurt," said Mom, inspecting us for the second time.

Delilah was standing in the gazebo at the front of our building, waiting. I approached, expecting to be chewed out for abandoning her so unceremoniously. Her face was hidden in the darkness, but her voice came across soft, gentle and clear.

"I'm sorry. I shouldn't have spoken like that." She waited. I didn't speak. "Can you forgive me?"

Her sincerity was unmistakable; however, I had already given our relationship a great deal of thought. I liked her, but I was searching for a lifelong partner. Our views regarding money and food were polar opposites and we were sure to clash again.

"I'm sorry too. Ah, the thing is, we're two different people."

She jumped in, "Do you want to lose this . . . friendship?"

Except for the breathing, we were silent for a very long time.

"Think it over," she said, then drove away.

Not long after, by a rather odd coincidence, I received an unusual phone call. It was Willy's mother who asked for a favour. He had recently broken up with his long-time girlfriend and would I check up on him.

The insurance company had offered to pay me the book value of the car since the repair was going to cost even more. I took the offer.

So without a car, it took a while to get to his place: a basement apartment where he moved after graduation.

I knocked at the side door several times before he answered. Haggard and surprised, he invited me into an apartment that looked worse than the one I shared with Fish, if you can believe it possible.

We talked about old times. I was surprised to find out his father had worked in the same refugee camp office in Zirndorf as Dad. Small world.

At first, he was reluctant to talk about the ex-girlfriend but with a little prompting, he spilled his guts.

"Look man," I started, "we can't let women manipulate our emotions like that." He filled my milk-stained glass with warm, flat Coke. I wasn't about to complain.

"Hey, *we* rule the world. We're boss!" I beat my chest with a fist for emphasis. Of course he and I didn't believe the last part. Males of our species have done a disastrous job of running this planet from time immemorial. Nevertheless, I was going to tell my buddy *whatever* necessary to snap him out of the doldrums.

It worked, and he agreed to go for a walk around the neighborhood.

The entire family was there to meet this 'tall, dark, handsome' guy, as Irene described him. However, under his pretentious façade I saw evil lurking. Some might say I was simply an overprotective brother.

My parents welcomed him into our home like Jesus arriving triumphantly into Jerusalem on Palm Sunday. He sat on our best chair with all but me catering to his every need. Surely, he sensed my reservations.

In the morning, we all headed out to do errands while Nebo stayed home alone. The last thing I did was to place a tape recorder under my bed and pressed RECORD.

An hour later I got back, hardly containing my suspense. The monarch was occupying his imperial throne, enjoying a cigarette and looking smug about it. Nobody had smoked in the house since Dad gave it up when Irene had the ECT. Controlling my urge to take two steps at a time, I went upstairs, shut the door behind me and pulled out the recorder, the reel still spinning.

I pressed STOP, rethreaded the tape and pressed REWIND.

My hand shook and heart pounded as I finally tapped PLAY.

I could hear my voice saying a casual goodbye and a door closing. Silence. Then I heard footsteps coming upstairs, like in a Hitchcock movie, to my parents' bedroom. Rummaging. Then he moved into my bedroom. First the closet and then under the bed, his hand searching. Not finding anything he returned downstairs. I had placed the recorder out of reach, just in case.

Gotcha! Now, what do I do with this evidence?

At the first opportunity I told Irene.

"You did what?" Her smile faded, obviously not pleased with my little surveillance, to say the least.

"I recorded him rummaging in our bedrooms."

"You had no right to do that!" Her eyes looked like they could scorch the ground I stood on.

Huh? Not exactly the reaction I expected or hoped for. I raised my hands and backed away.

"You better not tell anyone. You don't have to worry, we're moving right after the wedding."

On the day of the civic wedding, Nebo was dragging his feet getting ready but Irene was too busy with preparations to notice. I suspect, my parents didn't want to upset her so they said nothing about him.

Upon her urging, soon after, they moved to an apartment of their own.

I heard she was grabbing all kinds of overtime at the police station. Nebo stayed home.

* * * * *

This was year five, one last ditch effort to obtain a measly three-year B.A. and I desperately needed high marks in the final few courses to get a passing average. I was starting to question my intelligence but couldn't allow myself to dwell on it. Left behind with no friends as distractions, I *had* to get it done. There was no Plan B.

At home no one asked how things were, assuming I was pursuing my lofty dreams. As long as I was moving towards that pinnacle nothing was asked of me. They had no clue how little I was actually accomplishing—in fact, I was covering up a lie.

As a responsible adult, I felt obligated to pay my share of household expenses. At least a nominal amount. Rather than dipping into my retirement fund, I got a job as Simpson's Christmas help. However they soon hired me for a permanent position with hints of a career. All around me, veterans were doing the same mindless drudgery, day in day out. Their sole satisfaction: reaching for bottles of beer at supper and after work. Life of an alcoholic didn't sound appealing to me.

I don't recall much about this period—either I was too tired or too busy to keep memories or a diary. Through the daily grind of school, work and sleep, I was short on self-awareness and big on *not* giving up. If I had stopped to think about it, I would have realized I was burned out.

Back pain eventually led me to see the campus doctor and to wait for the psychiatric appointment, you read all about in the prologue.

Blindly, I slogged through the routine until the last lifeline to a degree drifted away over the horizon. For years I had nightmares about that period of my life—not being able to shake the dreadful feeling of failure.

On the last day of the school year, it was mid afternoon when I got home. No one was there. I turned to my TV addiction and slipped into a chair, accepting my fate, like Jack slipping underwater in his final scene of the *Titanic*.

PART II

ADULTHOOD

CHAPTER 6

THE RIGHT ONE

Toronto
April 18, 1977

A s luck would have it, the Boston Marathon was on and the winner, Canadian Jerome Drayton, sparked a flame of pride. The exaltation on each runner's face as they crossed the finish line, arms raised in victory, I also wanted to experience.

So unlike Jack, my head emerged out of the watery depths, spellbound by the dream of one day running the Boston Marathon. To that end, I was required to run a *qualifying* time in a previous race. To make the very difficult task remotely possible, it would need to be at the right season and on a flat course. Voila, the Toronto Marathon. *There's no better time to start something exciting than right now*!

Buoyed by newly found energy, the very next day I applied for and received a job at a collection agency. Not on par with IBM, but it was a job. The investigative aspect resembled solving a crime. Who wouldn't enjoy that? Detective G. Biondic on the case

The unpleasant part, pressuring people over the phone to pay up. Sure, some shirked their responsibility, but most did their level best and still couldn't make ends meet. My job was not to judge them, rather to meet a daily quota. By midafternoon most collectors, feeling the pressure, aggressively hustled their butts.

At 3:55 p.m., with 5 minutes left until quitting time the most senior collector would stand up to watch the seconds tick down.

At 4 p.m. he grabbed his hat from the coat rack and left.

This image spurred me to send a resume to Big Blue, IBM—any position there was preferred to the current one. As a major corporation IBM sought the crème de la crème, but still I wrote *two years university, no diploma.*

In spite of my lack of academic success, I was brought in for the aptitude and logic tests. Lo and behold, they hired me as a computer operator at the company headquarters.

A few days earlier Irene had come home unexpectedly, to tell us Nebo had returned to Bosnia for good with all the savings. Mom comforted her and I—very much tempted to say, "I warned you"—chose simply to listen.

Recognizing a need, she set up an appointment with the psychologist. I tagged along for moral support. At the end of the session he asked to speak with me in private, with her permission.

He told me she was holding up remarkably well under the circumstances, but that could change. If it did, I was not to take her anger personally. I should be supportive and yet not to tolerate her outbursts. Lastly, she was better off without Nebo because he displayed sociopathic tendencies. How did the doc know that?

As it turned out, the timing wasn't that bad for Irene and me. We found an apartment to share within walking distance to IBM. Nick, the Baron and Willy helped us move in.

Walking into IBM HQ felt right—*this is where I belong*—even though computer operator was a far cry from programmer. My partner Duane, a legendary programmer, had retreated (after a mental breakdown I suspected) into this tiny corner of the building to relax and share his views about the Bible and God. In an effort not to rock the boat I listened more than spoke.

But after a while the deliberate attempts to convert me to his religion without regard to *my* own religious beliefs, pushed me to the edge. My tolerance for proselytizing had been decreasing for years, through encounters with Jehovah Witnesses and other Christians seeking money and my soul. I had always engaged with these people in an open and respectful manner but on that one day I finally had enough of it.

I asked what God would allow millions of humans to suffer unspeakable and unimaginable pain for *eternity* in hell having the misfortune of not hearing about Christ, but instead let's say . . . Mohammed?

There was much more I had to say but Duane's usual cheerful demeanour turned heavy and downcast. Not my intention and I instantly regretted the outburst. I was taking out all my frustration on a really decent, well-intentioned person.

Why can't I be more understanding?

"Forgive me, Duane," I said. "Ah . . . I've been having a hard time lately. I really do appreciate your opinion and hope we're still friends."

We shook hands and left it behind us.

Visiting Dr. Rochman, the shrink, was definitely improving my mental health. After some initial difficulty, I identified two apparent-to-me truths: my memory and my ability to form mental images were in decline. Consequently, I had a genuine concern of not being able to hold a demanding, white-collar job beyond about the age of thirty-five.

He recommended: anxiety medication, meditation and an *easier* lifestyle.

For the sake of my health, I dared not push myself too hard. Between working as computer operator and running, I presumed my health would continue to improve.

Early retirement on my modest income was out of the question.

Irene and I got along well. On her suggestion, we took up disco dancing lessons at the community centre to the sounds of the Bee Gees, Barry White and Donna Summers. Once "I Will Survive" and "Born to be Alive" burst through the speakers, nothing could keep us seated.

In preparation for the Toronto Marathon, I trained after work at a nearby trail system. On race day—a sweat band, T-shirt, cut-off blue jeans and a pair of sneakers—did not land me on the cover of a fashion magazine. No surprise. Nonetheless, I did feel joy and a sense of accomplishment, from start to finish.

Mom's friend and neighbour, Dragica, told me she knew a nice Croatian girl and wondered if I'd be interested in meeting her? Sounded like an excellent opportunity, however, I didn't want to appear desperate. *I don't need help finding someone, thank you...*

I thought about the girls I met in discos and bars while I had the car: like this fashionably dressed Jewish girl who agreed to go on a date. The Pinto was impressive: shiny on the outside and garbage free on the inside. As a bonus, the gas tank was full. To give her the feeling of roominess, I pulled her seat way back. One look at my muscular machine and her parents would know their daughter was dating a classy guy. Or so I thought, until I realized she lived in Rosedale, the ritziest area of Toronto.

Stationed in their driveway was a Rolls Royce and a Mercedes Benz. God knows what was in the four-car garage. Being evaluated by the parents didn't bother me. I expected it. I brought up how the high interests were going to choke the economy, to impress them and to distract them from my wheels tucked discretely behind bushes.

No one smokes in my mobile sanctuary without asking, but she did. I'll be frank, I wasn't feeling a good vibe through the entire evening. When my date dropped the "my father buys my furs at" line, I knew without hesitation I was out of her league. At the end of the evening, it was mutually agreed this was not going to work out. No hard feelings.

If meeting women in drinking establishments was not producing good candidates, the daughter of a friend of a friend was worth a try. With my luck, she would be a cross-eyed, six-foot, 240-pound centre on a woman's football team. How would I extract myself from her clutches and try to explain we wouldn't see eye to eye—which would get me in *real* trouble with the cross-eyed thing?

She was standing motionless at the end of the subway platform. The only person there. The tapping of my Aldo leather shoes on the granite floor echoed across the vastness of the station.

This girl was nothing like my negative mind had conjured up. Maybe five feet one. Perfectly round eyes, upturned nose, red lips and white teeth you see in toothpaste ads—all surrounded by brown, curly hair. A short, trim figure lovingly wrapped in a tight cotton T-shirt and bell bottom pants. Impossible to turn my gaze away.

I sported a pressed navy-blue shirt, a subtle dab of Old Spice and daring white straight-cut pants. Squeaky clean and hair coiffed to perfection.

"Tereza?" I said, like I couldn't be so lucky.

"George?" she said in a playful tone. The glint in her eyes spoke volumes.

"In the flesh."

She chuckled at that.

I wanted to treat this beautiful edelweiss with care, so I gently extended my hand. Hers felt warm and velvety.

As agreed in advance, we went to a Tim Horton's coffee shop. Sitting across from each other, we spoke mostly in English, occasionally breaking into Croatian. Together with her mother, she lived in a downtown high-rise while she trained to be a medical lab technician. A younger sister had recently married.

Through the summer and fall, I took her to all the romantic places young couples in love go to: strolling through Edwards Gardens and Grenadier Pond and roller skating at The Terrace. Now that I think about it, the weather was faultless, mild temperature and pure sunshine as if by destiny. I took pictures of her with flowers and us hugging. On so many levels, a match made in heaven.

Serious subjects arose. She was turning thirty, so she wanted two children sooner rather than later and of course marriage before that. Cautiously, but honestly, I expressed a desire for the same although at a time when I was financially ready. I didn't tell her I didn't feel emotionally mature. How *could* I be if I still wanted to hang out with the guys? I wouldn't be all hers.

One Saturday afternoon we were in the kitchen, me 'helping' her study for an exam. ABBA started to sing her favourite tune

"Honey, Honey." She blinked at me with twinkling eyes, sending a thrill of excitement through my body.

One thing led to another with us ending up on the couch in the living room. I was unbuttoning my shirt just as the door clicked and her mother entered, far enough to see us. Red-faced, she excused herself and turned around. By the time she felt it appropriate to come back, we were in the kitchen *studying*, my shirt buttoned right to the top.

That year the Leafs finally had a Stanley Cup contending team led by Sittler and Salming. The masochistic fans, including the gang and me, loyal through the dismal decade, had real reason to cheer.

Speaking of loyalty, I had promised Helen—who Nick and I met on the cruise to Europe—a visit in New York City that December.

The reader may, rightfully so, disapprove of what I'm about to share, especially if I was in love with Tereza. Here's what I can say, I did do it and it's *all* true.

Knowing full well Tereza would not like it, I told her I was going by myself to Miami for rest on the beach.

The relationship with Helen, a literary minded and committed feminist, was basically platonic. We hoped for more, yet it never really went beyond a hug, kiss and holding hands—all because of me. I'll leave it to you, the reader, to psychoanalyze the reason why.

At first, she strongly objected to me opening a door for her. After a back-and-forth debate, she accepted it not as the diminishment of women but rather as common courtesy extended to everyone. The truth is I always did so for elderly, disabled and women but not necessarily for a guy, my equal. So call me a chauvinist. Also, we both hoped I could share her passion for poetry. But her gift of *Collections of Greatest Poems* was opened only at the *Dedication* and *Table of Contents*.

Upon my return to Toronto, I called Tereza right away.

"Miss you," she gushed. "Can't wait to see you with the tan."

"OK. Weekend?" I had forgotten about a tan.

"No, tonight. Don't you miss me?"

"Of course I do. Tonight it is," I said, trying to sound enthusiastic. Was she suspecting something?

Where do you get a quick natural tan at 5:30 on a Saturday evening, with everything about to close?

At the Mac's Milk convenience store the Chinese owner said in a thick accent, "I spen nuf house this place in week. I go home now." His one and only bottle of quick-tan lotion on the shelf promised an instant, natural tan.

Without reading the instructions, I splashed the liquid on my hands before realizing I had created a mess: dark, unnatural lines formed in the wrinkles and folds. *Fine, I'll just start again. Better leave enough for the face and neck.* Vigorous scrubbing with a soapy facecloth left my hands raw red; and the darn brown lines unchanged. *What do I do now? OK, I'll wear gloves.*

On the bottle it read "shake well before use." *Rats!* I had been too hasty. With hands trembling, I spread the remaining liquid on the face far more slowly this time even at the risk of being late. Without enough for the neck, I put on a turtleneck sweater. This may sound funny now, but it was very serious back then.

"C'mon up," she said over the entrance intercom.

"Can't. We'll be late for the movie," I said and waited outside.

"You look good," she said, when she came down.

"Thanks. You look beautiful yourself. Let's go," trying not to sound as jumpy as I felt.

Fortunately, the movie *The Jerk* (how appropriate, you're thinking) had started, so we made our way to the seats in the dark. Don't ask me about the storyline, I was too nervously scheming how to avoid detection.

"You haven't been you're usual self. Everything OK?" she asked at her building entrance.

"Ah, I'm tired from the trip," I said. But she wasn't buying it.

"Actually, I'm worried about what mess the replacement guy left for me at work." With that said, her curiosity was satisfied. A hug and kiss, and I was gone.

Nothing especially romantic, but at least I dodged a bullet.

A week later, the 'tan' had cleared up, thank God!

Four months later

The last appointment with Dr. Rochman was mostly an expression of my gratitude for putting this Humpty Dumpty back together again. Anxiety medication and group therapy was history. I was cured. My life was easily manageable and the future shone brightly: a dependable day job (IBM), a potential wife (Tereza) and an enjoyable pursuit (Ottawa Marathon with running friends and Irene; Boston the ultimate goal.)

One day Irene had an unpleasant surprise for me: she was moving out at the end of the month because living with someone who kept the place dirty and messy had become intolerable. To her credit, she did everything she could to keep it clean and tidy. For me, unless it was bigger than a pebble, it wasn't dirt. As for things lying around, I thought it made sense to have things handy—be it on the counter, table, chair or floor. No point wasting time digging in a drawer or cupboard for some commonly used item.

Paying the rent without her share was just a minor setback.

Tereza was feeling stressed out with the final exams. At least that's how she looked when I came over.

"You're going to be OK," I said. "You put in the time and you're smart."

"It's not just that," she said.

"What is it then?"

"Well, —"

"Go on. Tell me."

"Dravko, the last guy I dated . . ." I waited for her to continue. "One time, he picked me up in his arms and took me to the bedroom."

What? I didn't want to listen to this. *The past should be left in the past.*

"You've done nothing like that," she said.

The very last thing I needed to hear was about Macho Man and how wonderful he was. Was I jealous?

"Most of all, I can't wait any longer for a marriage proposal."
She really meant her mother and her but I completely understood
and sympathized with that part.

"I'm not quite there yet," I said, I had to, the situation was getting out of control.

Then the bomb dropped, obliterating everything real and imagined.

"This is over," she said.

I sat speechless, motionless, timeless. My face must have paled.
Looking stoic, I wasn't going to show how I felt.

"Please leave. I have an exam in the morning."

Outside her apartment, the door inches from my face, I deliber-
ated going back to prove I was as much as a man as Dravko.

The entire night I tossed and turned. *Only old-fashioned or in-
secure men in patriarchal societies insisted on having a virgin.
Even God, if taken seriously, required one.* I was glad she had wonderful experiences. *Every human has needs. Am I not interested in
her sexually? What's my problem?* The fact she was not with him
did not escape me. To be true to myself and her, I needed to do
things on *my* timetable. I wanted to be free to think and act without
influence. *None of this matters: the only woman for me is slipping
away!*

That morning I met Tereza in the Mt. Sinai Hospital lobby, on
my knees begging her to come back to me.

"My decision is final," she said before heading off for her exam.

Although it had been months, I called Delilah who was thrilled
to hear from me. That evening I found comfort in her arms, doing
the things Tereza wanted from me.

* * * * *

At the same time, Erlinda's new life continued.

Toronto
September, 1977

Not to everyone's liking, the atmosphere in the Emergency Department at the hospital was charged with intensity and the twelve-hour shifts thrashed the body. And yet, Erlinda sometimes revelled in it and other times just accepted it as a reliable source of income.

The debt for the flight to the States had been paid up long ago. Monthly, she mailed a money order to her stepfather with sincere gratitude for his assistance during the training years. Also, her adopted brother and six kids wrote often requesting money.

In general, Erlinda's life couldn't be better: a paid-up car, two-week vacation to the Caribbean or Europe and lots of friends. Some of the best times were living with classmates Nori and Hope, partying at home, going out dancing and visiting people and places. When they could comfortably afford their own apartments, they moved nearby, retaining their friendships.

Known as practical and good budget maker, Erlinda was nominated treasurer of the CPU Alumni, Toronto Branch.

Meeting the right guy didn't seem to be in the cards—the good ones were taken and the divorced always with kids and emotional baggage were of no interest.

Once financially and socially established, she charted a course for retirement. To start off, automatic pay withdrawals went towards the purchase of Canada Savings Bonds, a nest egg. The great dream shared by other single friends: build her own lovely Philippine house on top of a hill with a beach. Already, she had purchased the land. A live-in maid would look after her needs of cleaning, cooking and shopping. All this was based on good health—certainly not a guarantee—especially given the early passing of both parents. The dream persisted nevertheless. As Hope said, "We'll play mah-jong every day until midnight." To their hearts' content.

CHAPTER 7

CROSSING PATHS

Summer, 1979

O n the other side of Toronto, the general mood was vastly different—pleasant and positive. Mom kept the condo spotless with no strewn clothes to trip over, much more to Irene's liking. As always, Mom came home from work, power napped for 15 minutes before cooking supper; and on weekends there was laundry and cleaning other peoples' homes. As for Dad, well known at his work (Riverdale Hospital) as a prankster and a character—he spent spare time here or there; mostly there.

The person who received the most attention from Mom was her *baby*, Davy, an unplanned birth at forty. In his pre-teen years that baby grew rapidly to become tall and lanky. A Toronto Star paper route got him up in the mornings and kept him busy. The Biondics had full employment.

On Saturdays, after a late night of disco hopping with the guys, I had showed up to help with the very heavy edition—as though it would make up for my absence the other six days. I was happy to see he had several good friends from the building, which I felt let me off the hook. On rare occasions Davy and I played hockey, even if I couldn't skate all that well; and then we walked a considerable distance home, too impatient to wait for a bus.

Davy's heroes played professional basketball. Photos of guys like Larry Byrd covered a bedroom wall. One day Davy would be an all-star, he dreamed.

At this stage I wasn't much of a role model for either Davy or Irene. As their older brother, the one who was to pave the way, let's call a spade a spade, was a dismal failure. No university. No respectable job. No girlfriend.

In his teens Davy stood six feet tall and wrapped in sinewy muscles, the perfect physique for a running back. In a local football league he contributed to the team's domination three years in a row. MVP and nicknamed the Bionic Man, far cry from Little Igor.

Bestowed with natural athleticism, he played high school football and basketball and excelled in volleyball—a junior on the senior team.

One day bled into the next, I simply didn't care. At work Duane seeing that something was wrong, switched from religion to politics to perk up my mood. I buried my head pretending to be busy.

When I got back to my apartment, I locked the door and burrowed inside until the next morning—no energy even for a run. The phone was dead: it never rang which suited me just fine. Forgotten in a corner, the radio and record player collected dust. I couldn't stand any music, too afraid what emotions it might stir.

Not wanting to think or feel, I turned on the boob tube and ate cold cereal for supper. Just like breakfast, only switching Cornflakes to Rice Krispies. In the middle of the night, I turned off the TV and fumbled and stumbled my way to bed.

Clung to the hope that by some miracle Tereza would have a change of heart. Strong, mixed feelings returned, dominating my thinking. *Putting her goals aside, part of her must care for me. How can she be so practical, so calculating? It's a huge mistake. She'll never find anyone better.*

I resented that she gave up so easily on our perfect match.

* * * * *

Every Tuesday evening, Erlinda and a friend had been attending ballroom dancing classes. They met in the condo lobby and leisurely walked the 5 minutes to the nearby high school. The beginner class was inundated with women, so she felt fortunate to be partnered at times with one of the two male instructors. At a recent wedding she had sat out, watching elegant couples sweep effortlessly across the dance floor. Now she was taking the opportunity to learn.

* * * * *

As summer faded and I accepted, alas, a miracle was too much to ask for, a whole new attitude moved in. I vowed no women was *ever* again going to hold power over me! Virtually the same perspective I had pitched to Willy, but it's different when it happens to you, isn't it? Determination trumped dejection.

I commenced a regimented training program in preparation for the Toronto Marathon with the hope of qualifying for Boston. Further to that end, Dad moved in with me—no questions asked. What differences my parents had been none of my business. *Let them work it out.* Like civil war, there was no point other nations going in for their reasons and making things worse.

The new money paid for altitude training, like the elite runners, in Banff, Alberta.

By a stroke of good luck, I made friends and trained with Ted: a long-haired, bearded, teeth-missing character. Wildly funny. His hyperenergetic attitude—result of extra strong coffee and natural supplements—made me talk and smile, if not laugh.

That fall, I shot through three marathons in rapid succession, the fastest—with Mom, Irene and Davy cheering me on—clocking a respectable 2:53. Missed qualifying by three minutes.

On a different front, I registered for adult evening enrichment programs. Ballroom dancing, gourmet cooking and meditation. Great environments for meeting somebody compatible and increasing my appeal to the fairer sex.

My good buddies, Nick and the Baron were at the ballroom dancing classes as well, and by the second night we had steady partners.

For the winter semester, I signed up in both advanced and be-ginner classes, casting a wider net in the proverbial sea. My inten-tions were out in the open: just enjoying the freedom without ex-pectations or attachments.

In the beginner class, my regular partner Gabby was away for a few sessions, so I lined up again with other unmatched men across from unmatched women. I scanned the candidates stopping at an elegantly dressed Oriental woman, a lady with an aura of confident maturity about her. 'Oriental' in those days meant from East Asia, even exotic, with no pejorative connotation some bring to it now-adays.

I walked over.

By the end of the hour, Erlinda proved easy to get along with and easy to lead. Just another partner.

If the reader expected fireworks at this point, after the long buildup, sorry to disappoint.

For the New Year's Eve dance the class was going to a dance hall; Erlinda drove a girlfriend and me there. During the evening I danced with several women, but elicited a promise from Erlinda that the last dance was to be ours.

Even as we spoke I noticed the long, black hair spilling over the shoulders and her smell, clean and fresh like air after an April shower. Sorry again, I can't think of a more eloquent description. Gently I pulled her close, hand around the slim waist and slightly up the back to enjoy my most comfortable dance ever.

I felt downright creepy about what I was doing; and if it didn't work out, I was going to look incredibly foolish. At the entrance to the auditorium was a table with two sheets of student names, listed by surname, and their *phone numbers*. The instructor was away momentarily and other students were soon to arrive, so I had to act quickly. But I knew her only as Erlinda. This was not going to be easy. The instructor was coming back. *Think, George, think!*

At the end of the class, Erlinda and I agreed to go on a date.

"I'll call you," I said.

"But you don't have my number."

"Yes I do."

"OK smart guy, what is it?" she said playfully, placing hands on hips.

I carefully recited a number.

"Not even close, buster." She smiled.

"Now run it backwards," I said and turned to leave.

A bit of a delay before, "Oh my lord!" And with that, I knew I had her attention.

Our first movie was coincidentally, *The Jerk*. This time I was completely relaxed, enjoying the show and the company.

Typically on our dates, I dropped her off at her door and ran home, a daypack tight against my back and Walkman in hand. On one, it's safe to say, fortuitous evening I arrived at my apartment after our date only to discover my key was inside. Dad wasn't answering, undoubtedly somewhere else for the night.

I was locked out.

The closest person I knew was a female acquaintance in the next building. I explained my predicament over the phone. Quite understandably, she was not keen to let me crash at her place for the night. After a long day I was weary but not about to press.

Next, I rang up Erlinda.

"Fine. No problem. I'll get the sofa ready," she said with no hesitation in her voice. Trust me, I was listening.

When she opened the door, no guardian angel could have had a more sympathetic face.

The pullout was prepared, pillows and sheets perfectly in place.

Within the darkness I lay sleepy, and yet thinking about her beautiful body on the bed tantalizingly close in the other room. I felt a strong urge to join her. *If I did, what would it say about me? That I made up the story about being locked out. I was devious. A liar.* That's not how I wanted to be perceived. Besides, so far, I liked the path we were on.

In the morning, she didn't stir so I tiptoed to the kitchen for water. Spread on the table, a complete cereal breakfast—obviously she was a good listener when I told her my breakfast preferences—and a brief note ending with "Be sure to lock the door behind you. Erlinda."

Wait one moment. What just happened here? She had gone to work, trusting me with all her personal possessions.

139

The significance of that decision was impossible to ignore. An epiphanic moment. Any notion of dating other women completely evaporated in that kitchen, that morning.

Gabby, my first dance partner, called about a recent inheritance and invited me to spend some of it travelling. I politely declined.

Erlinda and I enjoyed doing things together: dancing at the historic The Palais Royale Ballroom and cross-country skiing that she introduced me to. Over a dinner I had prepared, we got to know each other even better. The gourmet classes came to good use.

I had been looking for a girl who could keep up with me, like roughing it in the wild outdoors. So I secretly put her to a test— camping in Algonquin Park—starting with a three-hour drive. Rented a canoe. With supplies loaded, I pushed off from the launching pad Erlinda at the front.

Not having roughed it before, she was willing to give it a go. She rowed, pinky sticking out and the other four fingers firmly holding the paddle. For two hours we rowed across Lake Joseph, portaged to another lake for more rowing; and landed on a tiny, uninhabited island.

She cooked supper while I filtered water and set up the tent. Early in the night, outside noises concerned her, "Could it be a bear?" and tucked in even closer to me.

By the time we returned the canoe, she hadn't uttered a single word of complaint—passing the test with flying color. Quite remarkable, for a woman twelve years older than me.

All my money was in RRSP GIC's earning 15% and since investment books emphasized diversification, I decided with great interest to expand into real estate. No, not an empire, but an entry level house. To make it feasible on my meager salary several things had to fall into place. First, determine an affordable price based on: a deposit (from my Registered Home Owners Savings Plan), carriable mortgage (preferably transferable), renovation costs, legal fees and moving expenses. Second, rental income from a basement apartment was essential for cashflow.

Erlinda suggested we live together and she pay me *rent*. Being with her all the time sounded enticing: the strength of our relationship would be thoroughly tested in a prelude to marriage. What's more, she offered additional financial aid with a loan of $10,000 to be paid when possible. I couldn't believe this woman!

"Fine," I said, "but on my terms." Is the reader following this wacky twist? I wanted, in writing, the principal plus going rate of interest to be due on a specified date and signed by me. She didn't think it necessary—she trusted me, but I insisted anyway. Considering that she offered, to some this may seem weird.

Within minutes of their meeting, Dad and Erlinda were chatting like they knew each other for years.

"Well then, let's find George a nice, little house," said Dad.

"*Ako Bog da,* God willing," Erlinda added, something she had picked up from me. Dad laughed heartily.

Hmm, he likes her already.

And so, with great enthusiasm we set out a house hunting. According to my high school urban geography, as I recalled, start in the right neighbourhood. Common sense, right?

Dad's broad knowledge of renovation was a comfort.

We viewed several properties.

Then, I took the comparable "Sold" and "For Sale" to do my own market analysis, not trusting the agent's honesty or ability.

Now I felt confident. With an understanding of the seller and his motivation, we had the best possible house at the lowest price: a one and a half story home in Scarborough.

Not long after, in the annual performance review at work, my manager expressed a concern: I wasn't displaying any initiative to climb up the corporate ladder. How could I tell him I felt perfectly content with the status quo? I had social, financial and psychological equilibrium.

Feeling pressured, I took a Production Control Operator position on the *night* shift at the main computer installation, a considerable distance away.

The intense, high-speed computer world operated under the sharp eyes of whizzes and geeks vying for promotion and not keen to help the new guy. A seismic shift for me.

My eyes couldn't keep up with the new scrolling monitors. At HQ I had used the old typewriter kind—no screen. I experienced growing dizziness, fatigue and slow cognitive processing. As the days passed, I became increasingly jittery and twitchy. The possibility of losing my job played heavily on my mind with house possession day looming!

Seeking a temporary reprieve, we took a vacation to Jamaica. Not one day too soon.

Erlinda, her voice soothing like baby oil over a blister, suggested that at some point I look for work elsewhere.

The lawyer went through the lengthy possession process and with final signatures out of the way, he informed me keys would be available on the big day.

To passers-by it wasn't much: a small, aluminum siding, detached house circa 1910. To me it was *my home*, purchased on my own initiative at the age of 27. And yet, I knew very well I could *not* have done it without Dad and Erlinda.

He and I scoped the outside and then, stepped inside.

It required work—lots of work—and he was eager to tackle it on the spot. Even so, something had to be established first.

"We start when you agree to let me pay you." It sounded harsh even to my ears. Now it's confirmed, I *am* weird.

"What are you saying?" He was confused.

"Whoever I get to work on the house will be paid, so that goes for you too." I disliked doing this to him but I had to.

"I can't take your money. I'm your father."

"And I am your *adult* son." The expression on my face must have convinced him not to call my bluff for he reluctantly agreed, clearly not pleased about the ultimatum.

Over the next few weeks we worked evenings and weekends, in addition to our regular jobs, building a tiny basement apartment just in time for the tenant to move in. The house was earning a small income.

Erlinda also moved in amongst all the noise and commotion.

Once half-settled in, I updated *our* living area as she handled the daily chores and sewed curtains to match the furniture.

Nights at IBM were dragging me down so much I dreaded everything there, and hence called in sick way too often. An absolute wreck in abject misery. Only Erlinda's loving embrace was powerful enough to sooth my frayed nerves.

When our place looked presentable, Mom came over for lunch. Concerned about propriety, I set up a second bedroom and presented it as Erlinda's. None of this was necessary if you asked her. Mom didn't even blink at the pretext, she loved the home's cheerful open concept. My culinary skills were put to use; on other special occasions, Erlinda and I teamed up preparing elaborate meals testing favourite classic recipes. For Christmas we were at Mom's, all except Dad.

Erlinda's personable nature made her an easy fit.

A new year, a new job, a fresh start.

The newspaper ad sounded appealing: downtown insurance company requires an energetic computer operator for shiftwork in a friendly environment. Their progressive approach of equal number of Blacks, Whites and Orientals did indeed help to create a friendly atmosphere. And as advertised, operators were always in motion.

Nevertheless, after a while I became aware again of my anxiety and memory issues. Every time I came back to work on Mondays, I struggled to remember 20 simple computer commands—ones I had entered hundreds of times before. Managed by reviewing.

My problem was linked to and affected by, exposure to a terminal, so I attached a standard glare-reducing filter. It helped somewhat.

But how long could I last in the industry with *this* vulnerability? Certainly not for a full working career. So I reintroduced my old target: retire at thirty-five by any means and by whatever smarts I still possessed.

Seven years away, the countdown clock was ticking again.

Would Erlinda be willing to go on this journey with me?

Speaking of journeys, she had talked about a wish to visit the northeast region of the States. At the first opportunity we loaded up her Volkswagen Rabbit with camping equipment ready to head out.

"Why don't you drive?" she said.

"Ah, I can't. It's your car," I said, not having driven ever since the Pinto accident. I still felt responsible.

"I'd like to share it with you," she lifted the left eyebrow invitingly.

So I got behind the wheel fully intent on not repeating my previous mistake.

Among the popular sights and attractions—Washington, D.C. was of particular interest for both its historical and political significance.

On the day of our return, the sky was powder blue and the sun a golden yellow. I recall sailing along a quiet country road enjoying a heart-to-heart conversation. Easy silence in between. Most of all, I recall the feeling of comfort.

The moment I had been wanting for years had arrived.

A glow swept over me like dawn in early morning and warmed every part of my being.

"I just thought of something," I said, inspired by the revelation.

"What is it?" asked Erlinda.

"I'll tell you one day."

She stared at me with open curiosity.

The packed elevator sped like it couldn't wait, up the CN Tower, at the time the tallest freestanding structure in the world and the most distinct feature of the Toronto skyline. In mere seconds it reached the observation deck. At the entrance to the restaurant, I requested a private table with a panoramic view.

While the restaurant revolved imperceptibly, we were treated to a bird's-eye view of our city, Toronto 'The Good': the islands on Lake Ontario, downtown skyscrapers and vast neighbourhoods. Familiar neighbourhoods where I grew up, worked, played and lived.

We ordered drinks and meals.

My entire focus now turned to Erlinda who wore a white, cotton, strapped dress sprinkled with pink and blue flowers.

How wonderful she made me feel.

Her playful voice danced in my ears. Her fresh smell I knew intimately, so feminine I wanted to inhale until I burst. Her shiny black hair, parted at the side and tucked behind an ear, tumbled in waves to her bare shoulders. Her eyes, oh those eyes, how I loved those joyful eyes that lighten my heavy heart. With the gentle raise of her eyebrow, I was willing to fall on a sword for her. And, a smile so bright it lit a path, my path, all the way to heaven.

I whispered instructions for the waiter to take a picture of us. My right hand slightly raised as I held hers in the other.

Then I asked the question all men who are in love long to say, "Will you marry me?"

My hand lowered and the waiter snapped the photo. She was taken aback, captured by the camera, even though we had discussed marriage on several occasions.

"Yes," slipped from the lovely lip. "Of course I will."

My search was over.

I rushed to the nearest public phone to tell Dad the great news.

"You called *me* first?" he said with a tremor. I had to, knowing how much it would mean to him.

Then I told Mom, who had just come home with Davy from a vacation, something I had promoted for months. After all the years of hard work, she deserved it.

"Nobody lives forever," I had reminded her.

Pictures of them on a Florida beach and at Disney World were proof it was money well spent.

Soon after, all the Biondics gathered in my parents' condo living room, looking worried. They had reason to be so. I had called for a rare family meeting and my own face suggested a serious matter was at hand. After a brief preamble, I cut to the chase.

"You know I love you *all* very much," I said.

Now they were really worried, so I tried to hurry up but struggled for the right words.

"This has been my family, but . . ." I stopped to gain courage, "it's time for me to have my own nest."

Their body language said, "Yes, so?"

"Should a time come where someone here has a disagreement with Erlinda I will always, *always* take her side, right or wrong." My loyalty was not to be tested.

Collectively they sat back with audible relief.

"That's never going to happen, dear," said Mom. "We want to see you and Erlinda happy."

"How can you talk that way?" said Dad quite firmly. "She's the best in the Biondic family."

He would refer to Erlinda with that expression right to the final days of his life.

* * * * *

With the warm summer weather at hand there was no better time to meet Erlinda's side of the *family*, her dear friends. There were many.

"Kindest, gentlest people you'd ever want to meet" is how Dad described the Filipinos, having worked with several at the hospital.

Barbecues, CPU alumni meetings and Baptist church services: we attended them all.

Wherever and whoever, I was warmly welcomed and accepted. Filipinos, and I, place the greatest importance on spirituality and strong family ties.

* * * * *

In those days Ontario Place, down by Lake Ontario, used to hold concerts. It was a marvelous location to sit on a grassy hill, with a pleasant breeze blowing your worries away as you enjoyed top notch, reasonably-priced music. A well-kept secret for several years.

On one memorable occasion Bobby Vinton performed, so Mom and Irene came with us.

They sat on a soft and green grassy knoll, the smiling sun caressing their beautiful faces. I had to take a picture. Had to.

The three most important women in my life, together, radiating joy and vitality, made for a singularly exquisite moment.

I'm such a lucky guy.

CHAPTER 8

MOTIVATION

Scarborough
November, 1981

T raditional weddings require far more work than many newly-
weds might imagine, and often turn into emotionally charged
events. For that reason alone try to get married only *once*, in spite
of the overwhelming statistics of failed and multiple marriages.
Who's invited, who's not, and where they sit takes more scrutiny
than studying the Holy Bible. Of course you could leave it to the
bride's mother just to make her happy. But hey, whose wedding is
it anyway? Should you forget, your lovely bride may remind you
in no uncertain terms, it's hers.

Erlinda and I paid for *everything*, but not without going through
a major dispute with Dad.

If you want to retain sanity and have some chance of a half decent time, start planning early: a year or more. Wedding planners
cost big bucks, so we took the DIY approach. You could pay
through the nose for everything, and mine would bleed with each
quote. Wherever you go you're either Prince Philip walking behind
Queen Elizabeth II or the assistant who writes the cheques. For the
millennials, that's what we used before credit cards, one step above
trading beads. Do you want your bride and everyone else to accuse
you of being cheap? One day, you could be on your deathbed praying to the good and merciful Lord to take you away, while she's

screaming into your hearing aid how you wouldn't cough up a lousy thousand bucks for the flowers. Think about it, my friend.

Fortunately, Erlinda and I were very much like minded, spelled FRUGAL. Having come from poverty, we absolutely wanted to avoid it . . . at all cost. For income tax purposes, November 27 was a good date: close to year end and yet not competing with Christmas. Our budget allowed a hundred guests, accepting that some on my father's side would get upset if not invited. Caterers create a fuss when someone brings four unexpected children and grandparents.

Erlinda is a Baptist and I a Catholic, so to avoid appearance of favoritism we picked United. A quaint chapel.

Warning! You may wish to skip the following two paragraphs for it contains scenes that some may find offensive. And for readers expecting scenes of explicit sex, you're out of luck. Sorry again.

Nick, the Baron, Willy and Kingston took me to an upscale strip place.

Thankfully, not a stag party where guys gamble and get roaring drunk. At these 'celebrations' some think it's fun howling jubilantly at hardcore movies of women being objectified and forced to perform unspeakable acts that make you want to vomit. Then a sleazy pimp brings a girl in a drug-induced stupor to grant guys 'favours' in the back room. You fight the impulse to pound the hell out of the bastard and cover the poor girl and take her to her parents. Others feel the same as you, and yet remain the silent majority, intimidated by peer pressure. You need to shower from the human depravity but it can't cleanse your mind of those images.

Enough of that. Back to the cheerful main topic: experiencing wedding bliss and stress, simultaneously.

Judy, Erlinda's close friend and nursing classmate put on a fun—by all accounts—shower with the Filipino friends.

Over the last few years, I became very good friends with Kingston. We had played billiards in Mom's building, talking about religion, politics and travel. It came as a pleasant surprise that his mother put on a second shower.

The day before tying the knot, I picked up my tux—white, double-breasted jacket padded nicely in the shoulders, and snug pants which to my surprise fit like tailor made. I felt handsome.

During the church rehearsal, I met Belen the maid of honour, a charming bundle of energetic joy and Claire, the shy flower girl.

Later on at our house, classmates Eve and Eva from New York joined Belen and Erlinda for a party. As per custom, I wasn't permitted to see the bride so they shooed me out the door to Mom's.

I had hoped to sleep in but there was much to do. Right from the get go, I was bouncing around between Mom's, our house and the hall: transporting things and people and constantly referring to a checklist.

Through the door I heard the girls chattering with excitement as they prepared Erlinda, putting on the dress, fixing the hair and applying makeup.

Late fall can be windy, cold and rainy if you're unlucky. However the gods were smiling upon us, for the day turned out warm and sunny.

In a room at the side of the chapel I put on the tux while Kingston, the best man, drove home in panic searching for his bowtie.

The giant organ thundered as Erlinda entered into view, escorted by Judy's husband Tany. She floated gracefully down the aisle—a white, satin gown trimmed with lace wrapped her svelte figure—radiating beauty and happiness. Using her own talent, she had transformed a simple gown into an intricate and elegant one, just as her Mom would have done if she was alive.

In front of all, we promised to each other to hold our union as most sacred.

Then, we faced the smiling and clapping guests to savour the joy. One person confessed to me (years later) she had suspected a husband could not remain faithful to an older wife. Perhaps the other only dissenting person in the church was Dragica who introduced me to Tereza.

There is no doubt in my mind that ultimately, this was the best outcome for Tereza and myself.

In the receiving line at the reception, Dad and Mom who didn't appear together much nowadays, jointly and proudly welcomed everyone. Nick, the MC, entertained with a mixed blend of humour and sincerity; just before supper, Duane my good friend from IBM said grace; Erlinda received a flattering speech from Kingston; and when a Croatian guest suggested some entertainment, the Baron stepped in with an impromptu Cossack dance.

Oh, what a relief to see everything go smoothly.

To end the evening, Erlinda and I danced to the romantic "Stranger on the Shore" just as I had imagined for this day.

Here's a note Erlinda wrote in our year end review:

> *Never noticed him at dance classes. He came towards me with so much hair, I wondered if there was a face underneath. I'll never forget how he held me at the New Year's Eve dance. He was polite, gentle and kind. It feels great that he is interested seriously in me for who I am, as I am. We share the same interests and values. He looks after me and is true to me. I no longer consider myself too old to marry.*

The real estate agent insisted over the phone to make the offer at that very hour, so we converged at Erlinda's work. Right there in the crowded Emergency hallway with patients moaning nearby, he slapped the papers onto the only empty stretcher.

My heart skipped a beat, Erlinda so scrumptious in a green, figure-hugging uniform, a stethoscope hanging from the neck. *Oh, she was going to get attacked tonight!*

"Hold it," I said quickly. While I pulled out the camera, she covered an elderly patient with an extra gown, unaware his back end was exposed.

"Let's get going," said the agent eager to seal the deal.

"This must be the strangest place you've done this?" I spoke.

"You'd be surprised."

After putting my John Hancock on the purchase of a suburban bungalow, a step up from the old place, I relaxed.

Not having seen Mom since Christmas, I drove to my parent's condo.

"Mom, I'm home," I shouted, letting myself in.

She was sitting in the chair next to the phone, looking rather stunned.

"What's going on?"

"A woman just called," she said. "She told me to drop dead. Imagine that."

"What? Who is she?"

"I don't know. But she asked for Marijan . . ." She stopped to think. "All these years it was cards. Now it's women." The muttered words faded away, so I got a glass of cold water out of the fridge for her.

Once revived she spoke, picking up speed. "I do his laundry and he runs around." Now in a rage. "No more. That's it. He and I are finished!"

The next day while she was at work, Dad came by to gather up a few personal things from the condo and left. Apparently, he had been living with the other woman for some time, as Mom suspected but didn't want to face.

When Dad called me at home, I tried to remain calm, not to take sides. He acknowledged they'd have to sell the condo, even though he hated the idea of greedy agents and lawyers getting outrageous amounts of their hard-earned money.

Mom worried about where she, Davy and Irene would go once the place was sold, so much so, that her doctor put her on medication.

Once I heard all that, I decided it was time to step in, even at risk of appearing to take sides. Erlinda and I agreed to help financially so Mom could buy out Dad. Staying true to who he was, Dad asked for much less than half.

Mom was relieved, but the damage was already done.

With the packing almost finished, we were looking forward to moving into our new house when Davy called.

Mom was in the hospital.

Worried out of our minds we rushed to St. Joseph's where the doctor informed us that she had had a stroke, affecting the left side of the body. I had feared worse.

Soon after, she was transferred to a convalescent home for a few weeks. We visited when possible as did Irene. Davy was there every day, even school days.

To lift his spirits (he was only sixteen), we watched him in a volleyball tournament. Leaping high over the net he released blistering spikes. No signs of emotional turmoil.

When I ran the 42k Toronto Marathon, Davy did also, on the spur of the moment, clocking 3:45; rather astounding for an inexperienced teen whose longest training run was 10k.

After rehab we brought Mom, still looking fragile, to our place for a barbecue. While Erlinda grilled the burgers, Mom and I sat in the living room out of the summer sun. Silence.

To start a conversation I asked about the exercise program for the left hand. After a short sentence or two and she was quiet again.

"In a few weeks you'll be as good as new," I said. According to the doctor most of the expected recovery *had* already taken place. She limped using a cane and wore a brace to support the sagging shoulder.

Out of nowhere, "You stole my jewelry, you bastard," she said in Croatian, visibly agitated. And then followed by a number of profanities all flying in my direction. For a moment I couldn't breath, it felt like a blade had been plunged into my gut and with each foul word it was being twisted.

Soon I realized the outburst was meant for someone else. The doctor had warned us about potential mental confusion arising from the stroke.

Concerned about how long Mom would be with us, here on earth, even though she wasn't even sixty, we had her over throughout the summer and fall. Contrary to the medical opinion, both her mental and physical conditions improved. She was not giving up without a fight.

The three of us lounged in the back yard, enjoying gentle hours among the luxuriant vegetables and flowers tended to by Erlinda. For those times, I am especially grateful and will always cherish.

That year the province and federal governments set up temporary incentive programs: a grant and an interest free loan for first time home buyers. I proposed that we and Irene buy a condo.

She couldn't see how that was possible, she had no savings, until I explained the attractive incentives available to her. Home ownership was feasible if she share it with a suitable tenant.

Irene was converted.

A two-bedroom apartment across from Mom popped up on the market and we immediately jumped on it, conditional on financing.

To our great disappointment, the unit sold that night on a firm offer.

Irene was livid that she lost the opportunity because of me. Even with the agent's recommendation, I had refused to remove the 'conditional on financing' clause.

Irene dropped the whole idea of working with me.

* * * * *

No day of the year triggers an introspection of oneself and our priorities as much as a birthday. On Erlinda's, we stopped to re-examine the original plan of waiting for financial security before having a child. You see, her biological clock was fast approaching midnight; we felt compelled to act without delay.

IUD was removed. After several monthly cycles of no luck, we decided to investigate. For my part it sounded easy enough. I simply produce a sample, after all, since my early teens I had been producing more samples than I care to count or admit to.

At the urologist's office the nurse handed me a jar and pointed to the washroom.

I stood over the toilet bowl waiting. Ho-hum. As a teenager I would have been shaking with excitement at the opportunity, moreover, now I didn't have to be concerned about ending up in hades. Strange, I showed no interest. *This is ridiculous.*

Ten frustrating minutes later, I sheepishly stepped out to the reception area.

"Can I go home and come later?" I said kind of mumbling through the word *come*.

"Sure, we understand."

Was I imagining things or was she grinning?

156

Darn it, I had thrown out all the Playboy centrefolds some time ago. Scrambling pathetically I found an Eaton's catalogue.

"Everything is fine," said the doctor. "You can't rush nature, you know." I wasn't trying to rush her, simply trying to check off a few bigger items from a lengthy "to do" list.

"If I was you, I wouldn't worry about it," he continued. *If you were me, I wouldn't worry about it either, but . . .*

To increase the probability of success, the doctor offered suggestions and sent us home on a serious *mission*: to procreate.

Her responsibility was tracking the ovulation cycle. Mine, to wear boxer shorts, not a huge ordeal at first glance; and yet, the thought of 'junk flying in the trunk' was unsettling. Think of driving without a seatbelt. What's more (some guys will understand this), when you sit down too hastily you risk irreparable harm and may be forced to abort the *mission* permanently.

(Reminds me of the Ono bird, well recognized by birdwatchers for its large, drooping testicles. Every time the Ono flies down for a landing, he can be seen frantically flapping his wings and heard fearfully shouting, "Oh, no! Oh, no!")

Back to us. The last two years we had behaved like two rabbits in heat, exploring along the way many Kamasutra acrobatic entanglements. Sometimes it started with me saying, "Oh karida, you make my blood boil" and kiss her fingertips and up the arm, like Gomez to Trish in the *Adam's Family*. Then I improvised, "You make my liver quiver and corpuscles pulse." She responded, "You're such a nutcase," but it was always worked. Now, regrettably, the whole process was reduced to work.

To raise a child in this world and still maintain household harmony, I felt that financial stability was essential, but on our salaries it would take way too long. My curiosity turned to an obsession. I proposed, not imposed, and Erlinda went along with buying an additional house. On paper it looked possible providing the basement and first floor covered the cash flow.

In a letter to Garth Turner, money columnist for the Toronto Sun and future Canadian finance minister, I asked for advice.

A subsequent book of his included my letter and his reply: "You're talking pretty grand plans for a guy with a very large truck barrelling down on him. So, forget the second house. You've got enough troubles."

Aha, you don't say.

With Dad's help we found a bungalow nearby.

By the end of fall, Mom recovered beyond anyone's expectation and visited us often. As always, she and I would wait in the living room while Erlinda prepared lunch.

On one particular visit we reminisced about the old days in Croatia. When she and Dad met, he was charming and ambitious, but in time his weakness for cards became painfully evident. One day she had had enough so she got ready and walked out of the apartment with Irene and me, ages 3 and 7. We got half way down the road. She stopped.

"Is everything OK, Mama?" I asked.

"Yes, sweetheart," she said. "We are finished with our walk." There was no way she could bring us up without a father.

Today, she was grateful for the nice homes and that none of us had turned to gambling.

"Lunch will be ready in a few minutes," said Erlinda from the kitchen.

"Do you remember that?" Mom asked.

I nodded. The secret was ours.

Did we share another, I wondered? A dim and distant recollection that rarely surfaced because of its horrible nature. Even now as I write this narrative, I'm overcome with emotion. Was it real or a nightmare, only she would know?

"Did you ever do any other kind of work?" I steered the conversation.

"Not really." She adjusted the drooping shoulder. "Except one summer I cooked in a lumber camp. I took you with me."

I dared not interrupt, I was so close to clearing up the past.

"You wouldn't remember that. You were very young."

But I did. My earliest memory.

Of sleeping close to her. And, in the middle of the night, appar-
ently, I wake to a sound from the window.
Perhaps she is very tired for she does not stir.
A menacing figure climbs by stealth over the window sill, and
steps into the bedroom shadows. And approaches.
My body is immobilized with fear. I strain to scream but . . .
Then blackness.

I must have been lost in my own world far too long, for when I
looked up, she held me in a searching gaze.

I couldn't answer that quizzical look, couldn't risk putting her
through the ordeal, if true. What was to be gained? So I hid my
revealing eyes. And hurled the scene into the deepest cave of my
mind, never to let it see the light of day.

"Come and get it," Erlinda shouted.

"And try to eat it!" I responded in jest and relief.

The summer of '83 was all about building, with Dad, a basement apartment in the rental.. Following the proverb "time is money," we worked every available hour of every available day to prepare the unit in time for the tenant's promised move-in-date.

I was picking Dad up at the subway when I spotted beside him a much younger, attractive woman. It was Indira, I instantly suspected, someone he was eager for me to meet. The problem: I most definitely had no interest as I had repeatedly hinted.

Now, he had me cornered, knowing full well I wouldn't be rude.

Courteous on the outside; Furious on the inside.

The Star rental ad for the main floor hadn't generated a response so we were overjoyed to finally interview a couple. A limo parked in front of our driveway; a chauffeur stepped out to hold a door open for the young couple dressed in business attire. Who would believe our luck?

Charmed by the Durochers, I replaced probing questions with pleasantries. Mr. Durocher wrote up 12 postdated cheques on the spot. Impressive.

After I deposited the second cheque, it returned a week later, not sufficient funds.

Being a successful business man he was hard to get a hold of.

"I hate to bother you…" I spoke up.

"Must be some sort of a mistake." Mr. Durocher spoke cheerfully. "To make it easier, I'll get you a certified cheque. It'll just take a couple days." I regretted doubting him, but several weeks passed before I actually held it in my hands.

"This is not certified," declared the teller at the bank.

"What do you mean? It's stamped certified," I said confused.

"If you look closely, someone handprinted *CERTIFIED*.

At the police station, the officer found four charges of forgery against Durocher. He suggested I go to Small Claims Court and that the Landlord and Tenant Agency could help with that.

Four months later, the tenants from hell disappeared, leaving in a bedroom heaps of garbage and dog droppings.

At Small Claims, we won a judgement but before the wages could be garnisheed, he skipped from his job as a limo driver.

Now that I've proven to be a gullible fool, the next story is actually *more* embarrassing for another reason altogether. I promised myself at the onset of these self-indulgent ramblings, to be honest with myself and you the reader. Since the shoe fits, I'll wear it.

In reading the newspaper regularly, I got the general impression a lot of violent crimes in Toronto were being committed by black Caribbean people. A running friend said it was mostly Jamaican gangs that moved up here to sell drugs.

Not wanting additional stress of *any* kind, I screened phone calls with one more variable, the accent. *All the Jamaicans in Toronto have our phone number. Why me?* I knew it was wrong because I felt like a sleaze, even though it seemed justifiable.

One caller passed the test and still, after the Durocher fiasco, I was on guard. A *luxury* car parked in front and a middle age, impeccably dressed, Black man opened the passenger door for a pregnant, stunning blond.

Not again.

At this point there was no choice except to answer the door.

He sounded educated, behaved with dignity and looked like . . . Sidney Poitier in *Guess Who's Coming to Dinner.* I kid you not.

I thoroughly checked the references, desperate to believe Mr. Poitier and wife were the real deal.

How did it turn out, I'm sure you want to know?

Well, they were the first tenants to receive a Christmas present from us: Erlinda knitted a hat and mitts set for the newborn.

We badly wanted them to stay. Don't believe it? Ask Erlinda.

* * * * *

Dad and Indira's relationship was more than a brief affair: in a few months they got married, a civil wedding. The only invitees, Erlinda and I, although my heart wasn't into it. Bursting-at-the-seams pregnant and a twenty years age difference meant this relationship wouldn't last.

However, Dad—ecstatic when Angela was born—showered mother and child with great attention and affection. At the age of 61 he was a young man again.

In the spring another miracle was in the making, probably conceived while we were on a winter vacation in Curacao. The first sign—Erlinda missing her period and feeling nauseous—followed by the obstetrician confirming our excited suspicions.

The sewing room was redecorated to a nursery centred by a crib.

Deciding on a name took days, if not weeks, given it should express a strong spirit. The finalists were Ayla, the heroin in *Clan of the Cave Bear* or Alexander, after the great king.

Erlinda's knitting needles clicked with joy making a hat and mitts; and I sat next to her like butter melting in the sun.

One morning about three months into the pregnancy, Erlinda called me urgently to the bathroom. Her face, colourless and grave, focused on a bloody fetus limp in her hands.

Following the obstetrician's instruction, I rushed her to the Emergency where they performed a D and C.

On the drive home we scarcely said a word until Erlinda broke the silence.

"It's so unfair," she said bitterly. "Women who don't want a baby have one. I *do* and can't."

"You're OK, that's all that matters."

As I pulled into the driveway she said, "We still got each other."

Mother nature had signalled—we had run out of time.

With the miscarriage, one door closed and another opened: my initial exuberance at work resulted in a promotion to shift leader. My manager, sympathetic to our loss, gave me extra time off from work. Seeking emotional comfort, we bought a red Horizon, more like a necessity in fact for the old Rabbit was rusting badly. I had to duct tape the fender to keep it from falling off. Seriously.

In need of even more solace, we took a cross-country camping trip to the U.S. southwest. It didn't start well: we were in a minor car accident. It was *not* my fault! I was making a right and an inebriated guy tried to pass on the shoulder in a No Passing Zone!

In spite of the unpleasant incident, it was the beginning of a life long love affair with the region.

Irene, Davy, Erlinda and I were lined up in chairs, deathly quiet and still, at the end of a corridor. Waiting. I couldn't see anything, hear anything, feel anything. Erlinda nudged an elbow to my ribs: The Emergency doctor was heading our way.

"There's no easy way to say this. She's gone. I'm so sorry for your loss."

Two shattering words: *She's gone.*

"But she's breathing," Davy jumped in. Someone moaned from a nearby room.

"The respirator is doing it for her. She experienced massive cerebral hemorrhaging." The doctor waited patiently for the words to sink in. "There's no indication of neurological activity."

No one said anything.

"There's nothing left to do now except turn off the life support. The decision is yours." He looked around at all of us.

Irene who hadn't spoken to me since the loss of the condo, stared at him in shock.

Davy slowly slumped forward until his head rested on his palms, as though it would roll off his shoulders onto the floor. In minutes his powerful body had shrunk by half.

"Turn it off," I said. Somebody had to.

"Yes, go ahead," Irene agreed.

Davy mumbled something unintelligible.

Before we all went our ways, I offered to have him stay with us. He had friends to meet, he said. I was about to press the invitation, then let it go.

When I asked, months later, he explained what had happened that day. He was acting as lifeguard at the condo indoor swimming pool when a woman shouted that Mom was in the women's change room "not feeling well." He found her lying semi-dressed on the cold, granite floor unresponsive. An ambulance had rushed her to hospital.

Everyone we could contact in Toronto, including Dad, came to either the church or wake. Nick and the rest of my school friends, the pallbearers, were particularly supportive to Irene and me.

163

In the eulogy, I almost choked up when I said the most important thing in her life was her children. A few women sniffed and then cried.

As those children, we decided collectively on an open casket. I approached dutifully, fearfully, eagerly, all mixed up. She wasn't really gone; and yet her face was waxy yellow and her entire body, even the lungs, were still, no less still than the pyramids in Egypt.

She loved Davy, Irene and me equally—always ever so happy to see us come home and to feed us and care for us. I longed desperately to hug her one last time before her spirit lifted to join her *own* parents. Forced myself to pull away. Was I disloyal, deserting her? It sure felt that way.

Erlinda and I jointly place one blood-red rose on the coffin, watching it gradually lower into the earth.

As the executor of the estate, Irene decided to sell their condo. Of the proceeds, a small fixed amount went to her, some to pay out my loan and the majority to go to Davy, barely eighteen. I presumed she was eager to sell because of her own financial difficulty: she had offered to pay a third for the gravestone but wasn't able to. So Erlinda and I did.

In my mind, I was best suited as executor. I would have arranged some kind of joint ownership of the condo between Davy and Irene. Or at least wait patiently until we got a stronger offer, so Davy would end up with more. It was very difficult to see Irene and Davy not get the maximum out of the situation, but when misunderstandings arose between them, I was relieved not to be a part of it.

Two things I needed to retrieve before they were misplaced among the packing: family photos (or a copy I could make) and the little rabbit wearing a red jacket and blue pants, I had given Mom as a birthday gift all those years ago. The second item held no value to anyone but me.

* * * * *

The shift leader position suited me perfectly.

The only challenge, managing different personalities, but by leading with a positive, can-do attitude we meshed beautifully. Having minimal screen exposure, my memory proved adequate. Besides performing the regular day-to-day trouble shooting, I proposed and volunteered for special projects; thereby, improving the operations department. Result: hefty bonuses.

My manager noticed all this and promoted me to network analyst, (even though my resume showed no education or experience in the area).

This change proved to be most unfortunate.

Within a week, work life flipped on its head.

Sure the paycheque increased but the downside was an abyss. Every time I stepped into a cable room full of electric wires, my hair bristled and I felt woozy. I tried rushing in and out as fast as possible, still the effect was unavoidable; the longer I remained the more severe the effect.

Ashamed and a bundle of nerves, I idled at my desk in the cubicle daydreaming: retirement couldn't come one day too soon.

If only I could have my old job back. How do I explain the why?

Once the condo sold, Davy moved in with Dad and Indira who purchased a house close to us.

As for Irene, we moved her to a little apartment of her own. When all her major furniture seemed settled, I left.

She complained to Dad I wasn't particularly helpful. I must have responded badly because he reminded me that we should all be mindful of her difficult situation and that I should patch things up with her. I wasn't listening.

In fact, as time went on, Irene and I became increasingly estranged.

The rental property was financially self-sustaining, creating momentum for me to take another step. The clock was ticking, and I fixated on advancing towards financial freedom. Once Davy received the inheritance, I suggested we go into a partnership on a house. He preferred the worry-free GICs. No bank would give Erlinda and me a loan because of the high debt ratio, so I offered him a rate better than the banks which he gladly accepted.

We bought a third bungalow. Me acting as our agent saved us the commission fee. With Dad's help we built an even better basement apartment. Honing on safety, we installed extra smoke detectors, an electrician checked the wiring and I insisted on a non-smoking tenant. Experience paid off.

A nosy neighbour reported the apartment to the city. But without my permission, the bylaw inspector couldn't get in. I pressed on, an ever-present tightness in my chest: the basement income was critical in paying the mortgages. No wiggle room.

My manger must have sensed I wasn't happy in the current position, so he mercifully switched me to change co-ordinator. The hub between management, technical support and computer operations. Preventing costly mistakes was critical and I aimed for perfection. I wasn't going to fail this time!

In pursuit of clear and timely communication, a cornerstone of a smoothly functioning computer installation, I cultivated a friendly yet professional relationship with every department.

As it happens time to time in an office environment, a couple of women made romantic overtures: an after-work drink. Perhaps they sensed my vulnerability. Exciting as it might have been, I found the comfort and familiarity waiting for me at home more enticing. Besides, Erlinda and I were extremely busy juggling work and managing five rental units, including the basement in our home. Except for a short winter vacation, it seemed all we did was work and sleep. Our lives had been like that, for the most part, since we tied the knot. Years. My early retirement date had already passed; nevertheless, I thought I was on the right track.

In 1987 the Boston Marathon committee loosened qualification times, giving hope to runners such as myself. With Erlinda's help,

I embarked on an in-depth training program. At the Toronto Marathon, I ran a disciplined race and even with the scourge of the left leg, a pain ignored till now—I qualified for Boston by mere seconds in a time of 2:59.

Finally, after ten years, I was going to Boston.

While surfing the emotional high I got a call from Kingston, wondering if I was still interested in building that empire. Recently, he and his wife Lucille had chosen us as godparents to their daughter, a role we took quite seriously.

"Where?" I asked, intrigued by the notion.

Ten minutes away (from his house), a commercial building was in the final stage of construction and the first group of units was available.

"What's the location like?"

Prime. Major street. Minutes to the highway.

We visited the sales office and walked through the three-story structure. The materials and workmanship were excellent and in spite of the pricey cost, it appeared a sound investment opportunity.

In a lengthy discussion with Erlinda, I was able to convince her to purchase the well positioned corner unit.

Kingston mentioned that Lucille needed office space for her company and that she would be a great fit for us. However, his dual role of landlord and tenant was a concern to me, but he assured me, it would not be a problem.

We were given the shell. Since he was busy at work, I drew up interior plans according to Lucille's specific needs. Then I lined up trades people and ordered much of the material.

Fair market rent needed to determined. When Kingston's initial estimate seemed very low, I offered a solution: we each research comparable units and then compromise..

His list—vastly different to mine—focussed solely on units in old mixed-use strip plazas in mediocre locations. Coming from an intelligent person, his specious reasoning was difficult to fathom.

I sensed an increasing tension between us. To resolve the wide discrepancy I suggested we asked the builder for an opinion. Even though the builder sided with my list, Kingston wasn't budging.

I was baffled. I don't wish to misrepresent his inexplicable actions, but what was I to think?

The conflict *had* to be settled, so I proposed we search for *another* tenant where his loyalty would not come into question. He promised to speak with Lucille.

Out of the blue Irene called asking for a loan, promising to return it plus interest in a year. *What happened to the inheritance? She has a well-paying job and low rent.* In fairness, the inheritance wasn't much. When I asked what the money was for, she broke into a shouting rage and slammed the phone down.

What are we, banks with limitless amounts of money? Money orders were still being sent monthly to family in the Philippines. Erlinda's stepfather spent his share on a gun, gambling and women, according to a goddaughter; Erlinda's half brother, too frequently needed help paying for his six children. None of them sent even a simple thank you or birthday card in return. "Nobody is going to take care of us when we get old, except us," I said. And on that note, communication with her family back home ended.

Rather than money, I sent a letter to Irene suggesting she cut spending and find a devoted lifelong partner to share expenses with. Her boyfriend didn't sound like the marrying kind. I was *great* at dispensing advice, wasn't I?

I found out much later—Irene had lost her job!

The following day I received a letter, this time from Lucille's lawyer, suing me for breach of contract. But no contract had been written up. The situation had become increasing dire and the nightmare had no end.

My lawyer advised us to sell our share to Kingston and be done with it, a legal battle being costly and not guaranteeing success. *It's time to extricate myself from this quagmire.*

In the middle of accepting his low ball offer I stopped suddenly: one line stood out. He sought an outrageous amount of compensation for work *he* had done on the internal plans.

My letter to Kingston stated I would consider the offer, if the labour for the internal plans was credited to me. I felt confident.

Printing on the plans was undeniably mine. He agreed. I sold my share with a small loss but gained a big lesson, albeit nerve-rackingly painful.

Resentment disappeared eventually, replaced by cynicism.

In need of something positive to focus on, I doubled my efforts to get in shape for Boston, three months away. My rigorous training schedule gradually increased the weekly mileage to a peaking at 160km.

A 4:30 a.m. alarm woke me most weekdays for a 20km run to work. To cope with mid winter cold I covered myself with a toque, gloves and layers of clothes including a bright yellow *Training for Boston* shirt, an inspiration from Erlinda. A layer of Vaseline shielded my face against the biting northern winds. On stormy days it was easier to run on plowed roads rather than sidewalks, although I dodged the occasional honking car, driver not expecting a runner at such an ungodly hour. Homeowners shovelling the sidewalk stopped to stare and shake their heads in disbelief.

If time and willpower were available, I ran home.

Weekends were allocated for long runs with a motley group of runners, the "Over the Hill" gang whose lively energy I fed off.

Mondays were rest days.

To drop to a trim racing weight, I followed strictly a no fat or red meat diet of 3,000 calories. A colossal mistake! With whatever I did or thought, I struggled, due to a condition called 'Boston on the Brain' that didn't allow for laziness.

Yup, that's me (282) worn out.

When it became impossible to do a weekend run because my skinny legs felt like 100 lbs. of concrete, I paid a visit to Dr. Kildare with the hope he would write a sick note for work. So I could run some more! It made sense at the time.

"How are you?" He looked disapprovingly at my sickly pallor and shrivelled body.

"A bit tired."

"No kidding," he said.

According to bloodwork, I had anemia: the result of a poor diet and excessive running. Erlinda had probably said something about it but do you think I was listening? Dr. Kildare recommended a well-balanced diet rich in foods I had been avoiding and *no* running for the next week, leading to race day.

"I can't. I'll lose all my fitness."

"Listen to me," he ordered, not letting go of eye contact. "If you want *any* chance at all of finishing, do as I say." He should know, he was a runner too.

I bit my tongue and behaved like a good patient.

On sacred ground in Hopkinton, outside of Boston, Erlinda snapped the picture of me in a running pose, 'START' imprinted beneath my feet.

Famous for being north America's oldest continuous race, the Boston Marathon whipped up the 20,000 runners to a tremendous level of excitement and pride.

The personal picture at the finish line showed an emaciated stick figure barely able to lift his arms in victory.

As I regained physical strength, a change was underway at work: A major project installing new software. The task all mine.

I spent countless hours in front of the screen, eating lunch in my cubicle, often calling home I'd be late for supper. An extra hour turned to two. And still Erlinda refused to eat until I was there.

How long could I keep going, living on the edge?

Anxiety, forgetfulness and irritability reared their ugly heads.

Any small misunderstanding with Erlinda I blew out of proportion. Then I turned inward, sullen for a day or two, before snapping out of it.

Unflappable, Erlinda took care of me as well as anyone could, supporting at every turn.

Out of desperation I drew a chart: a lifetime budget detailing our expenses and assets and a retirement date of October 30.

Counting down the weeks to sweet relief. Seven. Six. Five.

Whenever I could go no further, I turned to the two photos at the side of my desk—Erlinda and Angela (half sister) who we were deeply involved with since Mom left us—and then I pressed on.

The letter of resignation arrived on my boss's desk a month in advance, giving him ample time to find a replacement. Nothing resentful, just heartfelt gratitude to him for the opportunities presented to me

"What are you going to do next?" he asked.

"Oh, I've got several exciting possibilities. Nothing finalized yet." In truth, other than a six month rest, nothing period. To declare I was retiring at 36 would have sounded either ludicrous or boastful.

I *did* finish the project on time and in perfect working order, but at an enormous cost—my health.

On a far more positive note: Davy was getting married in two days.

Not having enough money for school, he had quit and got a job at a newly opened Vic Tanney's fitness club on the other side of town. To reduce commuting time, especially on Sundays, he moved closer to the club.

He met a wonderful Irish woman, Beth. They took their time, their romance following a traditional dating path getting to know each other. And obvious to all, they were in love.

Still weary, I managed to pull myself together with extra strong coffee and peach Schnapps—for the event of the year, Davy's wedding—presumably no one wiser of my mental state.

CHAPTER 9

RECOVERY

1988

O n some level I knew I had to do something. Erlinda had gone to work as always and what was I doing? Sitting on my not so fat duff for the third day since the wedding. Like a zombie, I'd shuffle down the hallway from the kitchen to the bathroom for no purpose at all and stand there, not thinking, just breathing, barely existing.

Retirement came to fruition and yet . . . I needed something more than breathing.

At the dinner table Erlinda spoke with such energy, it prompted me to bring up a subject: building a full addition to the front of the house. A *real* dining room and a roomier entrance would go a long way to increase our comfort, providing ample justification for the project.

"How long do you think it will take?" she asked, looking interested.

"Four months. If I stuck to it."

"You sure you want to do this?"

"I'm sure."

Before a permit could be issued, the city's building department required a set of drawings with the application. My crude hand-drawn plans, obviously not done by an architect, took the inspector by surprise.

"Anything wrong?" I asked.

"Ah, no. Nothing major. Just a few missing bits of information."

In the midst of breakfast, Erlinda answered a knock at the front door.

"Good morning Erlinda!" It was Dad.

"Good morning Marijan."

"How's the best in the Biondic family?"

"Good. You?"

"Not bad as long as I'm busy." They exchanged generous hugs. He spotted me.

"Come on George. Let's get something done today." His typical seize-the-day attitude. I must have been slow to move because he added, "God helps those who help themselves."

With no time to dither which neither of them liked to do, I gobbled down the food faster than intended.

Met him outside where he was sizing up the project and stroking his handlebar moustache. Call us the odd couple, him in a suit and me in a plaid shirt and sweat pants. We moved about, hands waving and fingers pointing.

At Beaver Lumber we stuffed supplies in and on top of the Rabbit; at the rear stuck out a red flag waving *stay back.*

With the backhoe having excavated the area, we had hammered in the forms for the footings. A mixing truck poured concrete as we raked it level, trowelling for a smooth finish.

On Erlinda's day off, we rose at the crack of dawn to wheelbarrow gravel from the driveway down a ramp into the pit. Just like with all other renovations, she was not averse to hard physical labour. In the middle of raking came an amused laugh from above.

"Erlinda, let me do that," said Dad, marvelling at her tenacity.

He took over while she made him coffee with milk. When she returned, we were hustling.

"Now we're cooking with gas," she said, an expression that he and I liked to hear.

What we could do ourselves—framing, wiring, drywalling and flooring—we tackled with keen interest and enthusiasm, mostly generated by Dad. Otherwise I hired the proper trades. Once the main construction was completed, we removed the old door and window. Dust spread into the kitchen and living room even with plastic covering over the openings, creating more work for Erlinda who, as a very clean person, found it difficult to live with.

After several months, the project started to drag out.

Angela was growing and learning quickly, so while Dad and I focussed on the house, Erlinda drove her for hula dancing and gymnastics. To be honest, I felt excluded and envious.

Eventually the addition was completed in double the estimated time and money. Nevertheless, I can say that the satisfaction of having contributed to the household, more than made up for what I missed out on.

Time for leisure opened up so I spent it guiltfree with the family, including Dave and Beth occasionally. By now I had grown to fully accept Indira, giving her warm embraces to assure her I held no ill will.

Picnicking at Niagara Falls, strawberry picking, attending Angela's first Holy Communion, we did it all. On special occasions we combined with Beth's side of the family for even larger gatherings; indeed, for the better part of the next decade that's how it was.

The problem with daily assignments at Office Overload: I was on call, no guaranteed shift, and received minimum wage—so I got back to running. Three times a week and Sundays, Crazy Legs (as he liked to be called) Larry, the gregarious entertainer, two others and myself ran rain or shine. To warm up we bounced for an hour in an aerobics class at Super Fitness. Then we took the same route every day, with the last mile always turning into a full-out sprint back to the club.

All the major races in the northeast (Boston, New York and Chicago) were a day's drive, and we went as a group, doubling up in hotel rooms. The friendly rivalry squeezed out the best in each of us but I had one distinct advantage: Erlinda supporting me.

Before the start of each race I meditated. In the early miles I ran slowly *(unintentionally)*: staying with the guys was impossible. Five minutes behind was as close as I could be without expending valuable energy. At mile 20, known as the wall because most runners slow down sharply, I somehow turned on the jets.

"Fly!" I repeated internally, releasing endorphins.

Invariably, over the last few miles I passed them respectfully—in good sportsmanship—but offering no true encouragement to stay with me. My best time 3:03. The strong finish I attributed in large part to carbo loading in the week leading up to race day.

In late fall, a severe jolt woke me up and made me take notice.

It was a typical day until Erlinda came home from work, worry written all over her face. I sat her down and waited.

In the midst of cleaning a table at work, she had pricked a finger on a used needle. Such an exposure could lead to any number of diseases transmitted through blood, including at the time the highly dangerous AIDS virus. To contain fear, even though it flushed like poison through my own veins, I assured her and myself it was probably nothing to worry about.

As soon as possible she went for blood tests. We waited, trying not to think about it but failing miserably.

Thank God, the results were negative. Once again, we could breathe—she was healthy as always.

* * * * *

What a year politically speaking! The Cold War was over: the Berlin Wall came down, the USSR split up to bits. A Russian setback. And for us, all troubles and fears were behind us.

That Christmas the celebrations were held at our place with everyone including Irene. Dad was particularly pleased. For once I felt strong enough to fulfill his wish for Irene and me to reconcile our differences.

Over the next two months Irene, Erlinda and I enjoyed many good times together. In fact, one evening I spoke with her on the phone until both my ears were red.

Happy days were here again.

176

For Erlinda's 50th birthday we put on a family celebration. Wanting it to be memorable, I gave her a garnet ring. What she did not expect was two more parties, with our western and Filipino friends. This time I gave her two unusual gifts—a little rabbit wearing a red and blue outfit and early retirement. The needle scare had been a warning.

She chose to ease into retirement by working twice a week in the fracture room, safer and less chaotic than the Emergency Department.

I couldn't sleep or do much of anything since the previous evening's emotional phone call with Irene. My concern, in large part, was the affect it would have on how I treated Erlinda. Life's regular stresses can strain a relationship without adding on top this conflict with Irene.

Right from the start I detected by the tone of her voice this was not going to be good. She needed me to make more time for her, perhaps every weekend. My attempts to explain how this was not realistic got shot down.

Furthermore, she wanted advice about something I was afraid my honest opinion would be taken as, all too familiar, criticism. Instead, I listened. Her anger turned to tears leaving me feeling quite helpless.

"I can't get any moral support from you." She slammed the phone in a final burst of anger.

A carefully crafted letter seemed to be my escape from the loop playing in my mind. Without accusations I wrote how I felt and that I couldn't be better or do more. Obviously, she was experiencing depression, so I passed on the recommendations Dr. Rochman had given me.

One hot, humid day, Dave and I came for an unexpected visit to Dad's. Indira, still in her night gown (she rarely dressed up on a day off), was late in preparing supper; Dad had gone to pick up Angela at a girlfriend's place.

Dave and I went to meet them as a surprise. At the apartment, the friend's mother told us they had left a couple hours earlier. *Where could they be and how is it we didn't see them?*

In passing the lounge on the first floor, I spotted Dad with a group of men playing cards. *Where is Angela?*

We entered the room to find her sitting in a corner alone; immediately, she ran to us for a hug. Like Dave, I was relieved to see her but furious with Dad still absorbed by the game.

"We're taking Angela home," I said quite firmly to Dad.

"Huh?" He quickly put the cards down, took his money and caught up with us.

The sun had set by this point and except for street lights it was dark.

"This is late, past supper time." I took a gulp of air. "You don't see Angela is hungry?" The words were spitting out of my mouth, louder and louder; Dave bombarded him with similar anger, an avalanche of pent-up emotion.

"You can't leave her like that. Someone could take her," I continued.

"I'm watching her," he said.

"You're watching *cards*!" Dave and I shouted at the top of our voices, not giving a damn who heard us.

Angela started to cry, so we stopped and stooped down to her level, sensitive to the potential harm all this could do.

"Daddy made a mistake Angela." I stroked her face. "This is not your fault. You're a good girl. Everything will be Ok."

Dave and I hugged her dearly while Dad stood nearby awkwardly silent. Ignored.

* * * * *

The hallway outside Beth's hospital room was crowded, everyone eager for permission from the maternity nurse to enter. Once given the green light, we rushed the door like an unruly Boxing Day mob at Best Buy hoping for a door crasher prize.

"Please, please, one at a time. And keep your voices down," admonished the nurse. After composing ourselves, we entered sort of based on seniority: Dad, Indira and Angela were first.

Then Erlinda, Irene and me. This time—more like worshippers approaching a sacred altar—heads bowed, we shuffled and whispered. To put us at ease, Beth welcomed us much too enthusiastically for a woman who had just given birth.

The Madonna sat up in bed not tired at all, instead, glowing with contentment. In her arms slumbered a swaddled baby, the first of his generation. Beside the bed was a happy father satisfied, as in the Bible, to be background to the main event.

They say a child should be exposed to germs to build a strong immune system. This baby should grow up to be Superman since everyone slobbered his head with kisses.

In lieu of frankincense, myrrh or gold (where do you get the first two anyway?) Erlinda presented Beth with a yellow quilted blanket personally hand embroidered with full name, birth date and weight.

Much too soon, the nurse interrupted the chatter—mother and child needed rest—ushering us out.

* * * * *

As satisfying as running was, I felt an urge to explore; travel seemed to be the remedy. One little problem. On a measly income from Office Overload we couldn't afford to go anywhere, so I opened to the idea of a new career. *But what?*

Having enjoyed filling out our income tax returns, I suddenly saw that the answer was as obvious as the nose on my face. After an intensive training course, I was processing personal returns at Canada Revenue Agency.

It didn't take long before my enthusiasm waned: I sat in front of a screen eight hours a day, every work day. My production slipped even with a handy cheat sheet at my side. Meet the weekly quota, warned the supervisor!

To make things worse, I sat next to an attractive Spanish woman with strong perfume and tight top and mini skirt—an unnecessary distraction. Some might say she was trying to seduce me by smiling and pumping her crossed leg in a suggestive manner. I could try to lie to you and say I didn't take much notice but, *Ay caramba*, I'm a man after all.

Even though the bankruptcy office was close to my work, I was late to meet Irene and the consultant.

He was excellent. Without apparent judgement he explained her rights; how the debts would be reduced and consolidated to a manageable monthly payment, without accruing further interest. The program could take up to a year; meanwhile, the harassing calls and letters would stop.

With that assurance we sat back, minds at peace.

Signs of her mounting debt went back well over a year. She had borrowed money from us and faithfully returned it in small installments as agreed; however, not without a struggle on her part. I hadn't been terribly observant. The last straw was threats by Bell to have the phone disconnected. Erlinda and I covered the small phone bill and trustee fee.

On our 10th wedding anniversary—and me in desperate need of a break from work, *again*—we rented an old RV for a trip to Florida. If the RV experience suited us, we had an option to buy, minus the rental fee. Sounded good.

At a twenty-three-foot length and a nine-foot width, it was a big step up from a compact car, nevertheless, we got used to driving it. Essentially, it's a bachelor apartment on wheels: kitchen (fridge, stove, microwave and sink); bedroom (queen bed and another over the cab); dining area and bathroom (sink, toilet and shower.) In other words bigger than a tent, yet small enough to give your partner a piece of your mind without shouting in the middle of a good quarrel.

Due to a very late start, obviously caused by yours truly—I've never known Erlinda to be late, must be that nurse's training back in the Philippines—we got as far as a supermarket parking lot in Niagara Falls, two hours away.

It was going to be a chilly night and I didn't know how to start the furnace, so Erlinda pulled out the extra blankets, the blankets I told her wouldn't be necessary.

"Florida is warm," I had said.

Notwithstanding the dubious start, we were hooked on this mode of travelling.

As part of the annual New Year resolutions, we made a seismic shift in our investment strategy—sell the two rental houses sooner rather later. Three compelling reasons stood out for the change of direction.

1) Income tax laws with respect to rental property changed unfavourably.

2) A recent bad experience. One of our basement tenants, an obnoxious weekend drinker, complained to me about two noisy boyfriends having moved in with the upstairs girls. I paid a visit to the den of inequity with a plan that could blow up in my face if not executed properly. Both girls, assertive, worked in a collection agency and could read people quite easily. Formidable opponents. We had been on good terms with them, but that could change on a dime if they got wind of the truth. Five of us sat in the living room as I presented my case: I needed the place for my father (a rare legitimate reason to seek vacancy). Without argument they agreed to move out in two months. Back in the car, my shirt was drenched with sweat.

3) That part of the city was gaining a reputation as an undesirable area, especially after the notorious serial killer Paul Bernardo attacked a girl on our street.

* * * * *

One pleasant spring day, Erlinda and I were in the kitchen babysitting little Richie. He sat quietly in his high chair, Erlinda feeding him apple sauce one spoon after another. *Adorable.*

I pressed RECORD on the camcorder. Somewhere in between spoons, he uttered a sound. We stopped to look at each other with smiles, mouths open.

Erlinda turned back to him and said, "Talk to me Ritchie."

A moment of silent anticipation; and then, he murmured.

Was it a coincidence?

"Talk to me Ritchie," she said again, more animated. This time the response was immediate and prolonged, and without a doubt—he was communicating.

Oh, the joy!

We jumped up and danced around the chair, hooting with laughter and hugging him and each other.

That afternoon in the garden, Erlinda was showing Beth (Richie on her hip) the vegetables she had planted. The lovely scent of purple lilac bushes filled the air. Dave and I, at the picnic table, were talking about work. This seemed like the perfect time to approach a subject Erlinda and I had discussed at some length. I proposed they live with us: main floor for them and basement for us.

"You don't mind the basement?" he asked.

"Nah, it'll be fine. I'll have to tell the tenant."

"How much do you want?"

"Whatever is affordable for you guys," I said, "but I will need you to look after the houses while we're away travelling. Take a cut for that also." I knew it would get easier for him in the near future with the sale of the rentals.

Looking for stability they asked for a year and half term. After the trial period we would all reassess what to do next.

For convenience I gave him access to our bank accounts and safe deposit box. At the same time, we wrote new wills with him as executor and Power of Attorney.

As planned, we all moved.

I sold one of the rentals.

Now came the fun part—preparing for the six-month 'Dream Vacation' in the RV exploring U.S. and Canada. At work my boss reluctantly accepted my Leave of Absence for a *once in a lifetime trip.*

If he only knew what the future held. Nobody could possibly have imagined it. Not even me.

6 months in a motorhome
U.S. and Canada
1992

There was no way we would leave
late for this road trip, Erlinda made
sure of it. With wanderlust flowing
in my veins and a leather steering
wheel in my hands, I felt ready.
The open road and the simple RV
lifestyle. *Yes!*

    For the first segment, my
buddy, Crazy Legs Larry joined us
to run the Boston Marathon.

    Most of the following are excerpts from Erlinda's log (italics).
My comments are in square brackets.

    Boston, Mass.
Left Toronto 7am. Arrived 9pm. Rain and cold all the way.
Attended Runners' Expo. [Met running legend Grete Waitz.]
Party for Canadian runners at Canadian Embassy.
    Orlando, Fla.
Played trivial pursuit [driving down eastern seaboard.]
Our first BBQ—hamburgers, hotdogs, wine and beer. Mmm good.
Got annoyed at George for suggesting to conserve gas by using ice
cubes in fridge to keep it cold.
Called home.
Watched last episode of Cosby Show and riots in L.A.
Supper at Olive Garden. Wt–117 lbs. No good! G and I ran 30 min.
around campsite. No ice cream or munchies for a while.
    New Orleans, La.
Dinner at Ralph and Kaco's—blackened Cajun fish—very tasty.
Boat cruise down Mississippi River to a plantation.
Jazz band at Preservation Hall.
Stopped at a church & said prayers.
    Galveston, Tex.
After 25 yrs I am back in League Hall [nurses' residence.]
Hospital is still there but they built an addition. More people.

Big Bend N.P., Tex.
Paddled [guided by Mexicans] *across Rio Grande into Mexico. Donkey ride to poor village of 80.*
    Uvalde, Tex.
Driving along 90W–temp gage up & smoke coming from hood. Radiator hose burst. A truck driver helped us. RV fixed. Left. A/C hose ruptured. Back in Uvalde. Fixed. Singing along way. Vast, dry, hilly, but scenic.

    Phoenix, Ariz.
G got a saxophone. I had a chuckle listening & watching him play. Sounds like a duck c a sore throat. He's learning fast tho.
[Honking forced Erlinda out too often, so I sold it.]
    Grand Canyon N.P., Ariz.
Guided walk on the rim c a ranger. [Jaw dropping spectacular.]
[Called home. Beth to give birth any hour now.]
[I'm at the trailhead. The night sky is sprinkled with countless twinkling stars. A camcorder, tripod and backpack—food, water and other essentials—hang strapped to my back. For the initial darkness in the u-shaped chute, I need the headlamp; a broomstick acts as an improvised hiking stick valuable in the steep, dusty descent—one slip could be curtains for me. With only the sounds of shuffling feet, I tread cautiously down the narrow switchback path leaving behind on the rim a Ponderosa Pine forest and the early morning photographers. The air is cool, but rising up the chute, warm currents relax my tense muscles.

Now on an exposed ridge, I stop to observe and absorb the serenity and unparalleled panoramic beauty: Under an open blue sky the canyon's vastness. *Ooh, aah.*

185

Down at the Tonto Plateau, it's a hot barren desert, except for the tall agave and wonderfully smelling creosote bushes. Here, at halfway point, the cowboy dressed guide and mule riding passengers get off to stretch the legs and use the outhouse. This is not a place to depart from the established route—the unprepared and foolish, and even the strong—have died in these canyons. Pockets of shade in the rare rock formation provide the only respite from

the heat. I guzzle the allotted first bottle of water. To protect against the scorching sun, my T-shirt is wrapped around my head. If you're lucky, the rangers say, you might see a mountain lion. I'm not lucky today. Also, they warn against what I'm attempting, yet I'm drawn in by nature's beauty, delicious solitude and the challenge.

The trail descends 4,500 vertical feet over 11km to a suspension bridge. Three specks floating down the now visible Colorado River turn out to be blue rafts.

Once there, it's a land before time; Where dark rock—almost half the age of the planet, that's long before the dinosaurs—towers; Where prickly pear cacti sleep; Where droning cicadas abound and scorpions crawl.

On the shore of the grey-green Colorado I plant the tripod securely into the sand, attach the cam, press REC and rush in front to speak.

"I dedicate this hike to Beth and the new baby who I presume has come into the world way up there."

When I pinch my arm the skin returns immediately: hydration is good.

Time to climb back up, before it gets intolerably hot.]

He did it in 7hrs. Wow! Glad to see him. Happy for him. Born Samantha, 7 lbs. strong.

"The Wave," Coyote Buttes, Utah

Horsing around. White Sands National Monument, N.M.

In a sudden flash flood, narrow canyon could be inescapable.
Buckskin Gulch, Utah

Zion Nationa Park, Utah

Bryce Canyon N.P., Utah
Storm, hale & sleet during our drive.
[Canyon of thousands of colourful, weather-sculpted pillars under a crystalline blue sky.]
Freezing cold nights. Car battery dead. G used it to run furnace.
   Las Vegas, Nev.
[Massive, themed hotels line the main strip and beyond—where casinos happy to assist you empty your pocket and bank account of that annoying money before you know what happened.]
Breakfast at "The Mirage," great ambiance. Show–good laugh.
G shaved beard.
   Death Valley N.P., Cal.
Very hot–110F. Saw Devil's Golf Course & Badwater
[Lowest point on continent. In the extreme summer heat, you rarely see anyone, so early in the morning we ventured out among the giant sand dunes—smooth curves like a woman's prostate body—careful not to get lost. Like a child I ran and jumped and danced (completely naked) Erlinda videoing the entire lark. Marvelous freedom. But beyond the next dune, we discovered a camera-crew shooting a commercial. Oops!]
G ran 30k out of the valley [Erlinda drove beside me providing water and cold, refreshing Coke.]
   Visited wineries and San Miguel Mission.
   Yosemite N.P., Calif.
Hiked to Vernal Falls–Mist Trail [Got wet climbing the steep granite steps.] *Gorgeous view.*
G & I had one of those verbal fights. He took off hiking.
River rafting. Caught in thunder shower. We enjoyed it.
Saw Grizzly Giant [2,700 years old Sequoia tree recognized as the largest living thing.]
G hiked Half Dome [The iconic smooth granite dome rises high above the valley floor.]
   Carson City, Nev.
Radiator fluid is leaking. Repair took 3 days (waiting for parts). Meanwhile visited Virginia City, western & mining town of 1860. Picked up RV. Cruise & AC not working now. Finally fixed. Total cost $1,600. [Ouch! Scammed?]

Lake Louise, Alta.
Very scenic on Hwy 93–mountains. Saw black bear and 2 cubs.
Hiked along the lake to a tea house, guided by ranger.
Strolled through the Chateau.
Engine caught fire again [Overheated. I put on the heater NOT the AC to cool the engine. Meanwhile, we the humans suffered.]
Drove awfully slow up hill. It's working.
Calgary
RV inspected. Manifold gasket missing & cracked. 3 days lost.
UPS parcel from home. Saw Samantha's pictures for the 1st time.
Picked up our spirits.
Yellowstone N.P. Wyo.
Geysers & mud pots.

The terraces.

Mount Rushmore, S. Dak.
Four presidents carved in mountain rock.
Stopped dying my hair. Grey looks good on me.

Mesa Verde N.P. Colo.
[A major archeological preserve of hundreds of dwellings in the eroded alcoves of a cliff, way above the valley floor.]
Climbed very long ladder and crawled narrow tunnel.
Natural Bridges N.P., Utah
[Why do painful experiences last longer in our minds than pleasant ones? Of course, extremely pleasurable or first-time events stay as well, but pain is king. At least it's true for me.

At the end of a hot afternoon hike, we encountered a particularly tall, wooden ladder. To test its reliance I climbed first and Erlinda followed.

Similar to this.

Reaching the top she is quiet and woozy, so I sit her down on a boulder in the shade. Her face is ashen and the eyes roll around and then shut. *Oh my God, what is happening!?* It's pointless to shout, no one is around and she is swaying now, about to lose consciousness. I sit next to her as support and pour drinking water over her head. Waiting and watching, the whole while talking to keep her with me. Slowly she revives.

On the return to the RV, terrible guilt draped over me for putting her in this risky situation—considering her parents' health history. I vowed: When we are hiking, *she* has to be at the front setting the pace, not me. So far that is exactly how it has been.]

Navajo Tribal Park
[Directly from our campsites, we witnessed majestic scenery where isolated monoliths of red sandstone reach up high above the desert valley. Made famous in the old John Ford western movies starring John Wayne.]
Las Vegas
Back for supplies.
Wt. up to 119. Jogging daily 45 min.
I lost interest in casino. Have a feeling G does not want me to do any gambling.
Glens Fall, New York
Hot air balloon festival–hundreds of cars and RV parked in an airport field.
[Amazing sight of dozens of giant, gondola-carrying balloons filled the twilight sky. Rainbow colours and multitude of shapes.]

Despite all the RV troubles, we found communing with nature in the national parks enchanting and well worth revisiting.

* * * * *

Several days before Christmas, little Richie was downstairs with us. To keep him amused I put a spinning globe in front of him. Dave joined us, cuddling Sammy in a big red stocking Erlinda had sewed for Christmas gifts. They waltzed and twirled around the living room to Sammy's delightful coos and squeals.

When he sat down on the sofa, he placed her on his lap with the stocking over his head, crooked and half covering his face.

Picture a big, burly father playing with a delicate bundle of joy—a beautiful image of contrasts, worthy of preservation. I reached for the camcorder.

"Look Sammy," he said, blowing the tickling tassel off his nose. This was so funny I could barely keep the cam steady. Sammy wasn't the least bit interested in her father's antics. Hoping for better success, he repositioned and called her name again, but she was completely distracted by my hysterical laughter.

Richie waved an arm trying to get our attention.

"Look Daddy, look," he said excitedly, his finger on a spot on the globe.

"Canada, Canada," he shouted. Dave went over.

"Oh my gosh. It *is* Canada." He said in amazement. I had to see it for myself. Unbelievable for a two-year-old!

Beth came by to take the kids to bed and to drop off babysitting instructions for us.:

Dearest Erlinda & George,
Hi, it's me Sammy, and I come with my very own instructions!!...

It continued for forty lines detailing Sammy's care, while Dave and Beth were to be away for the weekend. A similar note for Ritchie already hung on the fridge.

Our lives had taken a turn, either as grandparents, aunt and uncle or surrogate parents I can't say, but we would care for them like they were our own children.

* * * * *

35,000 feet above the Pacific Ocean
Japan and Philippines

In my hand, a heart-shaped card: individual pictures of us, the kids, Dave and Beth in the centre— and a hand printed message around the perimeter. The words belonged to a song Ritchie heard on TV's *Sesame St.,* "We love you. You love us. We're a happy family!!!" The tune played in my mind as Erlinda snuggled into me reading over my shoulder.

Japanese airline flight 21 was returning her to the land of her birth via a short stay in Japan. From the Narita airport we took the Shinkansen, a smooth and punctual express train, to Kyoto. When we checked into the ryokan, the Japanese style inn, we dropped to the floor and that's where we slept. On a mat.

The following morning, we woke up quite relaxed but still dis-combobulated by jetlag. What a treat to wear matching kimonos and bedroom slippers and—to be seated on the floor at a low-lying table, enjoying a breakfast of tea and rolls. Outside the open window, birds chirped in cherry blossom trees and an old lady swept the already clean courtyard.

If you ever wish to visit a temple, castle, shrine and Imperial Palace in one city, may I recommend Kyoto. You won't be disap-pointed. Even in our state of stupor we managed getting around happily to most sites.

In the next city Nara, the Tourist Information Centre hooked us up with a cheerful guide (free: a student learning English) to visit several pagodas, a giant bronze Buddha and a Shinto shrine by the ocean.

The kind hostel proprietor made a cardboard sign to take to the roadside. In literally seconds, we hitched a ride to a gorgeous mountain lake surrounded by dozens of blossoming cherry trees.

In stark contrast the Hiroshima museum and the remains of the A-bomb Dome looked ever so, so sombre. Nearby a teacher spoke to a class of young students, perhaps about the horrors of war. The perfect place for it. As a white western man I felt self-conscious but no animosity was directed my way.

After a restaurant meal of steaming hot soup and sushi, we stepped outside to heavy rain. A well-dressed gentleman passing by recognized our predicament and offered the second umbrella he happened to have. With deep gratitude, I pulled out some yen. He politely refused to accept it. I ask you, who in this self-centered world hands a new, high-quality umbrella to a foreign stranger? Decades later, it stands sturdy in the entry closet, a testament to the generosity of the Japanese people.

With a connecting flight in Manila, we landed in Iloilo on the large island of Panay, in central Philippines.

As I found out later, Erlinda was apprehensive about how I would adapt and what I would think of the Filipino way of life.

I, on the other hand, very curious about her past and quite happy to witness her reconnect with it.

The good-natured Napoleon, head of the Golmayo family, was waiting at the airport.

On a dirt road outside of city proper, the Jeep jostled over the ruts, through the tropical lush vegetation and heat, to Jaro.

Nap and his wife Lita, a dentist, owned a house large enough for an extended family of eleven: three parents, an ailing sister, children and two maids.

Once settled and rested, we joined everyone at a long table, Nap at one end and me at the other, for an elaborate feast and interesting conversation.

April, Nap's teenage daughter, escorted us around the next day by hailing a Jeepney, a colourful and ornate public bus.

Central Philippine University covers a vast area, landscaped with neatly trimmed hedges, tall palm trees and flowering azaleas and plumeria. At the entrance of the Rose Memorial Hall—the very building where ceremonies and graduations have been held—we read the inscribed plaque. A rebuilt library and butterfly garden were new additions, noted Erlinda.

The Iloilo Mission Hospital, a two-story building painted white with blue trim, resonated emotionally with her more than anything. She fondly recalled morning exercises on a grassy area next to a flag pole. In the entrance foyer, the director of nursing exchanged introductions before taking us on a tour including the new chapel.

I inquired about an apparently forgotten building visible through a window.

"That used to be the nurses' residence," said Erlinda. Upon my urging, we saw the dormitory bedrooms, now used for storage.

Erlinda grew up in the suburb of LaPaz, so she and I hopped into a tuk-tuk—a covered motorcycle with a side compartment for passengers. We found her elementary and high schools, but the entire street she lived on was gone. At the cemetery, we searched carefully up and down every row for her parents' tombstones, without any luck. It was too much to ask for.

The jammed bus went for hours over dusty, rough roads across to the other side of Panay. Relief from the oppressive heat came from an adjustable roof vent. All part of the first-hand experience. We laughed. The ride ended at the foot of a ferry destined for the exotic island of Boracay.

For the next several days, a bamboo hut much like those on *Gilligan's Island* was home. A fine-white-sand beach and warm, clear azure water. The perfect place to kick back and relax. Trying out something new, we rented a sailboat. The wind whisked us away to explore the shoreline and bat filled caves. In the evenings our *bodyguards*, the hut owner's sons, escorted us for a night of disco dancing at the Beachcomber.

In Manila, classmate Rhodora and husband Lirio met us. Outside the terminal the combination of heat, humidity and pollution hit us like an avalanche. To be completely honest, the streets of Manila were pretty much like in any other major city: noisy and congested with traffic and pedestrians. Overwhelming after Boracay.

But the moment we entered their beautiful home in an upscale gated community, we felt the calm and comfort. Their three children greeted us ever so respectfully. Manners.

Lirio and Rhodora put on a first-class party in the back yard—with other classmates Erlinda hadn't seen since graduation—for a loud and joyous reunion.

Upon our return to Toronto, a vase of fresh flowers adorned the kitchen counter. And a colourful, hand-printed card read: "Welcome Home Erlinda and George!!!"

CHAPTER 10

EXTENDED FAMILY

Mississauga

T he manager wasn't happy with my production and long va-
cations, so I switched jobs. Back to the beginning: remote
computer operator, sure it was something I could still do without
the health issues.

The department, if I can call it that, was stuffed into a corner of
an old building. My responsibility involved starting the computer
at 7 a.m. to activate the building's terminals. The perpetually late
supervisor Trish and sidekick Maria lounged in her office, like you
would at a cottage, debating where to go shopping which they pursued with a vengeance over the lunch hour or two. Fine by me, we
were overstaffed anyway, although you couldn't convince Trish of
that. Rob, the other operator and I did all the work, which wasn't
much to speak of.

Desperate to be productive I proposed a long-ignored inventory
project with almost no electric wires or screens. Rob was amenable
to anything that would help pass the time. A recent university grad,
he was itching to "break out of this prison" to a job with a future.

"Go knock yourselves out," said Trish, shaking her head at why
anyone would be actively *looking* for work.

One morning someone called inquiring when their terminal
would be hooked up as they were in urgent need.

"When did you submit the request?" I asked.

"Three weeks ago," said the caller.

It lay at the bottom of Trish's huge pile of 'to do' papers.

"I'll go hook it up," I said, eager to move.

"You can't do that."

"Why?" I asked. She looked annoyed by the question.

"Then they'll expect it all the time," she replied.

I bit my tongue. *Just collect the paycheque.* We still needed about $100,000 to retire.

As promised, Erlinda was at liberty to call it quits anytime, therefore the onus was on me to come in as the closer to pitch the ninth inning, for the win.

Dave made a point to take out the kids on summer's sunny days and find pleasure in sunny ways: Wonderland for the rides, Ontario Place for the water park—he got drenched mixing in with the kids who screamed, jumped and jostled with delight—and the zoo for the monkeys and elephants. The rest of the household plus Angela gladly tagged along.

One lovely summer Saturday, Dave was about to wash the old, blue minivan in the driveway.

"Daddy, I wanna help," said Richie in his endearing voice.

Beth was holding Sammy and I powering up the camcorder, so Erlinda took him by his little hand.

At the faucet, she showed him how to fill the pail and add detergent.

His father returned with a long handle brush.

"Here you go buddy," he said.

Enjoying her son's earnest efforts Beth adjusted his baseball hat and smiled.

Louis Armstrong sang, "It's a Wonderful World."

Later in the back yard, Dave inflated the round pool under a powder blue sky. The kids and Angela splashed, jumped and tumbled with glee.

Meanwhile, with a watchful eye from the picnic table, the adults pondered our future.

No doubt everyone got along, so we pledged to live together, but in a bigger house, for seven more years.

Dave took the opportunity to ask for a loan which came as a surprise that they were deeper in debt than I imagined.

The search was on for an affordable, two-family house outside of Toronto.

Finally we found a new development in Mississauga advertised as large estate homes in a safe area. *That's for us!* The bungalow model with a walkout basement, Dave and Beth didn't mind living in, seemed to be the best fit.

After working out the details, the sales rep called a week later for us to come in and sign the papers. *Why so long?* They knew full well we had three weeks to move out of the current house.

"Has he changed his position on the price of the entrance flooring?" I asked. He was already making a ton of money on the basement construction, so why a ridiculous markup on a few tiles?

"No," said the rep.

I was glad. I wasn't completely convinced the basement was big enough for Dave and his family.

"Then we're not interested anymore."

"If you change your mind, call us," he said surprised.

"I doubt it," I said and hung up. He did not know I had received another highly anticipated call an hour earlier.

A few days before, I had contacted a Remax agent, call it Plan B, about existing houses for sale in the area. The moment I said, "We're prepared to move on it immediately," she really perked up. It was time to take action. Erlinda and I inspected several houses before Dave and Beth gave their approval on our top choice. Although the walkout basement was unfinished, once renovated the house would be three times as spacious as the current one. Great. Having completed a thorough cost analysis, we put in an offer at 10% below asking with the following comment, "It's our one and only offer."

A counter offer came back. Obviously, the seller didn't take my warning seriously. I calmly mentioned to the agent we were also considering a builder home. Now she went to work for us, using all her writing skills to compose (with help from me) a convincing letter as to why our offer was a reasonable one.

First, I brought to her attention:

1) A quick closing of three weeks meant they could move on. (I knew that it had been on the market for four months.)

2) Winter was approaching and less likely to sell. Heating, taxes, insurance and management would be additional expenses.

3) The market had been dropping for the last 5 years with no sign of a recovery.

I knew the actual owner, a company, had bought it for an employee who had transferred. The employer probably never even saw the inside and wasn't aware of its true value.

"The house is yours!" said the agent, that morning.

The only business thing remaining for me now, persuade our lawyer to get the paperwork done in an unheard of three weeks.

No time to dillydally. Next on the agenda: finish packing. The living room was congested with boxes. Erlinda, typically a person who never stops till the work is done, did that day to speak to the ever-present camcorder capturing the momentous occasion.

"This has been our home for ten years," she started. "We have many wonderful memories living here. Now it's time to say bye to our good neighbours." Her voice lowered, "I'm sad it's coming to an end." Even in the loss of the baby, she had not been this emotional.

The mood changed when the kids came down to play in and among the empty boxes. Filling the room with noise and laughter. Erlinda encouraging all of it. Completely recovered, she broke into a familiar tune from the *Beverly Hillbillies,* "We're loading up the truck" and I joined in "and moving to Beverly."

The Jays' World Series game was televised at that very moment, so Erlinda called Dave with whom she shared a fondness for baseball, to watch with us.

I turned up the volume.

The excitement rose in the final inning when Joe Carter was at bat. Even I became a fan.

Everyone was hustling unloading the moving van and stacking boxes in the appropriate room. When it came to heavy pieces like the fridge and stove Dave was a mountain of strength.

In the evening, all the adults wanted to be there when the kids saw their bedrooms. Upon first sight, their eyes lit up.

"Wow!" said Richie, his arms wide apart.

They jumped into the green tent giggling, zipped and unzipped the door with excitement, crawled through a yellow plastic tunnel, and climbed up a red slide singing, "Little Tony."

One day all these things would be outgrown. For now this was the Golden Age when the kids and adults were enjoying as it was.

In mid-December, we drove to a tree farm to select and cut the perfect Christmas tree to fit our two-story family room.

As traditional carols played in the background and the fragrance of cinnamon floated from the kitchen, each of us hung their favourite ornaments, many passed down from the previous generation.

On Christmas day, we all packed into Beth's parents' living room. By now everyone including Dad, Indira and Angela felt at ease together. The conversation flowed freely, eventually coming to business. I mentioned my idea of starting a franchised juice bar that never went beyond a pipedream. Beth's brother, Fred, told us about Noni, a Tahitian drink consumed not for taste, but rather for it's healing benefits.

"Like what?" I asked, curious.

Although the list was lengthy to me it seemed unconnected. Fred was part of a growing sales team that followed a pyramid structure not unlike Amway, and was convinced now as a great time to get in. On the ground floor. The prospect of supplementing my day job with a stream of easy income sounded quite tempting, even so, not tempting enough.

When it came to commuting, I lived by the clock. Five minutes of delay meant hundreds more competing for a place in the swelling asphalt arteries. My autopilot kicked in.

I'm up at 5 a.m. and on the road at 5:45, Erlinda beside me twice a week. In the dark January mornings staying present and alert for black ice is essential—cars in the ditch are proof enough. Speed limit seems to refer to a minimum, not maximum, otherwise some-one is sitting on my bumper. With lunatics weaving through traffic, no wonder there's road rage. I make a mental note where I leave the car in the parking lot, an ocean of vehicles.

The subway doors are closing and some idiot does the Hercules thing like it's the last train to heaven.

Erlinda needs to switch trains, squeezes my hands and gets up. But that's not enough for me. So I pull her back to plant a brief yet firm kiss squarely on the lips—my way of saying have a great day, I'll miss you and I'm not taking you for granted. If someone is offended, I don't really care.

I recall one bitterly cold morning stepping outside the subway. A blustery polar wind, funneling between the bank towers, whips the steam rising out of the manholes. I zip up my coat and lean forward. In my path, a vagrant dressed in layers of tattered rags and surrounded by all his worldly possessions, sleeps over a grill for warmth. *Could this be us one day? Begging to survive?* The thought sends a shiver and I promise myself *not* to let that happen.

By the time I returned home eleven hours had passed. In the dinette Beth had the kids drawing and painting. Their artwork cov-ered so much of the fridge you could scarcely find the fridge han-dle. Finally a drawer was designated for the older pieces.

I tried to put in a of couple of hours each day planning the base-ment apartment, my masterpiece. Weekends were when actual physical work was done.

Once a week before bedtime, Erlinda slipped into the red bath-ing suit with the Aztec pattern—it was hard to take my eyes off her—and joined the kids in the tub. While she washed them they were active with fun and games. Using plastic animal figurines I recounted adventurous tale of battles and escapes on the seven seas. To keep their interest I varied the stories, made sound effects and gave amusing names to the animals.

When the water cooled off and they shivered, Erlinda quickly wrapped them in big, thick towels, all the while the kids were jumping and giggling.

Lastly, Beth gathered us in a circle to hold hands and sing Barney's "I love you, you…" song like a joyful night prayer.

One evening I was in the study, full of plans about the renovation, when Beth knocked on the door.

"How's it going?" she asked.

"OK, I suppose."

"Any idea when it'll be done?"

"Ahh . . . I don't know." I wanted to do it right. "Perhaps a year."

It dawned on me that I didn't have much to show for my efforts in the six months since we had moved in. I had felt no sense of urgency. The top floor was divided into west and east wings. Their wing had three bedrooms and two bathrooms. The main floor, almost as big, was shared. Somehow the girls prepared separate meals without bumping into one another. Except for the bedrooms, Dave and Beth didn't really have any private space.

So I quit my job to focus on the construction full-time.

A month later, the basement was finished, with some weekend help from Dad and Dave.

The floor plan similar to the main floor—incorporating the best ideas I picked up over the years—created a cheerful, comfortable environment. The window, I cut out of the brick, added to the already abundant southern sunlight. The result: extremely satisfying.

With all the new available time I joined Erlinda and the kids in activities, guiltfree.

The kids were getting attention from everyone.

Dave and the kids.

Erlinda now 55, completely retired. Dave got a second job—effectively working at *two* places over the coming three years.

Easter lunch was organised by Beth's mother, Edith, who had firmly established herself as a gracious hostess and great cook.

By now Dave and Beth were selling Noni. Erlinda was trying it for a year. The only holdout: me. Sighting a couple of testimonials from many available, Fred tried to convince me of its medicinal merit and all the money to be made. Even though he was well-educated, honest and sincere—in the absence of *any* large, independent and randomized trials—it sounded like . . . snake oil. The spirit of my high school teacher, Mr. Stewart, spoke to me. *Think for yourself, George.* And for that attitude I felt like an outcast.

In need of money, I naturally turned to a traditional job. Should be a safe option. Right? So I scheduled an interview in a downtown ivory tower. Two most unfortunate events took place.

Riding up the elevator a lens popped out of my glasses, *of all times*, and try as I might it wasn't going back in. My dilemma— keep the glasses on with one eye closed (if open it messed up my brain) or go without (my vision only one level above that of a bat).

I entered the office tentatively (glasses tucked in the jacket), sat in a chair (presumably the correct one) and waited for a verbal cue.

Uncomfortable long silence.

Either he's trying to figure me out or he's reading my resume?

Needless to say there was no follow-up interview.

The second misfortune was more serious. A case of food poisoning from the muffin I ate just before the interview. It resulted in 'reactive arthritis' to the entire body, especially the knees. For a whole month I lay in bed or on the sofa, making my way between the two with Erlinda's assistance. Periodically, doctors Sammy and Richie checked my progress. Sammy placed a thermometer in my mouth while Richie listened to my breath and heart with a stethoscope. My brow furrowed in fearful apprehension. The prognosis was good. I just needed rest.

What saved my sanity, day in day out, was the trial of football legend O. J. Simpson for a double murder. As the 13th juror I listened to the testimony and studied the evidence with utmost impartiality. His dream team of lawyers pulled the 'if it does not fit, you must acquit' stunt; and in my opinion, he got away with murder. Eventually, justice did catch up with O.J. and he spent years behind bars for another crime.

Speaking of freedom, I finally sprung out one spring morning on my own, an exquisite delight to the senses. The awakened pleasure tugged at my soul to live life to the fullest.

A few days before our *Freedom 55* road trip, surfaced a minor mis-understanding in regards to our living arrangement. Dave and I fleshed out the original terms as best as we could recall; and where differences on interpretation existed, we compromised. To prevent future occurrences I wrote down the details, including 'rent' of $800 plus half the utilities.

Our departure day started on the wrong foot: me searching two hours for the Canadian Citizenship cards.

Then, no more than five minutes on the road, a car flashed its lights and honked its horn. I pulled to the shoulder. *Ugh*! The road behind us was strewed with clothes. You'll never guess which idiot forgot to close the roof storage unit when he was up there.

By the time we got to London the dreaded 'Service Engine' light came on. Diagnostics at the dealership found nothing; nevertheless, it haunted us for the remainder of the trip.

To be completely truthful, I was miserable company to Erlinda most of the way to California, getting upset at the smallest thing. Occasionally retreating to sleep on the couch and pout.

Fortunately, the hike up the famous Half Dome in Yosemite N.P. squeezed the irritability right out of me.

For most hikers, it's a tough one-day endeavour even without the unexpected obstacle at Nevada Falls. The loud rushing river from heavy spring snowmelt threatened to wash out the bridge. We backtracked down to Vernal Falls bridge for the alternate route, an extra hour and a half. Then past forests of pine, fir and juniper and the tree line to the base of Half Dome. Of course, we climbed at Erlinda's pace.

For first timers, the idea of scaling the nearly sheer monolith, can be intimidating.

"I'm going up," Erlinda announced without warning. Previously, this is where she waited for me.

"What?" I was surprised.

"Well, at least I can try."

With a pair of well-worn gloves from a used pile, she grabbed the heavy gage cable secured with spikes in the rock and took a few tentative steps.

"Lean into the rock and let your legs do the work," I suggested. Directly behind her, I spread my arms and legs as a safety net.

The steep, smooth granite rock has narrow rest boards about every ten feet, where you encounter other two-way climbers, resting or frozen with fear. There's room only for *two*, so timing is important. Also significant is the need to spread your energy evenly, it's a long way up; and to breathe deeply since you're at considerable altitude.

At the top, the size of a football field, you behold beautiful Yosemite Valley, including El Capitan, the world's largest monolith. This is where experienced rock climbers come to prove themselves.

On the return I went first ensuring again Erlinda's safety. Once at the bottom, she raised her curled fists triumphantly.

"I did it!" she hollered and whooped with smiling jubilation.

That whole experience was, for me, by far the best part of the trip.

* * * * *

Trust me on this: early October is the best time for a visit to the Toronto area. The weather is perfect, mild and free of summer humidity, and glorious fall colours abound. Ideal for bug-free outdoor activities.

Uncle Marco and Aunt Maria came from Croatia not for nature, but to erect a brick garage with Dad.

In the backyard stood a vine covered pergola laden with ripe red grapes. Under it, after supper, Dad and Uncle Marco sat on white plastic chairs singing loudly. Wine glasses in hand, brows arched, mouths wide open, they harmonized a cappella just like in the old country. *Klapa.*

My uncle and aunt are short and stocky people, but strong and tough evidenced by thick, calloused hands that worked the farm six days and then folded in prayer on Sundays.

So when Indira told me after they left, her jewelry was missing, I couldn't make the connection.

"Are you sure?" I asked.

"I looked," she said.

"Look around some more," I urged.

A week later, she found it in a place hidden by her for safe keeping.

Another fun activity in our neck of the woods was hunting in yard sales. Typically, on the day before going out, Beth and Erlinda checked out the ads in the local paper and worked out a route. Erlinda and I used to do this but it became a girls' thing—the chemistry would not have been the same with a guy around. I knew that. They always came home revelling over the discovered treasures.

On the topic of bonding, Irene and I were on good speaking terms, the closest in years. Things were not going well for her though: difficulty finding a job and problems with the landlord. When she decided to move, I rented a van and with Dave and Dad settled her in the new apartment.

One evening Erlinda prepared dinner and Irene spent the night in the guest bedroom.

For a year I had considered having her live with us. Erlinda didn't mind but when I presented the idea to Beth, she left no doubt where she stood.

"If she moves in, we're moving out," she said, visibly upset. A 'no' would not have been a complete surprise, since Dave had showed lack of interest when I asked him. I let it drop.

A week after Irene's stay, Indira told me she had been grumbling about me.

Irene confirmed it. She felt I should have made the offer to live with us when she had been looking. As so often happened she shouted, cried and slammed the phone. Once again, when emotion impaired my thinking, I resorted to the less confrontational letter.

I reminded her it had not turned out well last time we shared a place. Besides, she required privacy, not possible in a house where everyone wandered around freely. To preserve our long-term agreement with Dave and Beth, I had an obligation to keep them happy.

The bottom line: we couldn't manage the house on our own for long; selling it would be a difficult process.

At Edith's Easter lunch, I caved in under the pressure and promised to give Noni a try, despite the fact it appeared to be a waste of money; a bottle wasn't cheap. After all I could be wrong.

In the end nothing perceptibly changed in terms of general health or well being. Perhaps like religion, just believe and you will be saved. I may burn in hell as a nonbeliever but at least I used my brain for what it's worth. And retained my integrity. There was no way I would knowingly prey upon the vulnerable and gullible with an elixir to fatten my wallet, period.

The biggest bash at our house was a celebration of Sammy's birthday.

Preparation started days before. The girls decorated everything with colourful balloons and ribbons and signs, even the deck and back yard. Plates of food for any taste covered the dining table, not the least was Edith's delicious cakes and pies. The girls had things well under control.

At the high point of the afternoon, Beth and Sammy sat in the middle of our family room surrounded by gifts and children, the adults looking on.

I was about to start the camcorder when I spotted Dave using his on the balcony. A better vantage point.

I leaned against the wall and avoided getting in the way.

·

CHAPTER 11

ADVENTURES

WhyNot Marathon
East coast

H ave you ever said to yourself, what's the point of doing
something, when the odds are stacked against you?

Well that's what happened earlier in the year on a sedate winter
day: outside the kitchen window lay a sundrenched, snow-covered
wonderland. The kids had come through and moved on downstairs
to watch videos from an ever-expanding animation library.
Erlinda, feet up on a chair, was sipping a hot Nescafe and engrossed by the tough weekend crossword; I, content with the sweet
aroma of the coffee, reading the newspaper. Once done, I passed it
on to her, about to plan the next trip.

"Did you see this ad?" she said. "They're looking for volunteers
to raise funds for the physically challenged."

"Who do they want?"

"Retired firemen and policemen and their wives." *That excludes
us.* Nevertheless, she applied (along with four hundred others) and
two days later we were accepted. *Huh!*

There's a number of things I've done that I regret, but doing
something *good* for someone is not one of them.

That June at Metro Hall in downtown Toronto the volunteers
gathered for the opening ceremonies. In front of a supportive
crowd and the media, the Lt. Gov. Gen. Romeo Leblanc, other dignitaries and sponsors spoke inspiringly prior to the lighting of the

paralympic torch. Emboldened by the presence of TV crews, I asked for an interview with one medal bearing paralympian. He willingly complied and even suggested to Erlinda where to stand with our camera while I fielded the questions.

At the airport for the flight to Sydney, N.S. the WhyNot Team, as we were named, introduced ourselves. And united with one clear objective—raise money for the physically challenged.

Our route back to Toronto involved The Torch being carried through towns by sponsored walkers, runners, cyclists and even a young girl on a horse. The Chrysler donated vehicles followed very slowly behind. Meanwhile, the capable volunteers approached pedestrians and went door to door for donations.

The mayors of the towns and cities spoke about what a worthwhile cause this was. Vim, our leader and foundation director, mentioned the volunteers, saying "we could stand proudly six feet tall." In a few days we knew his speech inside out, some even mouthed it as he spoke. By the end we had grown to "ten feet tall." A couple of guys, innocent pranksters and natural comedians, triggered uproarious laughter from the team with their antics. But not everyone was happy, primarily because of the motel accommodation and standard restaurants, and so one couple left for home.

Town after town, province after province, the public warmly received us; although Vim had to make a couple of changes to avoid conflict. In the largely francophone community Dieppe, N.B., we refrained from playing our English-only theme song over the P.A. system. Similarity in Quebec City we avoided waving and distributing Canadian flags. To be fair, the people were extremely generous donors.

Based purely on emotional impact, one particular day stood out for everyone. The caravan was advancing slowly between towns through thick fog and drizzle—minus any torch bearers and the Torch itself lay idle, flame snuffed out. Our spirits were visibly low, down to the last person, partly due to an argument with Vim.

A distant rumble, scarcely audible at first, caught our attention.

Curious, we parked the vehicles on the shoulder of the road and dragged our way single file through a forest. Up ahead beyond the trees, someone switched on giant speakers to play a stirring

Vangelis's tune from the *1492: Conquest of Paradise* movie; and a crowd cheered loudly.

One by one we spilled out into the open and climbed up to the top of a hill.

Below us: an incredibly zealous, young crowd of about forty, but sounding like thunderous thousands in a football stadium. Disfigured bodies in wheelchairs and on crutches, crooked arms waving, heads shaking as they howled, moaned and gurgled—and yet their eyes sparkled with life, joy and intelligence. Stopping at each face, I could *feel* how much they appreciated what we were doing.

This was Camp Papillon and whether they spoke French, English or Martian it didn't matter. Goosebumps popped on my arms, neck and shoulders—the air was absolutely electric. Standing beside me, everyone equally touched. Even big, burly men who in the course of their careers as firemen and policemen had seen it all, emotionally moved.

On Canada Day at Parliament Hill, in Ottawa, we were a few drops in a sea of thousands waiting over an hour for the Prime Minister to show up. Close to me stood a tall suspicious looking character, the right hand hidden inside his jacket, shades of Robert DeNiro in *Taxi Driver. Is he holding a gun?* My rush to judgement eased when I noted the earpiece and sunglasses: plain clothes security service.

You could feel PM Jean Chretien approaching as the physical pressure dialed up. Our representative handed him a gift, the Why-Not T-shirt. He looked confused momentarily, then wiped his forehead with the T-shirt and threw it back to her.

On the last day, we convoyed right into the centre of Toronto to ever growing lines of spectators. Perched on a van's roof for a better angle, I videotaped people waving as we passed by.

Like heroes returning from war—we marched up to the stage at Metro Hall 48 days after departure to triumphant music, applause and speeches. Proud we were, but the best moment was on top of that hill back at Camp Papillon.

A year later at the reunion, Vim still wasn't able to tell us how much money was raised. The answer I uncovered in a newspaper article: shockingly low. Rumor had it that he became a senator in Ottawa, and as for the rest of us, we went on with our lives.

The Saturday after Erlinda and I returned home, she and Beth were off hunting for treasures, Dave took the kids to Edith's for the day and I sat in the study surrounded by—walls of travel and race pictures—working on the next trip.

76 Days Around the World

That trip was only two weeks away and in hindsight I should have taken a month to re-stabilise and prepare, but I'm blaming Jules Verne for the unchecked fascination. More preciously, his novel "Around the World in Eighty Days" had inspired this overly ambitious endeavour.

There was much to take care of: itinerary, passports, visas, traveller's cheques, credit cards, and Euro-rail Passes. Affordability, always a major obstacle, was partly solved by—I'm admitting it now—an arduous, convoluted flight schedule of standby tickets. We trimmed the luggage to light carry-on daypacks. Mobility we had.

I popped over to Dad's to finalise details of meeting relatives in Croatia and to leave a little money for Irene. Angela opened the door and said he was busy playing computer chess downstairs. Then she went back to watching TV.

I stood in the entrance feeling uncertain what to think or do. Short on answers and time, I dropped the money on the table and left.

By coincidence, I met Irene in Dave's car when he drove me to pick up the airline tickets.

"What's new?" I said, taken by surprise. She was applying for a disability pension and taking classes on managing emotions. *Something positive, but the extra weight not so much.*

"Have a great trip," she finished, although I had never mentioned it. I felt uncomfortable: it didn't seem right that our lives were exciting and hers was terribly difficult. So I avoided talking about the itinerary.

Three days later, hiking high above the coastal city of Bergen, Norway, we sat down on a moss-covered boulder to lunch on Yogurt, rolls and apple juice while overlooking the ocean and city below. The trail had been recommended by a Norwegian resident as off the beaten path, at least to tourists. Even with heavy heads from jetlag, we were determined to appreciate the rolling terrain. At one point I lost my temper but quickly apologized and got over it without creating a prolonged disturbance.

The first train ride took us to the village of Flam on the shores of a lovely fjord. If you were looking for a stress-free place to retire this would be it, a community of about 400 peaceful inhabitants. The English-speaking tourist office suggested the youth hostel, a six-bedroom chalet style building. A pleasant surprise! Guests shared a spotlessly clean, well-accessorized kitchen and living room. The walls of bright, lacquered pine created an ambiance of calm. *Aah*. The room alone broke the $50 a day budget but it was worth every cent.

On my birthday, we silently slipped outside by light of early dawn to a perfectly serene setting. The narrow inlet mirrored the sky and steep cliffs. Feeling the pleasant coolness on our skin we strolled wordlessly wishing not to disturb the tranquility. Also out for a walk, an elderly couple with rosy cheeks stopped to chat. They owned a large raspberry farm, along with sheep and beehives; lived simply in a 250-year-old house passed down from one generation to the next. Seasonally, foreign workers helped with picking the raspberries.

To save on accommodation, we took the night train through Scandinavia. In hindsight, sleeping on a train at our age was not a bright idea.

When we arrived in Berlin, Germany a number of well-meaning people gave us directions to a hostel but we got lost anyway. Nervous, we roamed up and down streets late into the evening, keeping a watchful eye for anyone lurking behind bushes and trees. The reward? A clean, reasonably priced room with breakfast.

Determined to explore the city, we left our packs at the station and set out on foot—past nude sunbathers lying in a park, through the Brandenburg Gate and into formerly communist East Berlin, accessible after the collapse of the Soviet Union. Shocking is not an exaggeration in describing the Library and Monument to Victims of Fascism and Militarism. The black and white photos displayed suffering prisoners. The psych can take only so much before the body turns away. A wreath hung in memory of those killed trying to cross the Berlin wall to freedom.

In welcome contrast, the cruise along the Rhine provided a leisurely way to view the grapevine swept hillsides and castles on top. Beside the river, energetic cyclists whizzed down roads as though racing us. That night we slept in a former castle, now a huge youth hostel, in separate rooms with the company of . . . youth.

A free tourist bus took us into walled, medieval Rothenburg, charming town of cobblestone streets, flowers in the windows and quaint shops and restaurants.

On to Paris. I sat uncomfortably—for the entire crowded train ride—next to a man in serious need of a shower. Periodically, I stepped outside the compartment for fresh air.

After securing a hostel room, exchanging currency, and a quick bite, we headed off to the massive Louvre. Due to a lack of sound sleep, we wandered indifferent to some of the greatest art anywhere. A real shame. On that topic, Erlinda was embarrassed when we stopped for a drink and I ordered *one* expensive beer for the *two* of us. To make things worse, I got upset and felt out of sorts for the rest of the evening.

Over the following couple of days we visited on foot most of the Parisian sights, gladly holding hands in an effort to patch up the rift. Honestly, the only tourist site I truly enjoyed was Notre Dame cathedral where I lit a candle for Mom.

Soon things turned very sour, very quickly. Along the Seine River an enormous and vocal crowd was marching downtown in protest against illegal immigration. Feeling we needed a bit of excitement in our lives, we followed. To add to the existing police

presence several trucks zipped down a side street and quickly parked; resolute riot squads armed to the gills jumped out and rushed towards the crowd. No longer entertained, we picked up our packs at the hostel and alertly headed for the station two hours early. Machine gun toting, oversized soldiers patrolled entrances and halls; newly posted signs warned the public not to leave bags unattended. Thankfully, a timely train whisked us away to a more peaceful destination, the Swiss Alps.

A gentle jostle awakened us to a spectacular view from our window seats: starry sky, glacial mountains and the front of the train speeding through tunnels and over giant passes.

In Grindelwald the highly recommended youth hostel was full, so we continued up the hill to another one. Even though we shared a room with three others, we slept soundly, cozy under cotton duvets. Cool air wafted in through an open window.

This was the best hostel ever! Green and flower speckled scenery, a delicious breakfast and a staff helpful with choosing a hike.

Europe's longest (at the time) cable car lifted us up Mannlichen mountain to be followed by a walk back down. Needless to say, the camera worked overtime filming jagged, snow-capped peaks and verdant slopes of grass and forests. *Oh my!* The air felt and smelled invigoratingly fresh. Clanging bells drew our attention to cows and sheep grazing or drinking contentedly snow melted water out of wooden troughs. In tune to the surroundings, we sauntered for hours along a well marked trail occasionally crossing paths with Swiss couples in traditional lederhosen.

A very satisfying supper included bratwurst with sauerkraut and mustard, a cold Weininger beer, and apple strudel with ice cream. Here's a surprise. During the purchase of a souvenir spoon, we were short the equivalent of $2.20, so the cashier waved us through with a "don't worry about it."

We called home to catch up on family news. Beth said our kitchen sliding door had shattered from excessive solar heat. Of the three quotes she obtained, I asked her to take the middle one. And, Dave's long-time buddies took him for his birthday to Florida.

In Pozega, Croatia, a clerk at the bus depot called on our behalf my niece Mariana. (When she had visited Dad in Canada, we showed her Toronto.) Getting no answer, I wondered if Dad had relayed clearly our travel plans. Another lady overheard and drove us to Mariana's. With nobody home we were unsure what to do. Just as we were leaving, Mariana came around the corner, surprised to see us.

In minutes the whole family was there to welcome us—they had no specific arrival date. She was happily married. Her brother, a sergeant in the army, had received an award from President Tudjman for his part in the war from '90 to '92.

Just as Dad had predicted, when Tito died in 1980 the Yugoslav federation frayed quickly, with Slovenia and Croatia declaring independence. Bitter war broke out in 1990, spreading throughout Bosnia, Croatia and Serbia as evidenced by the bullet holes in walls seen on our bus ride to Pozega. I had suspected Dad sent money to help during the war. Fortunately, the UN came to restore peace.

The old neighbourhood—the house with the large metal door where I as a child played soccer—was as I remembered it but smaller. Everything was. The creek behind the house, where we dragged the crate, still flowed. Mr. Ambrosia had died three years earlier and his wife more recently. Sensing my mood turn gloomy, Erlinda stroked my back.

The only person in town from Mom's family, Aunt Kaya lived on a small pension in a modest apartment. At first hesitant to open the door, she finally showed us in. As we sat on the old sofa she talked about the early '90s when Uncle Niko and others moved out of Bosnia to safety in Trst. *Is she harbouring a grudge against me?* The responsibility to help them had rested on my shoulders and yet I had consciously turned my back, a decision that weighs heavily on me to this day.

After the emotional roller coaster in Croatia, we found ourselves in Venice, Italy on a brilliantly sunny day. In the renowned Piazza San Marco, seated at an outside table, we sipped $8 cappuccinos. Free from any stresses, we watched waves of tourists taking pictures and excited children chasing dozens of cooing pigeons. *Should we or shouldn't we?* To quote my father, "Hell, you live only once."

Assisted by the gondolier, we stepped in his boat for a ride through the canals. Sitting back, we soaked up the whole gently-floating experience. Time stood still.

Once back on land, we realized that catching the last train out of town was going to be tight. The more we rushed the more we got lost—normally a favourite tourist pastime here and not difficult in a city of irregular, narrow lanes on 118 islets linked by bridges.

We dashed into the station and split up: Erlinda checked the departure board for the bay number while I retrieved the packs out of storage.

Where is she? There in the last bay, naturally. Oh, oh. The train was moving. Go on, I waved, running to catch up. Just in the nick of time I grabbed the last bar and jumped on board.

Once re-united, we laughed shamelessly long and loud like a couple of unruly teenagers. Next stop, Rome.

Nothing was more mentally draining for me than handling 'business matters' because of the proximity to computers or electricity. But—like washing clothes and preparing food—it had to get done; and when in Rome the "Eternal City" it's no small feat.

'Business matters' on that day involved finding a reliable travel agency to book side-trip flights, developing pictures to send to families back in Croatia and calling Fouad a contact in Cairo. We squeezed in a few sights, the last being the Spanish Steps: for years a meeting place for foreigners. Erlinda noticed at one point a wide-open pocket on my pack—it had been picked. Luckily no loss as it had been empty. Somehow though, I found a reason to blame Erlinda which naturally upset her. After some soul-searching, I admitted it was all my fault. *Will I ever learn?*

Limited by time before our flight, we decided to see Rome's jewel in the crown, Michelangelo's St. Peter's Basilica, the most grandiose and extravagant Christian church. I was emotionally overcome by this vision, but not in the way it was intended. My spirits crashed, not soared, at the thought of how many and how long the poor suffered while the church leadership focused on this extravagance. Food for the soul, nothing for the body.

Twelve million people lived in Cairo; it looked like most of them were swarming in front of us as we gazed at the city from the second-floor arrivals window.

Fouad shouted over the cacophonous noise introducing himself and Rifa'ai, the driver.

Surrounded by traffic chaos the taxi crawled, two lanes becoming four; and drivers leaned on the horn apparently with each breath. We were dropped off at an elegant, well-located hotel, where the receptionist advertised himself as a highly qualified tour guide with a university degree no less.

The following morning we booked with an agency all our Egyptian travel.

Once on the street again, a mass of people swept us up in the wrong direction. We had to push and elbow to extricate ourselves. Upsetting. Also unsettling, women covered the entire body, except for peering eyes, with a black burka.

Oh, what a day! It started with an argument. The receptionist insisted on a ten-pound tip—to pay off his university degree I suppose—and a $10 U.S. room rate increase. Then our guide showed up an hour late to take us to the Great Sphinx and pyramids.

Rude nagging camel owners, trinket sellers and beggars blocked the entrance.

The guide allowed *ten minutes* to enter a pyramid—one of the Seven Wonders of the World—and a *full hour* at the carpet factory. Finally he dropped us off at the travel agency just before it closed.

The agent stayed late to give us the cruise papers and sent an energetic errand boy to bring us supper as we hadn't eaten since breakfast. Needless to say, we tipped generously. Another guide drove us to the train station and told us to get off the night train at *5 a.m.* in time to catch the Nile cruise.

When we woke up the train car was almost empty and seconds from moving on. It was *4 a.m.*

Breathless and rattled, we boarded the MS Symphony, determined to settle down and enjoy what lay ahead.

After the captain's welcome party most of us went on deck to lounge in the shade out of the scorching sun. The ship navigated up the lazy waters of the Nile, flanked by palm trees, grey-green shrubs and the inhospitable desert beyond. Perfect for a nap.

We docked near the Valley of the Kings.

After a short bus ride, our tour group walked through a hillside opening with giant pillars. Cool, echoing tunnels. Hieroglyphics marked ochre, stone walls.

We entered the ancient tombs of the pharaohs. Timeless.

At the end of the cruise, in Aswan, we bid farewell to fellow passengers and dropped back to reality with a heavy thud. While waiting, we wandered through a crowded, dusty market with rude-in-your-face merchants and kids in tattered clothes pulling my hand for baksheesh. On the ship I had contracted a case of stomach cramps and diarrhea; so when we turned a corner to a pungent smell of burning garbage and donkey dung, I vomited. Erlinda helped me clean up. Dehydrated even further by the sweltering heat, I guzzled a bottle of odd tasting 'natural water' before realizing it had been previously opened. *Not good!*

On the 15-hour bus ride back to Cairo, *loud* Egyptian videos played mercilessly late into the night.

The torment continued back at the hotel where a front desk clerk nagged for my bottle of Coke.

Just as I was about to scream, two angels descended to earth to lift my spirits. A young woman, Hoda, and her father, Mohamed, overheard me enquiring about directions to a supermarket—so they drove me there, if you can believe it. Back in the room, Erlinda was resting with stomach issues herself.

Hoda, a student of languages, and Mohamed, a well travelled banker, helped me select food and drove me back to the hotel. I swear to the truth of all this.

On the way to the airport, Erlinda and I shared with an older couple a taxi paid by us, in honor of my heavenly guardians.

Once back in Rome we enjoyed relative sanity. Forget my earlier comments, you *should* visit St. Peter's, Vatican Museum, Trevi fountain and Vittorio Emanuel II monument: wonderful examples of mankind's great creativity.

Cost of accommodation in London, England was not cheap. The best we could afford was youth hostel dorm beds.

I got up early to get the 'business matters' out of the way. The outcome: a muddled brain and a three-day flight delay because of a lack of standby seats. A foul mood hung over me like a wet T-shirt. Erlinda felt drained, partly by my nonsense. To combat my mental malaise, we decided to sightsee at a much leisurely pace. *Be positive, happy and a good companion, George.*

At Buckingham Palace a curious crowd enjoyed the pageantry of the changing of the guards wearing their red uniforms and tall, black hats.

The moment you enter Westminster Abbey you sense history: since 1066 almost all monarchs have been crowned here. This great Gothic church holds tombs and monuments of the country's literary, political and scientific giants the likes of Newton, Darwin and Chaucer.

At the hostel we played scrabble, me still behaving. *One day at a time.*

Our plane flew over Russia and Afghanistan and landed in New Delhi around midnight. Feeling vulnerable at such an unholy hour and in culture shock, we shared a taxi with Clayton, an American on his way to teach Christianity in Nepal. The cabbie offered a friend's place, but Erlinda and I chose a hotel recommended by *Let's Go.*

At 2:30 a.m. after hearing our several knocks, the night manager turned on lights and opened the lobby door to reveal people sleeping on the marble floor. Being cautious, I inspected our room and flushed the toilet. On a hunch, I pulled back the shower door. For display was a generous portion of human feces. Judging by the volume, the donor must have been saving it for an extra long time. Disgusting. We chose another room. Concerned about dirt, disease and DDT immune cockroaches, we slept in our travel clothes—at least Erlinda did, I wasn't that sleepy after all.

The next day, we met Clayton looking dishevelled and dazed.

"How do you like your hotel?" he asked.

"Not much. We're in another one now. What happened to you?"

"I stayed with a friendly local, talking and drinking. When I woke up, he and my money were gone. Oh well, I guess he needed it more than I did."

Compared to Cairo, New Delhi had less chaos but more wildlife: cows and even an elephant mingled with vehicular traffic. At a major intersection, a double leg amputee rolled fearlessly on a dolly between traffic lanes begging. So heartbreaking. On the other hand, quite publicly and without hesitation men walked up to a wall to urinate. With acrid stench and car exhaust fumes in the air, we lost interest in food.

A city bus tour included the Raj Ghats square where Mahatma Gandhi was cremated.

In front of the parliament buildings a flute playing cobra charmer allowed us a picture, then insisted on a $10 fee. Repeatedly and vehemently.

Our hotel concierge purchased (supposedly) round-trip rail tickets to Agra for a day visit of the Taj Mahal.

At its entrance we had to fight through the hawkers and beggars, to bestowing our eyes upon a fantasy vision. The white marble monument to love possesses the power to calm even the worst case of frayed nerves. In 1650 Shah Jehan brought 20,000 craftsmen from as far as Europe to build it in memory of his wife. She and the Shah lie in the vault beneath the tomb chamber. While relaxing on the smooth marble floor enjoying the splendor, we struck up a friendly conversation with an Australian couple, Allan and Lisa.

The four of us agreed to a dinner at a ritzy restaurant. At the end of the meal the waiter addressed me since I was handling the bill.

Gratuity was inadequate, he said. I was temporarily speechless, so Allen jumped in with, "Fine, then we'll leave him nothing!" Heads turned my way and the waiter refused to leave. A standoff.

Too embarrassed, I handed a significantly larger tip.

A man from the next table leaned and whispered, "No local would have done that. You just gave him what he makes in a full day."

On the return to New Delhi, it became apparent the rail tickets had been in fact *one* way, so we lined up to make a purchase. The moment the booth opened bedlam broke out like someone was handing out food to the starving in Sudan. If the seats were sold out, we could be spending the night God knows where, so I turned ugly as well.

Along the way we had to transfer to another train, perhaps due to limited service at such a late hour. We stood uncertain on a poorly lit, almost vacant platform. Nearby two young American girls were being harassed by two young men claiming to be plain clothes police. The girls joined us and together we boarded the next standing-room-only train.

Our guide book warned about pickpockets at the Delhi station, so the four of us prepared for the physical interaction. Once the thieves spotted us in the station's crushing crowd, they made a bee-line for us.

A day later and not a second too soon, the very early morning taxi was whipping up road dust on the way to the airport.

Suddenly without warning it stopped.

The driver informed us he was not permitted to enter the air-port—he was going to leave us there on a dark, desolate stretch of highway. About two kilometers short.

"I cannot pay you unless you finish our agreement," I said gently but firmly.

At the airport, I emptied my pockets of all the rupees to give to him, vowing never to return.

They say you either love or hate India. It should be no surprise to the reader, I hated the country and its people but to my great shame: that was *not* how I was brought up to be. Would I ever rid myself of that hatred, I wondered?

Hong Kong, another British colony but very successful economically, was to revert to China in 1997, so it seemed like an opportune occasion to visit before the communists messed it up. Although not far flying *east* from New Delhi, we flew *west* because of the cheaper round trip airfares—through London, Toronto, and Vancouver into Kowloon, Hong Kong.

We took an affordable room, or was it a closet, in a 20-story hostel prone to fires because of the exposed electrical wiring.

We called home. Beth was soon returning from a trip to Vegas.

In handling 'business matters' I booked side-trip flights to Beijing and Xian.

Famished, we resorted to the cheapest option, McDonald's. While waiting for our order we sat by a window looking outside. I felt the full weight of the grey, rainy day.

A melancholy mood descended upon me as never before, the cumulative result of hunger, jetlag, long exhausting flights and negative experiences over the last seventy days.

In the harbor countless boats and ships of various shapes and sizes wandered aimlessly.

"I'm leaving," I mumbled, looking straight ahead.

"What?" said Erlinda.

"I'm leaving home." I couldn't believe the words were coming out of my mouth.

"What are you talking about?" She was now staring at me.

"I'm not getting along with Beth and Dave."

A single raindrop clung under its own weight to the window-pane.

"Most of all, I'm a horrible husband." That much I knew.

"Oh George, I need you," she wrapped soft, warm arms around me and rested her head on my shoulder. "We can work this out."

She paused. "Look, after eating, let's go to the bird market."

We ate double portions of everything—enough to invigorate our bodies and spirits. Who knew McDonald's could have such a powerful effect?

The Air China flight 347 into Beijing, carrying mostly Chinese passengers, was a pleasant surprise. The flight was as good as any western one. The country had made tremendous progress in the twenty years since Richard Nixon visited. Skyscrapers sprouted and business boomed. The streets, still inundated with young and old cyclists, were cleaner and quieter than those in New Delhi. A courteous rickshaw operator took us to a good, affordable hotel where the staff expected no tips. How refreshing. Without any drama or delays a receptionist obtained tour tickets to the tombs of the Ming emperors and the Great Wall.

This incredible fortification is the only man-made structure visible from outer space, that's not to say I went up to verify it. I mean, some things you just have to take their word for it.

Language and writing were a distinct barrier, however, the tourist office made things much easier. After an interesting walk through the Forbidden City, formerly the emperor's residence, we entered Tiananmen Square, the world's largest square. (They say.) A military brigade marched putting on a show under the watchful eye of a giant Mao painting. Supposedly students, three young Chinese men inquired about Canada and life there, nevertheless, I shunned politicizing the conversation even if they were truly interested students.

A number of sincere Chinese people did help us; the following was particularly meaningful to me. Searching for some tranquility we went to a mosque. At the entrance we removed our shoes. As in any place of worship, be it a church or synagogue, you could feel the reverence; and so with respect, we knelt inconspicuously at the back; while at the front men bowed in prayer.

Calmed, we eased out to a walled garden landscaped with grey-green plants and stone carvings.

As I propped up against a stone turtle for Erlinda to take a photo, —two children, no older than four, approached me unafraid.

I glanced around.

How could the parents leave them like this?

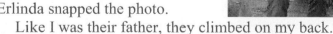

Adorable, innocent faces and eyes looked up at me.

They spoke something presumably in Cantonese.

Then the boy put a hand on my shoulder and the girl leaned into my chest and lap, at the moment Erlinda snapped the photo.

Like I was their father, they climbed on my back.

We horsed around and played.

* * * * *

The strength that powers Erlinda's body is quite remarkable: the day after we got home, she was multitasking. While the washer and dryer were chugging along in the background, she cooked meals and entertained the kids. The weather being cooperative, she enlisted Sammy to help rake the final vestiges of fall.

Baking a chocolate cake for Halloween used to be a big event. Next to her, the kids sitting on the kitchen counter would goof around, laugh and lick icing from the spatula.

There used to be great excitement getting dressed to go out. One time, showing everyone her princess costume, Sammy was looking around for Ritchie. She and I found him in the powder room sitting naked on the toilet, reading my "Calvin and Hobbs" book, oblivious to everything. "Maybe we should give him some pee-rivacy," I said.

Erlinda, in a home-made witch costume, and I had traded duties with Dave and Beth: half the evening we walked the kids through the neighborhood and the other half handed out treats at our door.

Within a week of our return, I was once again on the assembly line for a six-month term. Contract work suited our travel lifestyle. Often after work Sammy wanted to play and there was no shortage of games. In one we acted out a scene: I a misbehaving dog and she an admonishing owner. My runner's knee ached from being on all fours but I kept it to myself—knowing this stage with her would pass much too soon.

The most fun and enduring was hide-and-seek with Richie and Erlinda, in an ever-expanding list of creative hiding places. It helped to have a huge house.

One memorable day, in the middle of a game, Sammy pouted, "I'm not playing" and stomped off to her room. Richie looked up at us like a miniature adult and said, "I'll go talk to her." Amazing words for a six-year old. Before long both were back and the game continued as if nothing happened. Perhaps this behaviour originates in the nature of DNA, but I suspect it's influenced to a larger degree by the nurturing of parents.

233

Here's another example of what I'm talking about. I was in the study when I heard Beth say, "Go on." Richie entered with a shy smile, and in his extended hands a tooth that had wobbled for days.

"Wow," I said, "the tooth fairy will be happy to receive that." Behind him stood Beth, proud how her little boy was growing up.

In those early days, pre-electronics and cellphones, the kids were given responsibility to groom the family cats Fizz and Tots. With every passing year the bond grew and when the pets died the kids, with great sadness, buried them in the back yard. Sammy asked for another cat and Richie for a hamster. Thanks to him, Hammy always had fresh water, food and a clean cage.

The kids' rooms were generally left open and on one sleepless night, I could hear the pitter-patter of little feet. Happy Hammy in his cage on the spinner, cranking out the miles.

All's well on the western front.

* * * * *

One day in the middle of that winter, my manager called for me. As soon as I sat down in his office, he got to the point.

"We're letting you go," he said bluntly. I couldn't believe it. There had been no indication of a problem. No warning. Nothing.

"I see." I didn't see.

"Can you tell me what I'm doing wrong and I'll correct it?" I said, not accepting it as a final decision.

"I heard reports but I can't be specific." He said, eager to get rid of me.

Minutes later, I was out the door in shock and beyond indignant. *How dare they? I am an excellent employee.*

The only possible explanation I could come up with concerned a time in the dining hall when I asked quite innocently of a co-worker, "Do you guys have a union?"

I told myself it wasn't my performance, it wasn't personal; but that's not how it felt.

We needed money for more travel so I was not about to give up. Landing a job at the post office was not easy and yet I managed, promising myself to give it a do-or-die effort.

My route changed every week or two. Consequently, there were periods of difficult adjustment. Even in the face of a brutally cold winter and with a heavy mailbag straining my bony runner's shoulders, the mail got delivered.

I worked quite late most days and claimed the overtime to which my supervisor insisted, "You should be able to finish on regular time."

After twelve-hour days, I came home tired, disheartened and certainly unable to appreciate all the good around me.

On the day I quit, I asked myself out loud, "Why do I always have the worst routes?" The postie next to me replied, "Because that's what they do to all the new guys."

At this point in my life, I was running out of work options. *What's wrong with me? Is it indifference or laziness?*

I couldn't allow it.

Out of desperation I took on a job as a courier. "All you need is a car and willingness to work hard," said the hiring manager.

Mortified to be scraping of what I believed to be the bottom of the employment barrel, I kept it to myself.

My life had spiralled from NASA to courier, spelled LOSER. I clung to one positive thread, I was earning something, albeit pittance.

Once again, my working days were long, lonely and lifeless—I picked up the parcels and headed out, hopefully on a reasonably safe and efficient route while risking car and limb.

One fateful evening, I was to deliver my last package of the day and then go home for badly needed rest. Driving along a dark, deserted, rural highway I slowed to squint at the house numbers.

I carefully reversed and turned down a steep, curving drive. Dense forest on both sides. A dim porch light fixture my target. Then it happened.

For some reason, the car on its own free will was sliding down into the forest. Inexplicably missing several trees before coming to a stop at the bottom. That was when I heard the panting. It was me. I hadn't taken a single breath on the way down.

From my seat I looked around and sized up the situation. The slimmest opening suggested there was a chance to escape this trap. Yet when I pressed the gas pedal the tires spun uselessly.

I turned the engine off.

The Horizon and I were entombed like helpless insects in sap, only to be discover a million years later.

I closed my eyes.

The sun is rising and I can see clearly now.

An uneasy feeling burns within my chest as I drive along an Arizona road. My only comfort: Erlinda is back home safe and surrounded by family love. I know that if something should happen to this car, the reserve fund is there for her.

I pull onto a sideroad and continue, my heart pounding, right to the very edge of my favourite place, the Grand Canyon. One final view of its timeless beauty.

Determined, I floor the gas pedal and pick up speed. There's no going back now.

The smell of the ponderosa pine, juniper and pinon pine levitates my soul. I'm soaring like Thelma and Louise through the sky, free of pain, surrendering to the loving light that is accepting me, embracing me for all of eternity.

My eyes popped open—I had hit rock bottom!

CHAPTER 12

DISTURBANCES AND DIVERSIONS

I climbed over the seat to the back, got out and trudged up the hill to the highway; looked both ways before deciding on the house with all the bright lights. Judging by the loud merriment coming from within, a party was in progress. Nobody responded to my knock, so I entered.

In the living room, a group of well-dressed women, wine glasses in hands, were shushing each other to listen to the hostess.

"Look girls, a man," she said, "just what we need." They all turned to face me, smiling.

"Can I use your phone," I asked sheepishly.

"Sure hon."

My boss wasn't interested in hearing about my problems, "Just deliver the damn package," he shouted. Having picked up on the conversation, the hostess asked for everyone's attention.

"Let's help out this poor man, shall we?" she said. Several thought this a hoot, the wine having something to do with it.

The rowdy volunteers—arms gesticulating and heals clicking on the pavement—walked me with a bag of gravel back to my car.

By God, if the sexy squad was not able to assist the Horizon in first gear, out and up the hill! We surfaced cheering and high-fiving, miraculously without a scratch to person or vehicle.

Relieved, I expressed deep and sincere gratitude to one and all.

"Stay out of trouble and forests," winked the hostess as they waved good-bye.

"I'll try."

The time had come to take stock of my life and to decide what to do next, not that I had many options available. So it was back to the drawing board in the privacy of my study. *Can I retire on what we got?* Painstaking care to assuming, number crunching and prognosticating, produced a new lifetime chart. There was just enough, not a fortune, for the average lifespan plus an extra 10% for unforeseen eventualities. If we lived too long, we could always start smoking. Do you detect a hint of cynicism? The ultimate irony of life's conclusion—part of you wants to live as long as possible and another part doesn't.

Back to retirement. Happiness is what I was suppose to feel, not a fragile contentment devoid of any satisfaction or purpose. A far cry from a crazy rich Croatian with a real estate empire.

My 'retirement' went unnoticed just as I wanted it.

The house was full of excitement and nervous anticipation one September morn, the first day of school. The kids were following Beth in a straight line to the minivan, dangling on their backs Little Mermaid and Batman packs.

If they leave without us, I can only blame myself.

"Can we come along?" I shouted.

Beth mumbled something I assumed to be yes. They were in a hurry.

I scooped up Erlinda in the kitchen doing dishes and followed in our car.

As we all watched from the parking lot, Dave took Richie inside the new school, switching this year to attend classes for the *gifted*. A few tears rolled down Beth's face.

"Are you OK?" asked Erlinda.

"Yes. It's . . . I worry how he'll manage in the different setting."

"He'll be just fine," said Erlinda with a comforting smile.

Sammy's kindergarten was in another school and Beth had the pleasure this time.

Throughout the whole day Erlinda and I waited anxiously for the report on the day's events.

"Woo-hoo! Anybody home?" shouted Sammy from the front door. *That sounds good.* It had been a "fun" day and her teacher was "really nice." For months, she announced her return from school with those melodious words, *Anybody home?*

For his part, Richie was keen to start working on the project *What I did during the summer*, based on the household's trip to the U.S. southwest. On a poster, he included text and his photos of national parks. The project was marked *A+* and held a prominent spot in their study for months.

But as the year progressed, something changed. I sort of sensed it but didn't place any importance because it was so subtle.

One morning, for no apparent reason, the kids were in a quiet reclusive mood, so I tried to coax them and Erlinda into the production of a musical video in the family room. By a shrug of the shoulder Sammy seemed disinterested. That changed when Richie got on board. Dressed as a rock'n'roll band with wigs and instruments, we lip synced to "I'm a Believer" by the Monkees. We started subdued, gradually picking up energy and ending with wild fun chasing each other around the room. At the next Edith gathering everyone watched the video in stitches.

More change was coming. There was talk of next spring Beth going back to work, and Dave quitting the second job to spend more time with the kids and pitch in with the laundry and cooking.

One constant through those years: Erlinda was enjoying the kids and retirement.

* * * * *

Beth asked if Ernie could stay in the downstairs' spare bedroom for the weekend. Who is Ernie, you ask? Well, that's what I was thinking. She met this self-taught medicine man of a local indigenous community at a powwow. Apparently, not only was he highly respected for communicating with spirits but also possessed special healing powers: he cured a member of a white family right in their home. To further her existing belief in holistic and herbal medicine, she was going to learn how to be a medicine woman. She had attended a couple sweat lodge events.

"It's for one weekend," Erlinda reminded me.

After a brief intro Ernie spent the entire time downstairs. I left the security off at night so he could step outside for a smoke.

The idea that a stranger—to me he was a stranger—could be wandering around during the night was disconcerting.

After Ernie's second unannounced visit, I thought it best to be frank with Beth. She valued his expertise so I had to handle the subject tactfully.

"I'm not comfortable having Ernie in the house," I said. As I recall, the reaction was beyond anything I expected.

"You're a racist," she said. I winced inwardly from the accusation and the sharpness in her voice. "What are you afraid of? Always shredding papers." She waited for a response.

But to avoid provoking her further, I backed off. The truth is I *did* shred papers, those with our SIN, DOB and investment information.

"All you have to do," she said, "is lock up your valuables."

My initial resentment turned to sympathy. Lately, she had been looking uncharacteristically haggard and disheveled, an indication of a problem. At the same time, I couldn't help brooding defensively. *Aren't we all racist to one degree or another? Perhaps I'm more than I'm aware of.*

A few days later, Beth spoke to Erlinda instead of me about the matter. Beth had several suggestions: the security system could be turned on at night, Ernie would not go out for a smoke; we didn't need to feel compelled to speak with him when passing in the hallway; and I should learn to deal with my fears and insecurities.

During another four-day stay, Beth used the washer and dryer to do his laundry. Incensed, I blurted out to Dave on his way to work, "I'm not happy with Ernie staying here."

"I don't have time," he said, avoiding me from that point on.

Despite the tension, one unusually pleasant Saturday in April I asked Beth if I could take the kids cycling. Bad timing, she said, the next-door kids were coming over. But later, my neighbour mentioned his kids were away all that weekend.

Erlinda and I left on another summer trip, a badly needed break as far as I was concerned. When we got back, I sat down with Dave for a calm conversation.

I said I had installed a lock on the study door before leaving on vacation and asked Beth to slide any mail under the door. But most of it had been left out in the open in the family room.

"He was here only once," Dave knew what I was driving at.

"Just last weekend, he brought his wife and son," I continued, even though this was not news to him. "Ernie's visits are creating tension." He looked at me like, what do you want me to do?

How am I to explain my discomfort, if I can't understand it myself? So I dropped into a memory cave, true or false, from my childhood. A memory where in the middle of the night a menacing figure entered through a window.

For a while he was silent and then spoke like he hadn't heard me.

"She may want to move out," referring to Beth. Shortly after Mom's passing, Dave always presented a cheerful exterior and he wasn't about to wallow with me in this sorrow either. I believe with all sincerity, he did the right thing to ignore me.

"Speaking of moving," I said, "Dad is asking about moving into our spare bedroom." With so much going on I hadn't given it much thought till now.

Dave turned serious, saying "First of all, I don't like his kind of humor. The next time he says something stupid I'll let him know what I think." He was on a roll. "Anyway, where was he when I was growing up, huh?" He ended with this declaration, "If he moves in, we're moving out."

In need of friendly faces and feeling nostalgic, I invited the old gang for an afternoon of cards. It was time. For about two decades I had declined invitations from them to focus exclusively on Erlinda and work.

Nick was first to show up, having picked up the Baron on the way. The moment they came through the door, boisterous and smiling, my spirits lifted. I extended my hand for a shake. "Don't expect that Russian triple cheek stuff," I warned, a habit they picked up over the years. They laughed like in the old days and gave an unrestrained Russian bearhug instead.

Behind them Willy was pulling into the driveway—with a child. As they approached, I couldn't help noticing of mixed race.

I crouched down to her level, "What's your name?"

Being shy, so Willy picked her up, "This is Flora."

After two failed marriages, he was in a committed relationship with a West Indian woman. Obviously he cared about Flora as he cared for his own teenage sons from the second marriage.

Although his hair had thinned and crow's feet had formed around the eyes (not half as pronounced as mine), he still had the great gymnast physique.

Nick was physically unchanged, unmarried and childless, but in a very stable relationship with Shirley he met way back at the ballroom classes. They owned a large home, personally decorated with exquisite taste, great for entertaining. Not a shock, looking back at his teen years. As an auditor and a psychologist, they could afford the finer things in life.

Perpetual bachelorhood was Baron's destiny. Nothing short of the perfect woman, in body *and* mind and with a high sexual drive, could satisfy him. He had saved a substantial nest egg for retirement which he gambled with on the ill-fated Nortel, counter to Nick's and my vociferous advice. And lost everything. Now, he was rebuilding—working long, exhausting hours as a pastry chef.

We indulged in his delicious pastry and cakes, played cards and caught up on "What's new?"

We had a great time. But after they left, I came to a conclusion: our interests had gone in different directions, besides, we lived in different towns.

To expand our closer-to-home social sphere, Erlinda and I turned to volunteering at the theatre and playing bridge at the Seniors Centre.

You meet all sorts of people there, the vast majority being well intentioned trying to enjoy their Golden Years by participating in a variety of social activities.

On one particular afternoon at a bridge table, a woman we just met appeared to be admiring Erlinda. It was clear, at least to me, she was thinking, *You're a cougar to have hooked a younger man.*

Her partner didn't appear as complimentary. By the back-and-forth glances and the abrupt, "How did you two meet?" I knew what she was thinking, none of it being new.

My standard reply kept the conversation on an even keel, but I was this close (my thumb and forefinger are almost touching) to tell her:

When we met, I was hunting for a rich woman and she craved for a young man good in bed. Once we got married the truth came out—she didn't have the money to provide me with a comfortable lifestyle and I wasn't frisky in bed. And yet, almost twenty years later, we're still together. Figure that out.

The truth was that right from the start her age (even though I was quite practical), nor her race, nor her religion diminished her standing in my mind. As the reader knows, it was her personality that won me over. Race has never, ever been an issue between us. As a complex thinking being, I have much more to offer than my skin colour, and so I resent being condensed to skin colour by anyone, white or black. The human race is my preferred association. With the intermingling soon we shall all become *One*. What a beautiful world that shall be!

* * * * *

Bruce Trail
Southern Ontario

What better way to celebrate your 60th birthday than to go for a summer stroll: in Erlinda's case, the Bruce Trail—all eight hundred kilometres of mud, sweat and cheers.

Our new friend Wern, who we met during a bridge game, joined us for the first week.

What can I tell you about Wern? With the support of his recently deceased wife, he had fought through a brain aneurism and colon cancer, developing along the way a contagious zest for the outdoors and life in general. Whenever I called him to go for a hike, even at short notice, he responded unwaveringly, "I'll be ready in five minutes." As a former marathoner, he was in great shape for a seventy-year-old. His mind entertained with extensive knowledge and stimulating conversation and to top it all, he was one of the kindest people I ever met. One trait, amusing? He was very frugal, worse than me, if you can believe it. Understand, he had experienced the Great Depression when people didn't throw things out. Now, as a millionaire in a huge house, he devoted a closet solely to neatly stacked plastic bags and smoothed-out-for-reuse aluminum foil strips.

On the drive up to Tobermory, with Erlinda and I following in our car, he let the gas tank get nearly empty before filling it at *two* gas stations in search of a lower price. It was the only annoying thing he ever did. Truly.

For six hiking days we shared the cars and in the evenings a campsite or B&B. After Wern left us we struggled on, missing him, but continue we did.

Every Sunday we returned home to catch up on house chores. On one of those days the whole family went to support Dave in his first triathlon. He acknowledged our cheers with a wave and confident smile and powered on to a strong finish. Months later I went with him to Ottawa where he did even better.

Exactly five weeks after Erlinda and I started her endeavour, we celebrated with glasses of wine at the Queenston terminus.

In my hope of reviving a fading family relationship, we dusted off the trailer and took the kids to Algonquin Park. Enthusiasm prevailed on the first day, but we and the times were changing. The kids grew lethargic and distant, felt more by me than Erlinda, though they tried to put up a happy front. Even with toasting marshmallows by the crackling campfire, canoeing lazily on the lake or playing everyone's favourite Monopoly, once the malaise crept in like a thick English fog, nothing could clear the air. I realized on that trip, the 'Good Old Days' had slid to an unavoidable end.

Something else was coming to an end: our housing agreement. I told Dave that it was best to go our separate ways.

"Why?" he asked.

"As you know, it's been stressful since Ernie came into the picture," I said. "Honestly, I can't take it anymore."

He looked caught off guard, silently processing my words.

"I just assumed we'd renew for another year."

Three days later, Beth appealed to Erlinda—for the sake of the kids' schooling, they wanted to stay another year. She had another request: from now on any further dialogue on these matters would be between the girls. Clearly, Dave wanted nothing to do with it anymore.

"No way I'm going through this another year," I said to Erlinda, my head was shaking adamantly. And then, her twinkling eyes spoke to me, beseechingly.

"We should do it for the kids," she said softly.

My head stopped. *Oh God, give me strength.* The agreement was renewed annually for *four* more years.

Cycle 2000

The salesman at the bicycle shop looked around, "The only hybrid under $300 is that one." He pointed to a dusty blue bike in a corner, passed up obviously by discriminating cyclists. She was heavy but sturdy and with additional accessories she would do, not that I knew much about bikes. I explained what I hoped to do.

"On this bike!' He looked at me incredulously. "When?"

"In a month."

"What cycling experience you got?

"A bit years ago," I said.

With that, he called over his co-worker. While they whispered, I questioned the wisdom of the whole idea.

"Who are you going with?"

"Nobody."

They looked at me like I was in way over my head, in a mid-life crisis. Perhaps, to a degree, I was. Yet it was a lot cheaper than a red sports car and safer than a young blond, if Erlinda found out.

After running my 5th Boston, I had experienced significant knee pain for which a doctor recommended giving up racing. "Try something new. Be good to your knees."

One thing for sure, I had to burn off pent-up energy and all that negative emotion bottled up inside.

Into Thin Air: Death on Everest got me dreaming about climbing the mountain. Winter camping in -34 degrees—numbing cold in either scale—and a mountaineering course opened my eyes to a beautiful world of snow, ice and glacial travel.

The dream ended when my primal instincts had to kick in to save me from a deadly fall on a Colorado Long's Peak slope.

The cycling idea had taken birth on a hike with the Baron up Mount Washington, N.Y. By the time we reached the summit I had my answer.

"Start easy," the sales guy had suggested, so I picked a low traffic road, my bright red and yellow vest screaming to be noticed. Panicked by the sound of an approaching vehicle from behind, I tightened the grip on the handle bars. As it passed by, a gust of air shook my balance, and fear surged through my body.

On Sundays a cycling group went for a ride so one day I joined them. Pedal as I might, I couldn't keep up even with the slowest. They have light weight racing machines and wear snazzy, aerodynamic clothes, I told myself. There was no second ride for me.

After a month of preparing, I felt I was up for the challenge.

DAY 1

Even with the fall sunshine, a few snowflakes drifted about as I eagerly wheeled out the driveway and onto the road, yet concerned something might turn up at the last minute to deny me this great adventure. Erlinda whispered, *Come home to me safe.*

If I was able to stick to the schedule, fall colours should be with me most of the way.

Blue Bell, as I named the bike, was equipped with a mirror, bell and a safety flag. Straddling the back wheel, a pannier contained clothes, maps and toiletries; a fanny pack protected my wallet.

A rendezvous with the Baron was the kind of send-off I needed. In no hurry, we talked and talked. The sun and clear blue sky reflected off Lake Ontario as we followed the Lakeshore Trail.

In Oakville he turned around and waved goodbye.

From that point I was on my own except for Blue Bell, not much of a talker but an exceptional listener. By 5:30 p.m. the two motels I tried in Hamilton were full, so we moved on to Grimsby to spend the night.

DAY 2

Without restful sleep my brain was operating in slow motion the entire day. Strangely enough, I felt happy. Was it Lake Ontario on the left or the vineyards on the right? Or was it the liberation from high drama at home? Strange to think: I had become claustrophobic in a huge, six-bedroom house.

Even the crowds milling around at beautiful Niagara Falls didn't change my mood or deter from a quick photo.

"Where you going?" asked the Customs and Immigration officer at the Peace Bridge, border entry to N.Y. state, USA.

"Daytona Beach, Florida." By the expression on his face, I wasn't the first crazy person he met on the job.

According to my daily log, downtown Buffalo on a Sunday looked like a ghost town. Peaceful, and yet the adjacent Black neighbourhood, I entered guardedly. Hollywood movies had left an impression. Some of the local folks may not look too kindly to a hotshot white dude cycling down their streets for no good reason, I presumed. My fears evaporated: the streets lay largely empty except for the well-dressed church goers; they sure didn't look like they would cause problems for me.

For supper and breakfast I picked up at a supermarket: canned salmon, V8 juice, Gatorade powder, 3 yogurts and 3 muffins. My typical daily food. Exciting?

DAY 3

The temperature was cold enough to see my breath and the ears, fingers and toes felt it. Nevertheless, I was in a good frame of mind because of the colourful fall foliage and wide shoulders. Snow at the top of a long steep hill reminded me to push on without delay. Blue Bell started to complain about her back brake and gears, so I made some minor adjustments. I had issues too, it's just that I was less vocal: hand tingling and numbness from long periods on the handlebars, so I raised one at a time to rest—not the wisest move when vehicles pounce on you. To remedy saddle soreness, I stood up on the pedals when necessary which was often, right down to the last day.

DAY 4

New York's endless steep hills and rain were draining; thus I was ready to call it a day at a YMCA. Unfortunately, they were full but I perked up when they found a free room at the Salvation Army 8 miles away. If I got there by 4 p.m.! My shoulders slumped. *Rats! No time to waste.* With head down I pumped the pedals like a madman, on a four lane, sometimes shoulder-less road.

How dangerous, when I think about it now!

Since I was the only person there who needed salvation, the manager, Iris spoke to me—as I ate and drank, my head nodding with a full mouth. She spoke about her husband's brain cancer and how difficult it was looking after him.

While the room was being prepared, I went to the local library where I examined topographical maps for the best route going forward.

When I got back to Sally Ann, I couldn't believe my eyes: a clean bright room all to myself; the hot shower had new soap and a comb.

Around 9 p.m. Iris knocked gently at the door and whispered, "George?" I pretended to be asleep. Don't misunderstand me, I was grateful for all the kindness, but I didn't come on this journey to mess around, *if* that was her intention.

DAY 5

After breakfast, I thanked her with a warm hug and promised a postcard.

Two hills tested my resolve—a mile at 6% incline and another half-mile at 8%—but I persevered. Like a gentleman I escorted on foot Blue Bell to the top.

Habit, habits! They're hard to break. You would think, I should have learned by now not to leave finding a hotel so late into the afternoon. That day I suffered again. At 5:30 p.m. I discovered the next bed lay ten bloody (excuse my French) miles away. Normally I wouldn't ride on a major highway. For starters, it's illegal. But an accident backed up traffic as far as the eye could see, so naturally, I hopped on for a quick shortcut. At the wreckage site a managing policeman stared at me in disbelief.

"Get that God damn bike off the road, now!" Those were his exact words, not mine.

"Yes sir!" I gladly complied and pedalled furiously down the empty freeway, hoping he was too busy to chase after me.

My first of many encounters with man's best friend took place that day, but more on that later.

DAY 6

Picture if you will, cycling on unfamiliar roads in soupy fog with clothes wet from sweat. Can't be fun, right? Add to that a route circumventing Pittsburgh where the hills are long, steep and countless. I was a gentleman time after time escorting Blue Bell up the hills.

Speaking of my beautiful travelling companion: while I was devouring a McDonald's lunch, some shifty-eyed Casanova was ogling the curvature of her lovely frame. Panic stricken, I rushed out to protect my precious gem. *Where would I be without her*?

At one point in the afternoon I stopped at a house for directions to the nearest motel. A conversation with a woman at the door went way too long, ending with, "None in town. But you can stay here with me." Furious with myself for having been easily distracted and desperate for conversation, I missed a turn and got lost.

DAY 7

After another sleepless night and more horrible hills, I made a pit stop at a reputable cycle shop in Morgantown, West Virginia. Gunner, a local cycling legend, warned against going south: cyclists had been killed by logging trucks roaring down shoulder-less highways. Better to backtrack and head east through Maryland.

DAY 8

Oh, what a day! In the first part of crossing the Appalachian Mountains, I walked most of a two-mile hill. On the way up I injured the left knee cap and hamstrung, keeping it to myself, not wanting to alarm her. When we finally reached the valley floor on the other side, 5 miles from the next town, I noticed her front tire losing air. It took an hour and a half to repair the flat. Spent and demoralized, I sat on the ground seriously considering going home. Ready to admit it was one, big, mistake.

DAY 9

Thank God for the C & O Canal Towpath in Maryland—this flat, fine limestone path tunnels through forests, offering an easy, pleasant ride.

DAY 10
My nose bled, a first, and the head felt odd; yet, on the positive side, I slept well after taking a sleeping pill, also a first.

DAY 11
Fell twice. No harm though. *So*, so happy to hear Erlinda's voice that evening over the phone. Everybody was wondering where I was. I described the present predicament: the left knee was swollen and aching; the next day's route was on a shoulder-less hilly road; the forecast called for fog and rain; and Blue Bell's rear hub was grinding.

"What should I do?" I asked. She thought a long time, like she was solving world hunger. Finally, she directed me to the bathroom.

"What do you see?" she asked. In the mirror, a corpse like a character in the *Twilight Zone* was scrutinising me no matter how I turned my head. *My God, that can't possibly be me.*

"I don't look so good, Honey," I said, not wanting to scare her too much.

"Take the day off, like I've been telling you."

DAY 12 (Rest Day.)
Rain and fog the whole day. The knees' swelling and pain subsided once I took Ibuprofen and applied ice.

To my pleasant surprise, Myron, the shop owner in Harrisburg, picked us up at the motel. While he repaired Blue Bell, I stocked up on food.

With permission from my sweetheart to sleep, I slept lots. No pills.

DAY 13
A truly beautiful day, the fall colours ablaze in every direction. I felt great, powering across the Blue Ridge Mountains and the Shenandoah valley, up four continuous miles and along Skyline Drive in West Virginia. A policeman told me the nearest motel was 10 miles away in Zion X-roads—a dangerous place at night—I should hustle my buns. By now I was use to it. Hustle I did, like being on steroids and caffeine tablets.

The room had no phone, no working light or smoke detector, no lock (I blocked the door with the dresser and bed), no peace and quiet. A couple in the adjacent room argued until he threw her out in the middle of the night.

DAY 14

I was more than happy to move on.

Dogs. Dealing with them never occurred to me when this foolhardy adventure entered my thick skull. Here's the thing about them and my unique situation. Every day I was cycling many miles through unfamiliar territory, far from home and slowly enough that most wouldn't lose a breath catching me. Why chase me, anyway?

Perhaps 'man's best friend' was innocently curious about this strange person with a drawn face, advertising his presence with bold red and yellow clothes. Perhaps some were simply pretending to be hunting, others actually were. Perhaps some had a bad experience with a kicking cyclist and were now seeking revenge. Perhaps some simply enjoyed watching me sweat and cycle for dear life. If a cat can smell my fear, a dog should have no problem.

Two things I *do* know: if he's barking lustily, he's not practicing for a choir; if he's displaying those fangs, he's not taking me for a dentist.

DAY 15

Expecting a late arrival, I called the B&B and asked the owner, Elis, to pick up my mail—maps and Erlinda's letter—at the post office.

His wife was high on a ladder painting the front porch when I pulled in.

What a lazy so and so I thought about him, until I heard he was somewhat disabled by a back injury.

Felt bad about having asked him to get my mail. Elis, in fact, was a terrific guy, renovating the 1880 house as much as he could himself.

He kindly drove me to town to an ATM and a supermarket for a roasted chicken, I shared with them at supper. The meal finished with a prayer for my safe trip.

Over the phone, Erlinda told me she had been worrying because I hadn't called for several days. I read her letter in bed—her curlicued script, unlike my sharp print, so dear to me:

My dear Georgie,

Hope your legs are still holding you up. I miss you and think of you all the time.

I contacted some nice and very helpful people in St. Augustine about your airline ticket home.

Your Dad had a cataract operation. He needs a lawn mower, but bought a snow blower, his third. My hike with Wern and the club was great. Beautiful fall colours. He likes to be at the front of the pack, but you know me, slow and steady. Several people want to hear how you're doing. Some are shocked you're cycling to Florida. Sammy is interested which state you're in.

One side of the bed is awfully cold without you. I'm praying every night for your safety. I love you.

Erlinda

DAY 16

It was Sunday and yet, the three giant dogs—barking and sprinting across the lawn directly for me—were not observing it as a day of rest. My previously successful cries of "Stop! Sit" (or was it "Shop! Shit!) went completely unnoticed. Leaving me no choice, I dismounted, ready to fight with Herculean strength. Such was my fear. Fortunately for the canines, I didn't have to display my explosive powers of self-preservation—providence intervened in the form of a honking car. Confused by the appearance of this heavy metallic obstacle, my raging adversaries stopped just long enough for me to pedal away and yell behind to the driver, "Thank you, thank you!"

My problems weren't over for the day. A kind driver gave me a map of Raleigh, North Carolina.

"God speed," he said, like I was John Glenn rocketing to outer space. Speed I'd need, soon enough. My intention was to go around the international airport—because of the misleading road construction signs—I was going straight through. Disoriented and lost (again) I ended up on Interstate 40, a big no-no. For three miles I sped along the highway determined to take the shortest route.

DAY 17

Never underestimate the power of a smile, I say.

Blue Bell and I were sailing along on perfectly flat sideroads in the most welcoming sunshine.

Cotton plantations for miles and miles.

On the other side of the road, an elderly Black lady with a bush of white hair strolling in my direction.

When our eyes met she sent me the gentlest of smiles.

Peace and serenity swept over me.

I couldn't help pondering on how this descendant of slaves harboured no ill will towards me, a white man? How was she able to liberate herself from the horrible past?

255

DAY 18

With the terrain pancake flat, I was really motoring through the Black towns of the Carolinas. Very relaxed now. What trepidation I had about Blacks evaporated—if anything, they were friendly and curious.

DAY 19

Flying today: 160 km.

Day 20

For the first time the sun was strikingly hot. Drinking lots.

At a post office in Sumter, the manager Ethel and staff, who had been anticipating my arrival for days, welcomed me with a package of maps from Erlinda.

DAY 21

My nerves were rattled by the heavy traffic, especially trucks ripping by at 55 mph on federal roads with no shoulder. *Relax*.

In search of a bathroom, I entered Ft Stewart Military Reserve, Georgia—massive collection of military buildings, equipment and people. After I got sidetracked with a visit to the museum, a group of soldiers invited me for lunch to talk about my journey. *How nice of them*. I had to decline.

By the time I checked into a motel I was sunburned and late for food shopping.

DAY 22

Made it to Florida, but not without incident. Right after loading up on McDonald's buffet breakfast, I was ready to hit the road when I noticed a broken spoke. *Crap*! You're probably used to me using such language.

So back to the Days Inn where the owner allowed me to have the room until 11:30 a.m. The maintenance guy brought his tool box and watched. In haste I, like an idiot, inserted the spoke backwards and punctured the tube. *Double crap*! Feeling under the gun timewise, I told myself to calm down. At 11:15 and the repairs completed, I dropped an Alexander Hamilton ($10) to my kind assistant who I suspected wasn't paid all that well, and moved on.

DAY 23

To save time I skipped the morning shower. It's not like I was going out on a hot date. Beautiful coastal A1A seemed the best way around sprawling Jacksonville; but I ignored the scenery to crank out the thirty miles on a road without a shoulder, food or drink. After considerable exertion my reward lay historic St. Augustine, the oldest city in the U.S. dating back to 1565.

The airline tickets had not arrived according to Bill the tourist office person. "Call in the morning."

With time on my hands, a rare treat, I explored on foot the charming town and its well-preserved Spanish fort.

DAY 24
I wanted to get going so minutes seemed like hours. No tickets on the 8:30 delivery. Restless, I cycled around town. Finally at 11:30 the tickets arrived!

Once again on A1A, except now I could relax and enjoy the view: large homes and properties along the blue ocean; the smell and feel of the refreshing breeze. When I turned onto the John Anderson Parkway, I entered a totally different world: a quiet road all my own and surrounded by a beautiful tropical jungle.

At long last, after 2,850 km—I reached my set destination—Daytona Beach. If you have been reading this account you can well image my relief, my joy. From the hotel balcony, Blue Bell and I gazed at the miles of sandy beach and ocean.

All we had to do now was get home. Should be easy, right? Or as we say in Canada, eh?

DAY 25
Decisions, decisions! Should I sell Blue Bell and to whom? After several discreet (so she couldn't hear) calls, I determined selling would not be easy—besides, I didn't want to give her up after *all* we had been through together.

How do we get to Orlando? Where do I get a box for her?

A place only seven cycling miles away but first, one last picture of us and a Daytona sign to mail to the guys at the shop where I bought her. "We made it, boys!"

Where do I buy clothes suitable for air travel? My current threads were tattered and torn. A second-hand store satisfied my discriminating taste with an outfit for $11. Although I did have to tighten the belt and wear an extra layer not to look so emaciated.

Several buses later I made it to a motel in Orlando. Next door at a McDonald's—I'll never complain, "They're everywhere."—I celebrated with *four* Quarter Pounders and a *jug* of beer.

Unable to sleep, I got up at 2 a.m. to arrive at the airport, shall I say, slightly early. I loaded up with *five* bagels to be recognizable when I reached home.

The agent at the gate awoke me, "Your lucky day Mr. Biondic. We have a seat for you."

"Alleluia," I said, rubbing my eyes and yawning.

Oh, what a home coming! Erlinda had been waiting quite a while at the Go station's Kiss 'n Ride when I popped out. Someone honked a horn. I guess we had been holding each other a little too long in the middle of the exit lane. We had kissed but didn't ride fast enough.

At home, the kids were climbing all over me at first. Then Richie brought out the chess board and Halloween cake they saved.

While Sammy rubbed my neck, I spoke over the phone with Dave about my trip.

Supper, shower, sinful sex and sleep. SSSS.

* * * * *

As you know, the cycling challenge was brutally difficult, and yet I was extremely glad for the experience. While I somehow found the strength to face adventure, the adventure gave me strength. However, I *really* doubt I'll take on something like that again—I missed Erlinda, like the desert misses the rain.

After the initial surge of goodwill, life settled back more or less on the trajectory set before my escapade.

I hibernated that winter except for a little jogging. As the winter snow piled up and then melted in the spring, I felt a need to do something and the genesis of that something was an article in the *Runner's World* magazine featuring Marshall Ulrich.

An incredible athlete, Marshall had set records in adventure racing, climbed the Seven Summits (the highest mountains on the seven continents) and won Badwater: *The World's Toughest Footrace,* run in Death Valley.

In our travels through Death Valley, I had done some running noncompetitively, simply for the joy of it. Now, the idea of racing intriguing me so I contacted the race director. My five Boston Marathons didn't impress him much.

To be accepted into a limited field of 80 international participants, an applicant needed to meet certain qualifying standards for
one reason above all others: the danger factors of heat illness and
heat stroke.

For the first qualifying requirement I entered a 50-mile race in
Texas. Almost the equivalent of two marathons. With Dave's help,
I fared reasonably well considering I crashed energy-wise in the
latter stage, learning the importance of proper race nutrition.

We worked well together and had great fun.

The kids had shown an interest in hiking the Grand Canyon, so
with a bit of advice and encouragement they started *training*. With
loaded Little Mermaid and Batman backpacks they proceeded to
climb stairs from the basement to the second floor. Every third lap,
I checked their heart rates and Erlinda provided ice cold water.
They liked both.

"Way to go troops," I said when their energy waned; and on
they continued, knowing ice cream awaited.

That June, Dave and the kids joined us in the trailer at the south
rim campground. On the morning of the big hike, Richie stayed
with Erlinda on the rim, not wanting her "to feel lonely," three of
us headed down the dusty trail.

Each carried a pack but Dave held the most weight plus
Sammy's hand. She oohed at the scenery.

In the sweltering heat and sun we crossed the Colorado River
suspension bridge and came to the 'Welcome to the Phantom
Ranch' sign next to the stone mule corral. So for me to take a photo,
Dave picked her up and she placed an arm around his neck.

"It's nice to be here with my dad," she said wistfully, "who I
haven't seen much lately," and then placed her perspiring head on
his massive shoulder. My heart sank. I couldn't speak.

*He's trying to make up for lost time, Sammy. He loves you and
Richie more than anything in the world. You need to understand
that he's human, just like the rest of us.*

260

I missed spending time with him also. I recall a winter trip to Jamaica where *I* showed him who was the Mighty Moses (the childhood character) and *he* enjoyed a drink.

Admittedly, the distance between us was partly my fault.

All these years had passed with me self-absorbed and unaware of relationships evolving around me.

On the bank of the Bright Angel Creek we set up camp, shaded by a giant sycamore tree. The temperature reached 95 degrees so we dipped our feet into the refreshing water.

In the morning, we packed up and made our way out, stopping frequently and especially for lunch at Indian Gardens.

As we carried on, I felt a tugging weight.

"Why does my pack feel so heavy," I said. Sammy giggled.

"Come on mule," she said and giggled even more all the way to the top. Erlinda and Richie were there for the last mile.

After dropping them off at the Phoenix airport, Erlinda and I continued on to Death Valley to crew a participant in *his* Badwater race and thereby fulfilling my second requirement. At the prerace check-in, all the great athletes including Marshall, in the flesh. *Awesome.* But to be completely frank, I felt like an imposter: no right to identify myself as an ultrarunner. *Not really one of them.* However, I knew the knowledge gained as Paul's crew would be valuable in our race.

At the end of the race course Mount Whitney, the highest in the contiguous U.S., stood provocatively, leaving Erlinda and me no choice but to hike up. On the summit I suffered altitude sickness, so Erlinda took charge and led us down.

261

Ultracentric Ultramarathon
Dallas, Texas

For the third requirement, I applied to a race on an outdoor track. The objective: competitors run and walk as many miles as they can in the allotted 48 hours.

Staying within character, I developed several overuse injuries during the training—resolved by a chiropodist, physiotherapist and rest off course. The last few days I slept very little due to nerves and time mismanagement. No point making it easy?!

We planted a tent, table and chair close to the track and toilets.

Fourteen regional competitors gathered at the start line.

In the early hours I experimented with various food and drinks.

Result: nausea, until we corrected the electrolyte imbalance. Live and learn. Once recovered, I felt capable to alternately run and walk—forever.

On the first night, like some others, I tried to sleep a couple of hours on the cold, concrete washroom floor. But on a thin pad! Erlinda slept in the tent. Frustrated and too lazy to get warmer clothing, I returned to the track.

At some point my right shoe felt tight even though I repeatedly loosened the laces. As I found out later, the foot was swelling from an infection, cellulitis, slowly spreading up my leg!

I was in seventh position until late afternoon when Erlinda pointed to the leader board: second. *Wow*! I could hardly contain my excitement, hoping to hang on till the end.

At midnight, just as I was looking forward to decent shut eye—this time with a thicker pad and warmer clothing—I was thrown off balanced by Collin, the third-place person. After returning from his nap, he was motoring with startling speed. Concerned, I asked first place Butch sitting next to me, "What's up with Collin?"

"He's planning to pass you while you're sleeping."

Call it concern, call it fear—either way, panic rushed in like a tidal wave. Instantly I was awake and vibrating. My mind processing at fibre optic speed. *You've never been this high up in the standings. It's now or never, so think like a champion.*

Over Erlinda's objection, I drank a cup of coffee and returned to the track. Approaching Collin, I patted him on the back.

"You're looking strong," I said and then passed him careful not to reveal my gimpy right leg. The caffeine was kicking in.

Lapping him, I pulled up next to him.

"I understand you're looking to pass me when I go for a snooze." He chuckled.

"Here's the latest news, I'm not sleeping tonight."

Without any further words we raced shoulder to shoulder for about an hour. Once he realized I wasn't bluffing, he eased up, to my relief.

Butch ended up first, even with a stress fracture he told me about at the awards, and I second with a total of 164 miles.

Erlinda, and I on crutches, promptly flew home where the ER doctor told me the jolting news: any further delay in treatment of the cellulitis could have cost me my life.

Over the next eight days I was on Cloxacillin, a powerful antibiotic administered intravenously for maximum effect, and a diet to rebuild my immune system.

Before you go and categorize me as something unique, let me tell you there's lots of runners like me that aren't covered by main stream sportscasts.

My friend Charlie Upshall, a low-key person with a gentle wit and a disarming laugh, broke a Canadian 70 age record for six days by covering 500 kilometres. That was on two totally *replaced* knees—about a *year* leading up to the race. The surgeon never knew what Charlie was cooking up.

Women are supposed to be the weaker sex, but don't go saying that to little Ann Trason who won many times the women's division of the gruelling Western States 100-Mile Run. The course weaves through rugged mountain trails, across snow and ice fields and waist-deep rivers, and down into scorching valleys. In eight races she placed in the top six *overall*—and in two of them, she was beaten only by the male champion. Google her, if you don't believe me.

How about Uta Pippig who won the Boston Marathon while having her period. Women are said to be cantankerous at that time of the month but the finish photo shows a smiling face. If you look closely, there's drops of blood on her inner thigh.

Lessor known women have shown similar grit. In the middle of the night, Laurie McGrath and I were racing shoulder to shoulder on a narrow path through a dark forest. To stay awake she talked incessantly and it was really getting on my nerve. Silence suits me best, especially when I'm suffering, so I kicked up the speed. She moved back into her spot and kept yapping. *Darn it.* In the middle of a sentence she gently turned her head and a projectile vomit streamed out her mouth. Casually, she spat out the last bits and continued to get on my nerve. At the next checkpoint she left me in the dust. That's why she ranked top Canadian female that year.

And then there was Yolanda Holder, a slender Black lady, the fastest ultradistance walker I ever met. One race, she too was nearby, not talking at all though. And for a very good reason: with the head tilted back slightly, she was pinching the nose and breathing through the mouth. For half an hour she speed-walked like that. To shake her off, I had to run and quickly.

Seriously, I'm not making up this stuff.

Perhaps the last thing I expected to witness happened when I arrived late for a race. Most runners were heading for the start line; only one person and their friend stood between me and the registration table. Naturally, I was antsy but I *did* hear a pissing sound. *Huh?* The person ahead held the legs slightly apart and the arms were at the front. Although I couldn't see outright, I saw a stream from the skimpy shorts. The runner was urinating and the strangest part of it all: this was a woman. Obscured by the height of the table, she enjoyed just minimal privacy. The race volunteer and I exchanged glances in disbelief. My eyes must have been bulging for the woman's boyfriend said as they were leaving, "We didn't have time. She's going for a record." One issue of *Ultrarunning* detailed instructions for women on how to do it standing up, but to see it executed so expertly was something else.

Early that winter Erlinda was asked to babysit the kids. We smiled, pleased that for the first time in recent memory Beth and Dave were going away for the weekend.

Babysitting required very little nowadays—the Harry Potter series of books were the popular attractions. Thanks to the kids, Erlinda was reading them as well.

* * * * *

Badwater Ultramarathon
Death Valley, California

Badwater is titled the 'World's Toughest Footrace' for three compelling reasons: 135 highway miles, two mountain ranges, and hellish heat. Incomprehensible at first blush. *How is it possible? Doable if you have a week to complete the race.* However, the cutoff was two and half days.

To prepare for each aspect, I took a going-to-war approach. After reviewing articles about the race, studying the course for distance and elevation and researching the latest sports knowledge— I laid out a 6-month plan with charts and notes. The main points:
1) Pacing
2) Clothes and running shoes
3) Nutrition based on the sun, heat and air dryness
4) Schedules
5) Crew

Nobody enjoys being rejected. But since we were footing the bill for a crew of three, I politely reviewed and interviewed: focussing on physical durability, personality and compatibility.

Leaving nothing to misunderstanding, each member would be provided written responsibilities and instructions. Any chance of success required a smoothly functioning team effort.

My training regimen started in mornings at the mall before the stores opened. Wern, the fastest walker I knew in the area, and I— with a 30 lbs pack and dressed for winter—would climb up and down stairs. For further heat adaptation, I would jog on the spot in a sauna. All this, in addition to a 110 km weekly running program.

Compulsive behaviour? Perhaps. But I figured that's what it takes to get to the elite level.

On our drive across the country, Erlinda and I stopped at the Grand Canyon for *real* hill and altitude training. Before moving on, we hiked the rarely attempted double crossing of the canyon in two days. How should I describe it?

Using Erlinda's words, "We had fun but once was enough."

On the 4th of July Ben Jones, the race ambassador and the area coroner, held a running clinic for the novices right in Death Valley. He had acted as a medical expert in an academy nominated documentary *Running on the Sun*. Appreciated for his morbid sense of humor, the elderly giant became quite a legend by performing an *autopsy* in the middle of the race and returning to the course to finish in allotted time!

Over the ten ensuing days, our home base was the one-traffic-light town, Lone Pine, for years the headquarters of many movies filmed nearby. My daily routine was simple: run in the valley heat during the day, and then spend—a lonely night at the back of the van high in the mountains.

The much-anticipated day of the pre-race meeting arrived, the excitement palpable. By now my crew had arrived. Sitting next to us were brother Dave and our amiable neighbour Larry, I picked up at the Las Vegas airport. The last member Tony, an indigenous American with a jovial personality and ultrarunning experience, drove in. We mingled freely with many people including Marshall. This time I felt comfortable to say, "I'm an ultrarunner." *Having met all the requirements, I deserve to be here.*

During Ben's speech to the audience, he isolated me as the person who best exemplified what the race was about: perseverance.

In the predawn darkness of the next day, we drove to the start: lowest point in the western hemisphere, 282 feet *below* sea level. For the safety of participants, the first wave had already been released; one by one these golden gods galloped by.

At the start events moved quickly—a stretch, a visit to the outhouse and a team photo behind the Badwater sign. With a kiss from Erlinda and thumbs up from the guys, I was ready. For the U.S. national anthem and the countdown, I stood breathing deeply—savouring the moment—the crews' faces and the warm wind.

The gun went off, and so did our group of thirty warriors *immensely* proud to take on this monumental challenge.

Levitated by the wide blue sky, my body felt nimble, and yet powerful gliding over the dips and curves of the road. The lovely awakening barren desert radiated hope and optimism.

At Furnace Creek, a palm-tree oasis (mile 17) the crew topped up the four crucial ice chests in preparation for the Death Zone, so named for shade temperature of 120 F (49 C.)

Unfortunately, no shade existed along the looming 25 miles. If an athlete's water and salt intake are not adequate or imbalanced, it can lead to stomach sloshing, nausea and even death. Larry's soles peeled off—caused by the 200 F asphalt heat—so Erlinda gave him a pair of my running shoes. Humbled by the scorching sun I, like most runners, resorted to walking. *Survive.* To keep me moving through the shimmering heat waves the guys took turns pacing: entertained me with stories and songs, monitored my condition and shouted out my needs to those waiting at the van.

Every mile, the van pulled over and the crew, laughing and joking, worked in rapid precise succession providing me an ice-cold drink and water spraying my clothes and face for a refreshingly cool effect. All on the go. Without these measures I would have surely panicked. Picture being in an oven.

The time came when I was truly desperate for relief from the—sun, nonstop pace and reoccurring pain in the left leg. Relief showed up at the remote outpost Stovepipe Wells (mile 42): a motel, general store and gas station. That's it.

A journalist snapped photos of me eating and resting 'til he saw something more captivating: the great Scott Yurek submerging his torso in a tub of ice water. *Ooh, how can he stand it?* I cringed.

Historically, a quarter of the competitors quit right here, unable to go up 5,000 vertical feet to the first mountain pass.

About a mile up the course I was feeling fine, but nature was calling, a call impossible to ignore. So I found a ditch with relative privacy. After a struggle with constipation, I foolishly stood up much too quickly. Blood rushed from my head. Legs wobbled.

Luckily Erlinda, waiting nearby, grabbed me and helped back to the car.

In a few minutes with the sun dipping behind the mountains I got going, my head cleared and strength revived. At the first mountain pass I felt great!

Through the night, the full moon in the cloudless desert sky lit the way. Buoyed by the pleasant temperature, a nearby team started howling like wolves. My crew joined in the revelry. Without losing a beat I pushed hard through the valley hoping to tackle the next mountain and reach the pass *before* sunrise.

But first, a giant prehistoric caterpillar on the edge of the road. I was ready for it. Stories of such hallucinations from lack of sleep was something runners joked about after a race. Upon getting closer, I recognized it as simply a row of sagebrush.

To remind us there was *more* suffering in store, the baking sun was back with a vengeance.

I passed a female competitor trotting over rocky ground off the asphalt roadside, claiming it was cooler than the pavement.

Who was I to question?

The time came (mile 100) when my withered body grinded to a halt. No muscle or fibre could be willed to move.

Just before I collapsed, the crew carted me off the road. Tony and Larry poured energy gel and electrolyte down my throat; Erlinda repaired an ugly blister; Dave cut a hole in the shoe to prevent further rubbing; and I slept for the first and only time. There had been laughter when I insisted, "No more than ten minutes, guys." They snuck in twenty.

Marshall passed by offering help from his crew.

"We'll be fine, thanks," I said.

Before long I was on my not-so-merry way. A mile from Lone Pine, race headquarters, we met Ben checking up on runners.

In town (mile 122) our mood lifted as dusk flooded the sky with pink and purple. To ready for the home stretch, the third *hill*, the crew worked enthusiastically. Dave mentally calculated the pace we needed to get in by midnight, giving me something to take my mind off the strain.

Mile after mile past the aromatic sagebrush I chanted the mantra "I can do this." Guess what? It was working!

All five of us held hands crossing the finish line, surrounded by cheers, cool air and the dense towering pine forest at an 8,200 feet altitude.

Credit: Chris Kostman

How should I describe the feeling? A magical moment that transcended the physical world. I melded emotionally and spiritually with my marvelous crew—*Erlinda, Dave, Larry* and *Tony*—that gave so much of themselves; and the starry *cosmos* that provided a singularly unique place for it all to unfold.

As Erlinda drove back down the mountain, I kept fading in and out of sleep while mumbling, "Let me drive, I'm OK."

Everyone laughed. I didn't get the joke.

Later at the awards ceremony, the results became official: we placed 9th just ahead of Marshall. But for full disclosure, a few weeks earlier he had climbed Mount Denali in Alaska the coldest mountain anywhere.

Off to the side Ben spoke to me in private, "You're not done. Finish it." From the lowest elevation to the highest in the contiguous 48 U.S. states. Like I said, he had a morbid sense of humour except he wasn't kidding this time.

I hope you, the reader, are still with me. The adventure is not quite over.

After a few hours of sleep and carried by euphoria, I was alone and hiking onwards from the finish line in the dark pine forest, up 11 more miles and 6,300 vertical feet. Climbing past campgrounds and the tree line to the very last campground. *Regular* hikers were waking up to start their final ascent of the peak, still distant but enticingly visible.

Marshall was already coming back down. We exchanged words of encouragement.

Narrow, rocky switchbacks brought me higher and higher, above the flight of any birds, the air so thin I was panting for oxygen. *Chin up. Onwards.* Powered by Puccini's incomparable aria "Nessum Dorma" flowing and swelling in my mind, I pressed on the last few yards. My skin tingled. There, right there, at the summit of 14,495 feet—just as the orchestra reached the top of the crescendo—I caught my breath.

While I rested on a boulder, I scanned the Inyo Valley plunging thousands of feet below; Badwater out there about 100 miles away, impossible to see, but I knew its location having travelled from the start on my own two legs.

I handed my camera to someone nearby. With one hand over my heart and the other pointing at the lens, I said, "Take one for my wife." Successful athletes will tell you it's imperative to control your emotions during competition. Now I was at liberty to let go of my feelings: my eyes watered with love.

Seductive as the sunny summit was, I had to return to safety way down below—before a potential afternoon storm of lightning, hail and snow arrived.

Altitude and a miscalculated shortage of food and water sent me stumbling, adrift in a dreadful catatonic stupor. Somehow the legs took my beaten body down the mountain for I remember none of this segment.

Just before nightfall, the entire challenge was finally completed.

* * * * *

From the time Dad, Indira and Angela moved to be near us, we visited them quite regularly, always having a pleasant time.

One spring day just as Erlinda and I made ourselves comfortable at the kitchen table, it became very obvious something was wrong. Indira was not her usual jolly self. She told me that she wouldn't need a ride to work Sunday mornings. For a while.

"Why, what's up?" I said, hesitant to be cheery.

Her doctor had discovered a malignant lymph node near the right breast.

Oh, no! Both Erlinda and I got up and hugged her, me with less gusto than normal, watchful for any tenderness. Not wanting to show his feelings, I suspected, Dad started washing dishes.

The treatments would last several months, for which she needed a suitable wig.

* * * * *

Camino de Santiago
Northern Spain

In recent years a wonderful Spanish trail was attracting walkers with its variety of architecture, climate and landscapes. Originally a medieval Christian pilgrimage route, it exploded to grander prominence when UNESCO designated it a World Heritage site.

Why should *you* walk the Camino? If you have an unresolved issue in life, do it. If you wish to engage with intriguing people from around the world, do it. If you enjoy a physical challenge, do it. If you want to connect with nature or the creator, even if you're not a Christian, Camino de Santiago is calling you.

Erlinda and I registered at the pilgrims' office in St. Jean-Pied-de-Port on the French side of the Pyrenees Mountains.

For comradery, the municipal hostel—a stone building crowded with like minded 'pilgrims'—seemed like the best choice of lodging, bunkbeds notwithstanding. Erlinda liked a lower berth and I an upper.

272

Hey, not so close.
That's my wife.

It was early morning and the narrow, wet-from-washing cob-blestone streets were free of tourists, the only sound being the clicking of our walking sticks.

Then the rattle of a storefront grate rolling up. Two young friends going home drunk. The smell of baked bread led us to a bakery where the baskets overflowed with warm, crusty baguettes. Chance to top up the fuel supply for the 27 kms over the mountains.

Soon the road out of town turned abruptly steep and because of our substantial backpacks, we slowed considerably. Recently, a couple of pilgrims strayed off of the trail in thick fog. News of their discovered bodies lent an uncomfortable feeling as we carefully headed up the re-opened route. Heavy fog shrouded us as well, but we could hear others not far behind. At a fork we took time to choose the more trampled path. Finally, we broke through the fog to enjoy a panoramic vista: green hills, cow-grazing pastures and the occasional distant farmhouse.

Higher up, it got cold and windy. Out came the thick fleece tops. The terrain was barren, so we were lucky to find a suitable boulder to sit for lunch of sandwiches and rolls. Tasted great.

In due time we crossed into Spain and reached the monastery in Roncesvalles. Pilgrims were sitting and lying sprawled from the first-day ordeal, waiting for the registration office to open.

About eighty of us crammed in a cold and damp stone hall and eagerly reached for the limited supply of wool blankets. Faced with no hot water, the majority wimped out from having a shower. To-day, the monastery has a new building with clean, warm dorms so you need not suffer as much for your sins. As in all the coming towns, the church service included a pilgrims' blessing.

Generally speaking the trail was well marked; Along the way friendships formed as we often encountered the same people.

A thin, elderly man—down on his luck judging by the clothes, sandals instead of shoes and a flimsy little pack—kept reappearing.

"*That* guy's never going to make it," I made a bold prediction.

Every day after securing a bed in a *refugio* (hostel), we hurried to a supermarcado before siesta closing.

Then we relaxed—lying down and elevating our weary legs.

Later in the kitchen Erlinda cooked a one-big-pot meal.

Nearby sat the thin, elderly man (Robert) *sipping* his supper: black tea. So she invited him to share in our bounty.

His stomach rumbled, "Absolutely yes."

Robert
and
Erlinda

Robert was an American Jesuit whose last mission was helping the poor in Honduras. A well-educated man who spoke five languages, he was full of engaging conversation: decline of western morals, need for family ties and God's presence in nature and within each of us—not necessarily in heaven.

At times we lost contact with him for days.

One evening, Erlinda and I occupied a table with two brothers Jacque and Pierre about our age from Quebec, Canada. They were bottoming a bottle of wine, as we were, so our tongues loosened. The topic of Quebec separatism came up. Out of curiosity I asked, "Why?" They spoke of instances where they were mistreated by anglophones, purely on language differences. Not wishing to perpetuate the vulgar ugliness, I won't repeat the details here except to say I completely sympathized. I decided that if something positive could come out of the *pilgrimage*, this would be my opportunity. For Canada.

Jacque had worsening ankle tendinitis, so I offered suggestions and Voltaren, an ant-inflammatory cream. Within days the pain disappeared. In return, they shared their wine and lives: Jacque's wife would be amused to see him doing laundry; Pierre missed his wife's beautiful body, outlining its curvature with his hands. We all laughed; and that was the beginning of many jokes and playful ribbing as we made our way westward across Spain.

Returning from Santiago.

Dog tired.

The Camino wound through vineyards, fields of wheat and red poppies, and past blue columbine and fragrant yellow bushes. Every town and every village, quaint and interesting had a church to pray in, a fountain to drink from and a *refugio* in which to eat and rest. And every city had its attractions and distractions.

Life in the *refugios* (private and upscale accommodation was also available) was often crowded, creating potential for friction. It all came down to what frame of mind you brought to the Camino. When one snorer stopped another jumped in, simply for continuity I suppose. Other times they harmonized like a barbershop quartet. Earplugs were worth their weight in gold.

Not all friends were the two-legged type. The mid section of the Camino—the Castilla region is flat, dry and with great distances between towns—is best suited for solitude and reflection. While exiting one town, we were followed by a black and white mutt with a pink face and chest, someone painted.

"Go home." I pointed my hand sternly to show him I meant business. Unfortunately, he didn't understand English for he followed us. After several attempts to shoo him away we let him tag along, under the assumption he would give up soon enough.

However, a special affinity grew between Erlinda and Ralfy as she called him. She had stroked his head which was a big mistake and asked, "What's your name little doggy?" Another big mistake. He replied "Ralf." It sounded like that, but with a Spanish accent.

Like he knew her for years, Ralfy followed obediently beside her; when she stopped, he stopped. At the end of the day, 20 kms later, he was still with us. Not able to gain permission for him into the *refugio*, we left him bowls of food and water at the gate.

A big, vicious dog was roaming around early next morning in his place. Although concerned about Ralfy we had to push on. Shortly thereafter, we saw in the distance a black and white figure, with a touch of pink.

"Ralfy!" Erlinda shouted. At the sound of her voice, he jumped up three feet of the ground and scampered as fast as his little legs could go. You should have been there to see the joy of this loud and lively reunion. Absolutely overpowering.

Naturally, we continued our adventure with Ralfy. At times he diverted with ears flopping to chase a butterfly or to lap water in a puddle. About another 20 km down the road, we noticed his left hind leg limping. We talked about it with him, his round innocent eyes staring up at us intently, trustingly.

In Sahagun we knocked on a church door but neither they, nor the hostel, wanted him. With assistance from City Hall we called the *Servicio de Animales*. Hiding behind a window we watched the vets check him over and take him away, after repeated assurances he would be well taken care of. We sadly continued our journey.

A note
from
Robert

Not until we met Robert and the brothers did our spirits lift.

Walking 25 km day after day for a month without stopping can be physically and mentally draining. After a *particularly* long and steep climb through a eucalyptus forest our thoughts were on food and rest. As we crested, a tour bus opened and camera swinging tourists poured out. A woman caught sight of us and shouted, "Look, pilgrims!" as though sighting a rare species in Africa. The group ran for us, tripping over each other like the Keystone Cops. Erlinda has *always* been a polite person and yet when they came, she covered her dishevelled hair and shouted, "Get away from me!" A woman recoiled, "My lord, how rude."

On the last day we marched through the glorious sun-filled streets of Santiago de Compostela—Beethoven's "Ode to Joy" surging in my soul—to a huge square in front of the impressive baroque cathedral. Noisy jubilation and heartfelt congratulations echoed among the many met along the way. Almost all arrived not as saints, but with renewed spirits—even with or rather because of the miles of aches and pain and the wonderful experiences. Eyes filled, questions answered.

A South Korean woman we had met at a communal supper was beaming with happiness. Back home she had a husband completely devoted to his business and unable to say he loved her, no matter how often she said it to him. That day, she had an emotional phone call, he spontaneously expressed how he missed her and then said three magic words she longed to hear.

Jacque and Pierre beside me. Erlinda holds pilgrim diploma.

For the service inside the cathedral: standing room only. In our pew Jacque and Pierre sat beside Erlinda; on my side a vacant spot I was saving for Robert, we hadn't seen for days. Further on, cried a man.

"Tears of joy? "I said uncomfortably.

"No," he said. "Three months ago I stepped out of my house in the Netherlands and onto the Camino. I never spoke to anyone and never saw anything, except the ground in front of me."

Sadly, some can go through life the same way.

The grand service for the pilgrims was about to commence. On a premonition, I weaved through the crowd and stepped outside looking for Robert. There he was thin and in rags as always. We hugged and joined our group inside.

A few weeks later a letter arrived from Jacque and Pierre. They were happy to be in the loving arms of their wives, they wrote, and to let them know when we planned to go on the Camino again.

* * * * *

A couple days after returning home I got the strangest call. Ever. Indira was on the line. It started with the usual pleasantries as you might expect after being away for an extended period.

Before long she got to the purpose of the call; that's when the conversation turned, I'll say it, weird. She felt in danger, suggesting someone may try to kill her and asked if I would call daily to check she was still alive.

"Why would anyone do that?" I said, trying to be open minded regarding this highly dubious story. Her mother had died recently leaving behind a large property inheritance in Kenya.

"So it's about land?" I had heard about a property her mother owned.

"Yes."

"Who would do this to you?" I couldn't bring myself to say "kill." If it was her siblings as she implied, we had heard only good things.

"Any of them. All of them." she said.

I named them one by one including Ronald, her favourite. There was a "yes" after each name.

I promised to call, and I did, but reminded her about our upcoming trip to California.

Erlinda and I discussed the situation. A well know rivalry had existed in the beginning between her and a sister for Dad's attention, but surely not enough to kill. And when Indira gave birth to Angela, a white baby, the sister did also within a year, even though she was married to a non-white. This we all knew to be true.

Granted, money can motivate the rare person to perform terrible acts but, the probability that *all* her siblings conspired against her was zero. I didn't have the heart to tell her that because of what it would surely imply.

In about ten days their house was up for sale. There was no time to get involved as we were getting ready for California.

John Muir Trail
California

To prepare the minivan for the long voyage, I pulled out the back benches and built a platform to sleep on and provide storage underneath. Leaving the trailer at home gave us mobility.

Before the real adventure started, we stopped off in Death Valley to crew for Wayne, a big tough Englishman. An unusual number of runners did not finish that year and many crews took ill also. The heat got to Wayne early; he ended up in the hospital requiring a massive 6 quarts of IV replacement fluids.

With the minivan left behind in storage at Lone Pine, we bussed to Yosemite N.P. to backpack the John Muir Trail—215 remote miles and 43,000 feet of total elevation gain in the High Sierra mountains. Definitely not suitable for the weekend warrior. With four food drop-offs in place, we felt ready to tackle the 20 days of cold, hunger, injury and wildlife—bears, rodents and mosquitos.

But *not* ready for the level of hunger that grew daily, a consequence of burning calories at an unbelievable rate at altitude.

I think I can hear you ask, why? Well, beyond the thrill of the challenge, we were enamoured by visions of immersion into the sweeping, breathtaking landscapes: countless alpine lakes, granite cliffs and deep canyons.

And ah . . . perhaps we were a *bit* naïve.

Seven mountain passes.

Camped mostly alone.

Everything tasted great.

Cozy with packs and clothesline.

However, I should tell you in our defense, we followed the trail at a slow, steady and safe pace. On the last day we climbed to the summit of Mount Whitney, oblivious to the huge power outage on the east coast. Again, the final words go to Erlinda, "Once was enough."

* * * * *

It was settled: the family housing agreement was coming to an end in a year. From the time discord took hold, Erlinda and I had spent as much time away as possible. I hoped the last dozen months would be stress free for me to focus on preparing the house for sale.

Dad's house had 'no action' as yet, so they talked about dropping the asking price. I stepped in to turn things around. Following basic staging recommendations, Dad and I decluttered, cleaned up and painted a couple of dated rooms. The old dining room light fixture was replaced with a chandelier purchased at the Restore for next to nothing. Dad went along with whatever I suggested and within days they had an offer they were about to accept.

"Play it tough," I said, "you'll get another $5,000." They did.

One day I picked up Indira to drive to work. Having finished the cancer treatment, she was back at the pharmacy. On the way she was letting off some steam about Dad not doing much around the house and the gambling.

Perhaps I was harsh, I don't know, when I stated what appeared obvious.

"You can't expect him to change now. He's an old man." She seemed to be fine with that.

But the thing that set her off, "You knew all this when you married him." Those last few words really hit a nerve.

Filled with anger she said nothing more. For a long time to come we hardly spoke.

Just before Christmas, they moved with Dave's help to an apartment building close to her work.

Erlinda prepared a lunch specifically for Dad while the rest of us—Dave, kids, Irene and myself—played Monopoly with him. A side effect of medication, he had gained a lot of weight, a stark contrast to the spry and strong figure he had been his entire life. Now, with a bib to keep his shirt clean he looked like a baby, except very old, wisps of white hair around the ears. What's more, he was docile.

Each of us doted on him with affection, especially Irene who no longer harboured resentment. By giving his Monopoly properties to her, there was no hiding: he still favoured her.

I worried about him so a few months later I visited at the apartment. The place was a mess: boxes stacked, strewn and unopened since they had moved in.

"Take whatever you want." He pointed to things piled up in the living room. After a back and forth battle, I accepted a landline phone they hadn't used in years.

As I left Angela came out of her room.

"I'll need that," she said and took it.

Downstairs in the lobby, Dad and I talked more openly—one of us with fear and the other with frustration at the powerlessness over the situation. He accompanied me slowly to the car and looked up at Angela on the balcony watching us.

"I'd better go," he said. "She looks sad."

* * * * *

285

Ultrarunning magazine published my article with its self-deprecating humour about contrasting styles of running.

Monica and Me

Ultrarunners possess one common trait: an all-consuming passion for running—giving rise to confidence, we can do anything we set our minds to. Beyond that exists a spectrum of personalities.

Even though we flew into San Diego well in advance, my nerves were stretched taut as a bowstring. The race director emphasized in the pre-race meeting not to enter the course before 8:00 a.m.

At 6:15 my wristwatch beeped. I hardly slept the whole night but its alarm was set anyway; seconds later the clock radio sprang to life with its reminder; then the phone rang. It was comforting to know hotel's wake up service was operating well. All this too much? Hey, why take chances?

At 7:50, waiting at the track entrance our supplies stacked seven feet high, I was chomping on the bit to get the one and only decent spot to plant our tent. Who's got time to socialize when everything needs to be properly organized to avoid that frantic, middle-of-the-night search for some critical item? After a good stretch I dashed to the washroom. On the way, I almost bumped into Monica, *The* Monica Scholtz. A figure of radiating calm meets shoulders hunched and hellbent on reaching the washroom.

Once the race started, I settled into my groove, free to enjoy the easy strides and smooth breathing. The first lap was 3 seconds fast, within the acceptable range. Good.

Erlinda, my completely reliable wife, had her hands full looking after this high maintenance runner: all the food mixing, record keeping and whatnot left no time to herself.

Coming from behind, Monica patted my shoulder.

"Go Canada!" she cheered. A Canadian flag on my T-shirt displayed my pride but we both felt quite at home here with our American friends as much as anywhere in Canada. After she passed by, I couldn't help noticing the unflagging energy and unflappable spirit. She chatted, laughed and even hugged friends while floating around the course effortlessly. Her friendly smile betrayed a secret—it revealed a happy, well-adjusted human being. I'm more serious, pursuing my primary mission: crack the prestigious 100 miles in 24 ours.

Monica is universally recognized as an elite athlete and yet she didn't look it. A mass of curly, black hair topping a curvaceous figure. My hair is short, but not too short, purely out of concern people might think I'm a bit extreme. Still, being aerodynamic and lightweight is a big issue with me. Only the lightest shirt, shorts and shoes (a six-month-search could produce) would do for a skin and bones body like mine. If you enjoy counting ribs, I'm your man. Family and friends insist I must be ill, but I know it's my edge to a better performance.

However, my body can handle only two long ultras annually. Monica, on the other hand, has done an incredible twenty-three 100 milers in a single year. I'm perpetually complaining about an assortment of injuries; she seems indestructible

A leg cramp crept in, soon accompanied by doubt. Too invested, too determined, I had to find a solution and fast. Salt tablets and a quick massage, 5 minutes max I insisted, and I was back on the track.

In the dwindling hours my legs protested: Hey, whoa there, tiger! We've had just about enough down here. How long do you think you can keep this up, anyway? Are you listening? They say you should listen to your body. Hey macho man, you're going to do some irreparable damage to us or God knows what other parts of your body. There's talk of a mass, sit-down strike, for your information. Please no more! Let's compromise with just a 5 minutes walk. OK?

Over the remaining two hours, Monica was still flying and I still struggling on, having passed 100 miles.

So, should I be more like her? Certainly some fine tuning is in order but I believe it's generally best to be yourself. After all, no one is better at it than you.

* * * * *

Time was running out on two main priorities: preparing the house for sale and finding a home for Erlinda and myself. But a couple of hurdles sprung up. That's life.

Dave asked from us a considerable sum of money for the purchase of a condo still under construction. Having witnessed Irene's money mismanagement and bankruptcy, I first needed details about his financial situation. Reluctantly, he told me the credit card was maxed out. *Ouch*! I had presumed he was saving money over the last twelve years by virtue of the very low *rent*. Also, there was debt he apparently wasn't aware of.

With me having asked one too many questions, he dropped the whole subject of a loan.

In this hour of need, Dad would have expected me to help him. *I* expected me to help him.

And still, I had failed him. It hurts to this very day.

The second hurdle came in the form of a note from Beth left on the kitchen counter. She was requesting a to-whom-it may-concern letter. Erlinda and I were to confirm that they lived with us. Easy enough. Now came the difficulty: that we "knew their relationship broke down five years ago and that although they resided in the same house they have been living separate and apart during this time and at no time did they ever reconcile."

We knew she moved to sleep downstairs, according to her, due to "Dave's snoring" which I accepted at face value.

Lastly, "It is our knowledge that during this period of time they had both entered into outside relationships and that Dave presently was in a relationship where he spends 3 or 4 days of the week at her place."

The truth was: we didn't know any of this because they had become very private, and he did not appear to be away at all.

Here's what I *could* say—"Nobody in the house, except Erlinda, was particularly happy."

My emotions oscillated between discomfort and anger.

Make rational decisions, not emotional ones. Questions popped into my head but since we weren't communicating, they couldn't be answered. Ultimately, Erlinda said we should write the letter for the sake of the kids. So we did.

For a good portion of that winter and spring, I focused on the main objectives.

The house had to be at its presentable best—to the point I became a pain in the neck for Erlinda. When she wiped the bathroom mirror, I re-wiped it because of a small water mark in a corner she missed.

I fussed obsessively over every detail, even cleaned the cats' litter box on one occasion, irritated that nobody co-operated at the level I expected. Hardly exemplary or appropriate behaviour.

All my efforts paid off monetarily: the house sold for one of the highest prices in the area; and I negotiated an unheard-of commission rate with the real estate agent.

While all this was going on, I trained for Badwater II.

Supported by another Dream Team which included an Olympic record holder, we shaved two hours off the previous performance.

To top it all, Erlinda and I managed to buy a beautiful home.

With professional movers and without fanfare, we moved out.

PART III

LATTER YEARS

CHAPTER 13

EMPTY NEST AND HORNET'S NEST

Aurora
2004

W hat does a dream home look like for a middle-class family in a Greater Toronto area? How about this: a spacious, two-story, solid brick house on a quiet cul-de-sac in a desirable neighbourhood; landscaped front has a pink magnolia in the center of a thick green lawn; purple clematis climbs the garage wall; inside, Florida kitchen overlooks a private back yard with several mature shade trees and beyond, an exclusive golf course.

　　That was our home.

In no particular hurry and at liberty to express our personal taste, we arranged the furniture to create a warm, intimate feeling. Our favourite artwork, select paintings and Erlinda's needlepoint hung in just the right spots. Cleanliness and order prevailed, days of a messy bachelor apartment now ancient history. Tidiness was my new watchword. After lengthy discussions, we chose colour co-ordinated material for Erlinda to sew curtains. In general, her turf was the kitchen, sewing room and yards; mine was the study, basement and garage.

Once home sweet home was decorated our lives moved along free of financial stress and emotional strife. A hush descended upon us. Indulging in nostalgia, we spoke about the 'Good old Days' and how terribly we missed the kids. Always in a playful mood when she came home, she would shout, "Anybody home?" like Sammy used to do. Sparking joy and enthusiasm from both of us.

Generally, in the evenings we cuddled before the TV watching shows like *Survivor,* our favorite.

Wednesdays were bridge days, rotating homes with Wern and 'sparkplug' Susan. She had visions of romance. But Wern confided to us that as lively as she was, "No woman could possibly replace his wife, Emy," especially when Susan explained her tardiness one time saying she had to "shit, shower and shave."

Those tranquil and somewhat mundane days were the perfect opportunity to arrange a year of travelling for Erlinda's 65th birthday. The next-door couple offered to look after the house so there was nothing to worry about.

All the plans were put into jeopardy when Indira, who still spoke with Erlinda, mentioned perhaps by the slip of the tongue that Dad was in the hospital.

Immediately I drove to Toronto.

Having identified myself to the nurse at the office, I asked to see him.

"You can't," she said, reading his chart.

"I'm his oldest," I said, about to explode in disbelief. "None of us knows what's going on."

"Only his wife, who brought him in, is allowed."

Shouting would be useless so I calmed my voice although still furious inside. "What's he in for?"

"Depression," she said. Not a huge surprise to me, but requiring hospitalization?

"Bad enough to be here?" I asked.

It didn't appear like I would get an answer.

"Please, please," I pleaded, hands clasped in desperation. She studied me. A long pause before she spoke again.

"Attempted suicide," she whispered.

"How?"

"By hanging."

I passed Indira wordlessly on the way out, our eyes briefly making contact.

Two months later, I picked up Dad in front of his apartment building. A few blocks away from Indira's bungalow. He had called me out of the blue for help with his divorce. As we headed to the lawyer, I didn't let on knowing about the hospitalization—it was unfathomable that he had done what he was accused of. Rarely do you meet a man with his assuredness and strength, even in his situation. No, I wasn't buying it.

Dave was already in the lawyer's office waiting.

The divorce papers sent by Indira, divided very inequitably their assets: Dad got only $35,000; She got the house, ten times greater in value. Before he signed, I jumped in.

"This is not fair. You should get half."

"Absolutely." Dave was nodding.

"Dad, your pensions are good for now, but one day they may not be," I pressed.

Even though the lawyer completely agreed with us, Dad said he didn't want any more arguments with Indira.

"Let her have it," he finalized.

I had hoped for more, a more substantial inheritance for Irene.

And so most of Dad's money was held in trust by Dave, me as backup. Eventually to go as inheritance to Irene; the rest, a good start towards a car for Dave.

To my relief Dad moved in with us 6 months later—even with his four pensions, he had been unable to make rent and creditors were after him. Inexplicably, the money had been disappearing!

I helped file for bankruptcy.

Erlinda set up a bed with fresh linens in the spare bedroom, placed toiletries in the extra bathroom and washed thoroughly all his clothes: smelly from body odour and urine.

Unable to look after his own hygiene, I gave him a tub bath. During WWII a truck ran over him, according to one of his tall stories, and now proof: 20 cm scar crossed the abdomen.

On Dad's birthday, Dave invited us to check out his new condo and introduce his girlfriend, he met when he bought the unit.

In time, Dad's health improved and with less need for medication his weight dropped back to normal.

To keep him occupied, he and I played chess, but once he lost he had enough; without a challenge I grew bored.

When Wern and Susan came over for bridge, it was hard to watch Dad play solitaire. They weren't his kind of people, he said. His kind lived in Toronto.

One day I was immersed in something, and Dad heading out to Toronto by public transit. He enjoyed meeting people that way.

"Watch your wallet," I shouted looking up from my work.

"I'll be fine." He patted the back pocket and snickered.

Two hours later he called, "George, I can't find my wallet.

Darn it. Almost *all* his ID was in the stolen wallet! As you can well imagine, it took hours upon frustrating hours to get it reissued.

Camping and B&B
East coast

An east coast trip had been in the works for months, and from the get-go, Wern seized the opportunity to come along with us.

For his part, Dad wasn't keen sitting in a car any length of time because of "leg cramps." He reassured me he and the house would be just fine.

"A trip of a lifetime" is what Wern called it even though he could afford to travel anywhere in the world. On route, Quebec and the Maritimes had lovely campgrounds and B & Bs.

At Peggy's Cove, Nova Scotia, we found a quiet bench next to the iconic lighthouse. Warmed by the sun, we savoured the re-nowned fish and chips and scanned the vast Atlantic Ocean. Not looking for anything but finding a schooner and tranquility. It was a wonderful moment—to be comfortable with the silence, and I said so. No one disagreed, letting silence stretch.

Having enjoyed the East Coast Trail over several days in New-foundland, we embarked on a hike of Gros Morne Mountain. Up ahead, Wern was trying to hop from one slippery jagged rock to another with limited success. I knew why. A brain aneurism had resulted in a slight limp and notoriously poor balance. As a re-minder from the day before, a forehead Band-Aid covered the cut he received when he tripped on a root. What was I to do?

"It too dangerous," I said.

"What is?" he asked.

"It's too dangerous for you to go up," I said, yet trying to be compassionate.

"But I've been thinking about this for ages."

"I'm so sorry Wern. I couldn't live with myself if something happened."

His disappointment showed.

God! Why do I have to be the reasonable one, the bearer of bad news?

Most people would have held a grudge against me and yet, I'm sure of this, he never did. He was that kind of human being.

When we retuned home the house was a mess and more importantly, Dad had been eating from a can instead of Meals on Wheels. The time had come to breach that sensitive subject: a retirement home.

"Let's just look into it for down the road. Not for now," I said. "*You* pick the ones you like." I pointed out all the great benefits like someone cooking and cleaning so he could have fun with people his age. "It's *not* a nursing home," I tried to remain calm. Beyond not being interested, he was agitated by the whole discussion.

Talk of a will—if something happened to him the government would call the shots without it—went nowhere. As a last resort, I suggested he place me as joint owner on his bank account where the pensions were deposited, so I could pay his bills if he couldn't. Since he didn't like that either, I suggested Dave instead. It was exhausted just discussing the matter.

One day—after visiting Beth, her partner and the kids at their house—Dad told us he and a Croatian guy were moving to a bungalow in Toronto. No doubt he was emboldened by the increase in pension savings while living with us.

My fears had materialized: we had lost him! All I could do now was to call CCAC for home care.

* * * * *

The next summer, on my way to Dad's, I was surprised to see Wern at a bus stop, instead of taking a taxi or calling me. He was going home from the hospital after having fluids drained from the abdomen. News to us. The ravages of chemotherapy years ago had caused his organs to fail. For months the stomach looked bloated and he had been losing weight, going back even before the east coast trip. And yet he had never said anything. Quite the opposite—he was always good-natured.

By the time I dropped off Wern, I was late for moving Dad *again*. An attractive, middle age woman with a Russian accent was orchestrating the whole thing. So this was the Julia Dad had met on the subway. Charmed by the force of her personality Dad, Dave and the housemate were accepting her domination. There's no other way of describing it. Absolutely astounding. She must have sensed I disliked being ordered around and kept her distance.

As for Dave, the truth was he was angry. Dad had been asking lately for money from their bank account without explaining how it was spent. To stop the drain, Dave wasn't going to answer his calls for awhile.

This seemed like a good time to ask Dave about Irene's inheritance, that Dave managed. It was Dad's personal business, he said and refused to say anything more on the matter. I was totally baffled. As his backup, according to the written loan, I couldn't see how I would be able to fulfill my duty if something happened to him.

I hated to admit Julia was efficient and effective in moving Dad's things to an apartment across the hall from her.

"Don't worry. I'll keep an eye on him," she said, a responsibility that belonged to the family.

Even though I was racing locally a lot that year, I felt obliged to call CCAC to check up on Dad's home care. For some unknown reason, Dave and I were *replaced* on the contact list by a neighbour, Julia Smith.

Bell provided me Dad's new listing. After numerous rings Julia answered: He's sleeping. He's fine. I visit him daily.

Later when I knocked on Dad's door Julia opened it. For a moment she looked flustered then recovered her composure by introducing her mother Jenny, a sweet and, if being honest, gorgeous woman for her age. The two were helping Dad and gave me the impression I was getting in the way, but soon left to let us talk.

Dad was trembling and in a daze. "I'm in big trouble," he muttered. "Nobody calls me."

Perplexed, I called Erlinda at home to call us back.

Seconds later the phone rang barely audible from across the hall in *Julia's* apartment—she was screening his calls! A chill raced up my spine and my heart pounded as Dad looked at me imploringly.

I took hold of him tight to my chest and whispered into his ear, "Dad, don't worry." He was listening.

"I'll be back tomorrow to get you out, I promise. Be strong for me until then." He nodded and soon stopped shaking.

I met Julia in the hallway. "I think he could use some sleep. Thanks for the microwave oven and everything you're doing. I'll be back on the weekend." *Did she suspect anything—I did leave him behind without a fuss?*

When I got home I made several calls. The Advocacy Centre for the Elderly said *he* had to call, not me unless I had a POA. Irene suggested calling Dave even though, "He's busy nowadays."

Dave still angry, didn't want to get involved. Dad hadn't called to tell him "what's going on" since he moved next to Julia. I explained Julia was pre-empting the calls and we had been replaced by her on the contact list.

"Ok then, what do you want to do?"

"Get him out fast. Two trips with my van."

"That's shit," he snapped, a first for that kind of language.

"Fine." I needed him. "What do you suggest?"

"If you get a truck, I'll help you." The truck sounded like a better idea indeed.

U-Hall had a small truck available for the next morning. "Don't be late or I'll give it to the next guy."

I called Dave to confirm he was still on board with the move.

The police could provide assistance at exactly 10 a.m. for one hour only, no more.

At 9 a.m. we picked up the rental, poised for anything.

At 10 a.m. the police officer met us in front of the building. His role: stand beside the truck to keep the peace.

The first thing we did was hug Dad, "You're getting out right now." He looked reassured.

We worked silently and swiftly.

"What's going on?" said Julia when she opened her door, shocked to see us speeding by ignoring her.

"You can't do this," she shouted.

An expression used by former prime minister Pierre Elliott Trudeau came to mind, "Just watch me." My skin tingled.

Still on schedule I drove us and the loaded truck to Sunnybrook Hospital Emergency to see a social worker.

Dad ended up on the psych floor of Baycrest Hospital and his things in our garage, all thanks to Dave. I could *not* have done it without him.

Relaxed now that he was safe, there was just a little cleanup left. I notified the CCAC case manager that Dad didn't need further care. She explained, we indeed were originally on the contact list and an Intake person, Dimitri (a Russian I suspected) had changed it. Also, Dad's chart described how a caregiver had overheard a woman yelling at him, "Your family doesn't care about you. They don't even call."

When I reached the building's rental office in regards to him moving out, they asked about the other person on the rental agreement, Jennifer Smith.

Among the papers in our garage, a bank statement showed Jennifer Smith opening an account with Dad.

Disaster averted!

* * * * *

Dressed and on the way out Erlinda said, "I'm going to pick up supper."

"You could have done that with me this morning when I went to the bank," I said, frustrated.

"I didn't think of it."

"If our communication was better, we wouldn't be wasting time and gas like this." A point I had been making for years.

"I've got to go. What do you want for supper?"

"It doesn't matter to me. What do you want?"

"Chicken."

"But you like Chinese," I said.

"You like chicken better," she said

"But I want what's best for you."

* * * * *

He was sitting pensive in his room at Baycrest when we arrived.

"How are you Marijan." Erlinda embraced him.

"OK, Erlinda." He looked better.

"George," he directed my attention with a wink and dart of the eyes towards a ceiling camera. "The police are watching me. They're going to take me away."

"We won't let that happen, Dad. I'll talk to the doctor."

I came back from the nurses' station. "The doctor says the police have *no* right to come in here. You're under his care."

With a bit of prompting, he was out in the hallway showing off his speed, a few laps around the ward.

At that time he needed several things looked after: urological appointments for a bladder problem and a hearing aid, a nursing home to move into, and the Public Guardian trustee required his personal and financial information. Dad had been evaluated as 'incompetent' to make his decisions and he didn't have POA.

With limited records and no authority for me to obtain his information, it was going to be very difficult. And I had to keep Irene and Dave updated.

Dave didn't want to apply for Power of Attorney in case he had to defend his decisions to the Public Guardian. I assured him it wouldn't be so bad—I was going to dig up the financial details for the trustee and look after his physical needs—all he had to do was manage the money.

Wern sold his house to move out west to live with his son Gord and daughter-in-law. A hectic time for him and in spite of his dire health he somehow kept a positive outlook. Before he left, he gave us a large Bateman painting that hung above our mantle for years, a reminder of his amiable and indomitable spirit. Today it adorns a hospital admitting area, comforting the ill who go by. Wern called often, until Gord delivered the inevitable news.

About that time, Erlinda started volunteering at the Seniors Centre as a receptionist, in part, I suspect, seeking a respite from my mumbo jumbo.

Baycrest called requiring Dad's room: find a nursing home of our choosing or have CCAC place him in whatever was available. Most were depressingly dreary, patients often forgotten, and the few good ones had long waiting lists. He didn't like any we saw.

With holidays closing in, it looked hopeless. But I kept pestering CCAC daily for any new openings. As luck would have it, one popped up on the other side of town mid-afternoon Friday.

"It won't last," said the CCAC rep. Inside two hours I inspected it and called back, "We'll take it!"

The Christmas miracle—a clean, bright private room with a bathroom and a very conscientious staff; And he loved it!

Once a week I would drop by, first for a progress report from the nurses: "He's funny and no trouble at all."

I would stroke his bald head and kissed it before shaving him.

A quiet corner in the lounge was our place to chat nestled in armchairs. His favourite sweater—the thick, grey one Erlinda knitted—kept him warm and comfortable. The first time he wore it, he had put on a fashion show for the family, strutting and grinning proudly.

I spoke about the latest news on people and politics, and consulted with him concerning a current real or imagined home repair.

He reminisced with stories of the days long gone. I was the perfect toddler playing quietly in a high chair with a stuffed rabbit.

I had started to speak a little late.

For my 4th birthday he took me to Zagreb to see the circus. On the return, we were at the train station waiting when I had to use the bathroom.

I remembered the incident.

The train was coming and I worried we would miss it because of me.

"Heaven help me," I said, "I have to pee." He broke out into a hearty laugh back then in '56 and now.

I learned back then that if I made him laugh, he wouldn't get angry.

"I'll tell the conductor to hold the train for us," he had said.

Before I left him in his bedroom, he always asked that Dave and I make peace with Irene, something I couldn't promise for either of us.

On a final attempt to spell out details of Dad's financial and living will, I invited him and Dave to our place for a discussion before going to the lawyer.

I became concerned when the solicitor insisted on speaking privately with Dad. He determined that Dad was not of sound mind to form the will. On the positive side though, Dave had the POA

For some reason, Dad's bank statements were still coming to my address. The pensions were building the savings account for Irene's future. *Wonderful.*

Several years earlier he and I had gone to the very classy Mount Pleasant Cemetery, where Mom was buried, to take care of his funeral and cemetery arrangements. He chose to pay everything up front and left me to manage it.

Now, a cheque arrived for accrued interest on his advance payment which I forwarded to Dave.

In the wake of Dad's diminishing abilities I, unconsciously, doubled my efforts to squeeze everything out of life. At the end of a long, highly-competitive season of Ontario races, I joined a group to run an *unsanctioned* Badwater, all 135 miles, crewed solely by Erlinda and a female friend.

On our travels we rarely checked email. Fortuitously, we did on this one occasion. The manager of the Canadian National 24-Hour Team needed one more male for the World Championships—in three days! We had just finished crewing a friend in the *official* Badwater race. Given the urgency of the matter, a deadline of one hour remained for a response.

"I didn't know I was on the list," I said over the phone. One runner had turned ill and I was, based on previous race results, top of the sub list.

"Are you interested?" he asked, but didn't need to as far as I was concerned.

"Definitely."

"Any injuries?" he wanted to know. Injuries, always an issue because of the tremendous stress and strain ultrarunning places on the human body. What could I say after the grueling Ontario races and Badwater a week ago?

"Nothing to complain about," sidestepping the question. This was for Canada, not the egotism that motivated me so far. Time to rise to the occasion.

Our scheduled plans had to be delayed.

We flew to Drummondville, Quebec in time to march behind the Canadian flag in the Parade of Nations. Patriotism, a powerful motivator, swept over us.

Except for a quick bathroom break and clothes change, Erlinda and I did not stop the entire race.

Of the six-man team, I was the second best Canadian male with 195 km (121 miles) well ahead of the runner representing Croatia. Not bad for a day's work.

Our car was still in storage back in Las Vegas, so we took the next flight, foregoing any celebration or rest.

* * * * *

"Don't let your animal-loving neighbour see you with that trap," said the exterminator I called for a quote, "he probably thinks it's going to stress out the poor thing."

"Well the poor thing is stressing *me* out." I wasn't kidding. Winter was not that far away and the squirrel, I prefer to think rat, was scratching out a home in *my* attic directly above our bed. It was probably fornicating every night which is more than I could say about myself in those dizzy days.

"You might consider releasing it at your neighbour's house in the middle of the night," said the expert. "Just remember, they are excellent at finding their way back."

That neighbour was Jerry who walked his dog twice a day as far as *my* front lawn to watch it relieve itself. *My God, the park is only two doors down! Why doesn't he hold its delicate derriere shut tight until they get there?* Then Jerry turns around, nose turned up, and goes home satisfied just like his precious little treasure. Leaving me with enough crap by the end of summer to fertilize an entire farm.

"Don't you worry, I can handle this," I said to the pro as if he would worry about me. I wasn't willing to part with $300 for a 5-minute job.

After three hours of—climbing up through the closet, crawling nervously along the beams, itching from the insulation and sealing the hole before the rat returned—I still wasn't going to admit I should have left it to the *expert*.

The funny thing about old age: there's scarcely anything funny about it. Perhaps the writing was on the wall, but I'm short-sighted. Things turned serious when Dad couldn't urinate and the visiting GP had to install a catheter. Then his kidneys stopped filtering; the resultant toxicity created mental confusion and fatigue. An ambulance was supposed to take him to the specialist, but the evening before they cancelled. I explained the situation to Dave over the phone.

"Let him go, George," he said to end the call. I placed the receiver down on the cradle and stared ahead.

"I can't," I whispered to the air.

With staff's permission, I loaded him gingerly into the car; and drove to the hospital, talking to him the whole time.

The corridor was hot and chaotic, so I nabbed a stretcher for him to lie on.

After an endless wait the doctor showed up. He pulled back the cover. A truly sad and disturbing sight: the tip of the penis was ripped and bloody. In Dad's confused state, the nurse had told me, he yanked out the catheter.

"I can't work with this mess," yelled the doctor furiously at me, since I was the only person there. "Get him out of here!" He stomped off not hiding his exasperation, leaving the room dead still, dead quiet and Dad exposed.

With utmost caution I dressed him, sat him in a scrounged chair and wheeled him to the entrance. I had to get the car but no one was around.

"Just stay here. I'll be really quick." I ran like he was on fire.

After all that, not a thing had been accomplished. I felt completely helpless. Defeated.

In a day or two (my notes are unclear) an ambulance *did* pick him up, his situation having deteriorated even more.

Erlinda and I arrived at the ICU, a crammed room of whirling machines and flickering monitors and four beds separated by white curtains. An oxygen mask, unable to hide the ghostly whiteness of his face, had slipped and contorted his nose. I adjusted the mask. His breath was slow and shallow and his eyes glassy, half shut.

Only now, I truly noticed that somewhere along the way he had aged . . . no longer indestructible.

"The doctor said you can get out in a couple days," I said for his sake and mine. "Everyone's been asking about you."

We stayed until the eyelids closed completely. Pressure built up in my eyes, but nothing came. During our drive home, "In the Living Years" by Mike and the Mechanics played in my mind. Still no tears.

The next morning they called to say he had passed away.

The very first to arrive for the funeral was Irene, followed shortly by Dave and his partner. Not far behind were Beth, her partner and the kids. When Indira and Angela showed up, we kept it civil, thankfully. Paying their respects came staunch Croatians, true Canadians, white, brown, black, rich, poor. No matter what his faults, Dad saw the character of the person first.

As the casket lowered into the ground, I spoke to him one last time. "How will I ever do anything without you?"

You always could. You just needed a little encouragement.

The key turned too easily in the cylinder, I noticed as my stomach growled from hunger. *Two hours to supper.* Behind me, dark ominous clouds covered the sky, and in the distance the sound of rolling thunder. The air felt hot, humid and heavy.

"You didn't lock the door," I shouted from the front door.

"Oh," came from the kitchen.

"You can't let that happen," I insisted, entering the kitchen. "Somebody could just walk in and you wouldn't know it.

"My hands were full."

"What's the point of a security system if you leave doors open?" Frustration and anger started to well up from the chest to my head.

"You're always watching me, like a hawk." Now *she* was upset.

"It's my job as your husband to protect you," stating only the blatantly obvious.

"Yes but I'm walking around on eggshells afraid of making a mistake." She sounded like she was about to cry. It was time to pull back even if I was right.

Just before supper, I was rummaging for something in the basement's dark crawl space next to the electric panel. *How am I suppose to find things when she puts them away without rhyme or reason?* The storage area was a huge mess; and I was shouting to let her know it, without letting up.

Deep silence upstairs. Then she came down, a very grave look on her face. And *still* the severity of the situation did not register through my anger.

"I'm leaving you, George," she said, scarcely discernable.

"What?"

"I can't take it anymore.

CHAPTER 14

PATH TO PEACE

He who has a why to live can bear almost anything.
FRIEDRICH NIETZCHE

2008

"Where you going to stay?" *After all* **this** *is your home.* My breath sticks in the throat.

"I'll find a place." She grabs a suitcase and goes upstairs.

I'm watching her disappear and wondering if I'm having a nightmare. *No, it's real. Much more than a little warning after a spat. But how can this be happening to* **us**? *We have shared so much, come so far . . . and yet I was blind to the emotional pain I was causing. The horrible truth, now—I'm losing her forever.*

Suddenly, the windows are shaken by a tremendous crash of thunder.

Jerked out of my thoughts, I realize that my legs can't support me from the heavy void, so I rush upstairs and drop to the living room floor with a thud. I'm gasping for air.

A bolt of lightning illuminates the room and then the sky closes its eyes and rain pours like never before.

"I'm so, so sorry" I cry out and weep uncontrollably.

How long? I don't know.

A gentle hand touches my head, slides down my neck and rests on my shoulder. The healing power of touch. Erlinda kneels to my side and wraps her loving arms around me.

"Oh my poor, baby." In her soft voice there is kindness. Forgiveness.

In the immediate aftermath we decided to downsize. Too soon she would turn 70. Enough of weeding the lawns on her knees and cleaning a four-bedroom house. Enough of constant upkeep, sometimes at inopportune moments and in precarious positions. Clogged eaves needed to be cleared every late fall when winds were fierce. She held the ladder while I climbed two stories high to scoop cold, soggy leaves—six feet at a time—the full circumference of the house.

A 5-story condominium complex yet to be built answered our prayers. Occupancy two years away. In the interim, we parked our things in a tiny shoebox of a condo: to take a cruise or road trip or trek the Camino. Travel untethered.

To get through the worst of winter, we parked ourselves in a mobile home in Phoenix, Arizona. The snowbird lifestyle. Just by chance about a month into the vacation, a nurse on the premises took Erlinda's blood pressure. A dangerously high reading! The hospital ER staff brought it down to normal, but our health insurance company pushed for us to go home for further testing.

Terrified, I drove us two days solid (except for sleep) across the country. Extremely careful and vigilant for any change in her condition, I checked the BP hourly. All the way, a huge snow storm chased our tails.

The BP proved to be nothing serious—manageable by a change in diet and low-level medication.

So much for the snowbird lifestyle.

Since I had been registered for a race back in Phoenix, Erlinda urged me to go, reassuring me she would be "just fine" for a few days. I flew in on time but my luggage went missing.

At 3 a.m. the motel front desk rang, informing me my luggage had just arrived in the lobby. I scrambled to prepare food to last the full 24 hours of the race.

Having competed recently in the Commonwealth Championships, my fitness was still good and I finished 4th in a relatively easy field. More importantly, it became abundantly clear, should I ever forget, my past success was based not on *I* but rather on *We*.

I parked the car around the corner a block from the site of the new condo. Right from the beginning when it was a giant excavated area, we had been following (from behind a fence) the construction process. Now, presumably, most of the interior was completed and yet for 'safety reasons' unit owners were not permitted on site. Nevertheless, I wanted to check it out—we had a lot of money invested there.

To look like one of the construction crew, I bought at the Thrift store: a helmet (the broken inside strap had to be taped to keep it from sliding off) and steel toed boots (needed tight lacing and thick socks to hide the fact they were two sizes too big).

The first problem, find where to enter the building. My heart raced as I had no idea what to expect. *Act like you belong here.* The elevator door slid open. Its operator looked at me. And smiled.

"Where to boss?" he asked.

I can't believe it's working. Looking serious, I said with authority, my voice an octave lower than usual, "Third."

"You got it," he said.

Better not to say anything more. When I get out, turn right like I know what I'm doing.

The hallway unfinished and dusty; the doors wide open and unnumbered. I tried two units before recognizing our floor plan. *Our future resides here.*

Close inspection showed one wall did not meet our alteration request for which I eventually sought compensation. The sales rep would whisper, "Fine, just don't tell any other purchasers about the reimbursement."

On the way out the building, I smiled, "Thanks buddy." No point being a complete jerk.

What a relief to get out of the 'work' clothes.

Steep and narrow switchbacks. Approaching Ooh Aah Point.

Cruising. Santorini, Greece.

Kayaking and snorkeling. Moorea, south Pacific.

Hiking the Abel Tasman Trail, New Zealand.

Time for R and R after the travelling.

That year the World Championships were held in France and due to an early injury, I did poorly. Spain being in the vicinity, we set out on the 7th Camino. Initially we considered taking a few recovery days but I managed with hiking poles propping me up.

In July, we moved to start a new life in the two-bedroom, walking-distance-to-everything condo—the place we hoped to call home right to our final days.

A highly touted race caught my interest. I trained with friends primarily on the soft surface of the Bruce Trail as an injury prevention measure. And yet, in a moment of inattentiveness, I tripped and my knee landed on a rock. For ten days I could hardly walk.

Should we proceed with the race? Yes, provided I can recover enough to walk it. After that I am definitely hanging up the running shoes. Injuries have caused enough suffering. Besides, I wanted to spend quality time with Erlinda, instead of always training—and I couldn't do it out of a wheel chair—as a doctor had once warned. So I switched to running in a pool for safer training.

I was keenly aware of behaving myself—giving Erlinda room to breathe and choose without unsolicited advice. Not easy when every instinct in me screams to protect her. What mattered: we were quite happy. We entertained family (except busy Dave), friends and neighbours. Being content, we didn't want any kind of drama.

Funny how things can change.

Ultrarunning published my submission (similar to the following) with the editor adding to my original title, "and a Love Story."

A Swan Song and a Love Story

After 30 years of competing, I (we) retired in May. My wife, Erlinda, applied on my behalf (unbeknownst to me) for one last hurrah. "You can walk and be free of any worry. We'll have fun!" she said. I liked fun.

A target of 300 km and middle of the pack seemed reasonable to me. The race objective was to cover as much distance as possible in the three given days, starting December 29. Hence the title, Across the Years.

The course (in Phoenix) looped on a one-mile desert path around a large private estate.

In hearing range to our tent, conversed two running greats: John Geesler, the U.S. 2 Day record holder and member of the powerful 24-Hour National Team; Jeff (Ironman) Hagen, famous for years of consistently placing in the top five. In awe, Erlinda and I introduced ourselves. I expressed my sincere admiration for Jeff's published racing strategies, strategies I adopted. Feeling awkward about autographs—I asked for a photo with them.

Back home, Beth followed the race online and repeatedly sent positive e-mails, promptly printed by officials and hand delivered.

The first day was fairly cold and rainy for which I was not prepared clothes wise. *It's desert country.* To stay comfortable, I changed clothes every couple of hours; this meant Erlinda kept exceptionally busy drying them any way she could. Our tent neighbour shouted, "You got the best crew ever." "I agree!" I replied.

With the clay trail turning muddy and weighing down the squishing shoes, runners became wary of slipping.

That night when the rain was at its heaviest, I slept two hours under layers of blankets. Upon my return, I chose to run 4 minutes every hour, just to stay warm.

The second night the temperature dropped to below freezing. After a half hour nap, I increased the running to 8 minutes per hour.

By the third day everyone was badly beaten down by the adverse weather. I just happened to be sitting on a bench next to John.

Misery likes company. Our guards were down from weariness, so we had a uniquely personal chat. Feeling privileged that he would share a vulnerable side, I admired him even more. Beneath all his success, the surface, dwelled much more than a running machine.

Luckily the skies cleared, it warmed up and our spirits lifted. However a different kind of drama was about to play out.

Eight hours into the race, we had been 25th, as expected, and a huge 50 km behind John, the leader. At this point, quite unintentionally, we started climbing up in the standings, partly because I was one of the fastest ultra walkers in Canada. When John was struck by a mysterious condition, he switched to easy walking; and a door opened for the rest.

Two days into the race, I respectfully passed John and Jeff into 3rd place, 19 km behind the leaders.

Erlinda had been working tirelessly preparing food and drinks, drying clothes and shoes, and whatnot on limited sleep. As a surprise to her, I decided to go for the gold. Ahead of us were two interesting runners: Ed (charismatic and sociable 48-year-old American) and Andreas (33-year-old Swede with striking looks and an Olympian physique, sure to catch any woman's eyes). Then there was me (little, skinny wannabe at 58—well past prime).

The likelihood of attaining this ambitious goal was based on several factors. Both were experiencing problems whereas I, oddly enough, felt fresh. Secondly, I've always been a strong finisher. And lastly, when Erlinda helped a weary runner, he revealed a secret he overheard: Ed and Andreas had formed a pact to finish together. I concluded, if I passed one perhaps the other might stay back.

Shortly before midnight I cranked out a few quick miles to narrow the gap to within striking distance. Race organizers encouraged everyone to stop and celebrate the New Year. While Jeff, myself and our wives shared a bottle of wine, I was itching to get back to *work*.

Ed and Andreas were walking casually, confident first place was secure when I joined them to state my intention. Obvious puzzlement took hold.

"You got to get past us," said Ed.

To avoid a painful battle I proposed we split first place in un-heard-of three ways.

"Why should we? We have a big lead," said Andreas.

I tried to be convincing with my reasoning and finally suggested they at least think about it. As a show of strength, I stated unequiv-ocally the offer was good only for the next little while. It sure seemed like an idea at the time, I won't use the word *good*. Emo-tions and sleep deprivation overpowered rational thinking.

Their resentment was palpable.

Anyway, if John came back to life, none of us stood a chance.

While I got a drink, they checked the leader board. Eight km separated us. They must have felt a need for urgency because they immediately switched to jogging. Hustling to catch up, I moved beside them. Andreas's coach threw him a bottle he grabbed out of the air (on the run!) and took a big swig. Wow, is this guy ever cool! Then like three restless thoroughbreds at the gates of the Ken-tucky Derby, we bolted out.

Their reply was unmistakable. By any standard the acceleration was ridiculous and yet with foolish bravado I said, "This is fun." Strangely enough, I meant it.

"What's going on?" called out a surprised Erlinda from our tent.

"A race for first place," I shouted with gusto. This was equally her race and she deserved to come along for the ride.

They kicked up to another gear, determined to punish me, to snuff me out like wind to a candle flame. Where did I get the nerve to infringe on their territory, to want more? Me, a nobody.

As we hurtled by—spectators stopped to stare with raised eye-brows, murmur under breath, and study the leader board. Flashing cameras were capturing the showdown.

I felt young again! Endorphins rushed through every vein in my powerful body. *But for how long will this surge last?*

This much I knew: I was willing to endure a lot of pain for Erlinda as she had for me.

Shoulder to shoulder, kicking leg to kicking leg, pumping arm to pumping arm we battled for 8 km at their pace—until suddenly and without warning, Andreas dropped to the ground.

"Oh, my leg!" he cried out. "Go with him." But true to his word, Ed stayed with his friend.

With kilometers to catch up, I pressed on never looking back. I didn't summon strength. It flowed naturally. Through the darkest hours of the night while apparently everyone slept, I ran, under the watchful eye of the race director. Ran to the steady beat of my heart.

At about 6 a.m., convinced I had an insurmountable lead, I stopped. I could hear Erlinda encouraging me to keep moving. When I turned around to face her, she wasn't there. I had lost my mind . . .

And so in a state of delirium I wandered alone, but for fear, not knowing where I was or what I was doing.

Most fortunately, the glorious sun rose and my head cleared. Now with revived energy I pursued a new goal: 400 km.

We ended up 16 km ahead of the two friends.

At the awards ceremony, I shook Andreas's hand as a gesture of no hard feelings. He was happy to set a Swedish record and Ed received sponsorship from a shoe manufacturer. And I, the oldest (in a large field) to win the race.

That night in the serenity of our hotel room, Erlinda and I lay completely spent. We talked about the unscripted turn of events. As our minds drifted into oblivion she whispered, "Promise me you'll consider this race next year."

A smile flickered across my face and faded.

We did return and if spectators or runners expected another miracle, it was not to be. I got injured and based on medical advice left early.

Still, my competition days weren't quite over.

* * * * *

The phone conversation started pleasantly enough. Full of promise. I told Irene about a cute dog, Daisy, I was walking late every night for an older neighbour. What excited Irene and me was the dream trip to the Grand Canyon. Her flight and insurance would cost her $400, I summarized, the RV and food being our responsibility.

With that, her mood shifted abruptly and drastically.

"You should know I can't afford that." The words stabbed. "I assumed you were paying. *You* invited me."

"I thought you said—" I began in an effort to calm the situation before it got out of hand, but she was unstoppable.

"Let me tell you something. You think you're a nice guy? Mom, Dad and one of your friends didn't think so." Struck the jugular.

"I can't handle this," I said

"That's because you're f***** up." The knife continued to slice. "Be a man. All these years, I'm suffering cause of you."

For once *I* lay the phone down first, but gently. I couldn't let the blood splatter all over onto everything. Especially Erlinda. After all my progress, I wouldn't allow it.

Two months later a package arrived, two books and a letter:

Dear George,

I regret the way I expressed my feelings and am truly sorry that my words caused you such pain. That was not my intent. I know you meant well.

I want you to know that I love you...

For quite a while she had been under tremendous financial strain to pay rent, food and so forth. But her situation was turning around: she found an affordable bachelor apartment; a community course was teaching her how to manage problems; a switch in medication was helping enormously.

The two books were gifts she hoped we would enjoy.

All great news, but how long will good health last.

I called and we spoke at length. This time it was different.

Curious about the past, and yet not wishing to open wounds, I asked very carefully about her dark, secret past.

After years of misdiagnosis, she was found to have clinical depression. She thinks it started at age eight.

"How did the relationship with Dad go so wrong?"

When she entered the teens, he used to send her to get his Croatian newspaper where the owner would ogle her every time. "Dad should have known what kind of person he was." On one occasion Dad wanted her to take a cheque downtown, she assumed to settle a gambling debt. For the first time she outright refused. Then, when he suggested she pick up extra money serving sandwiches and drinks at his club, she lost any trust in him.

All of that she wanted to forget.

I asked no more. Pavelic (the monster who attacked her way back in high school) never entered the conversation.

She accepts her lot in life and is focussing on a positive future and hopes to enjoy an easy close relationship with us. On her fridge is a quote she aspires to live by:

Forgive, not so much as people need forgiveness,
but you need peace.

What courage and strength she showed through the years dealing with her illness! I couldn't have done it.

* * * * *

The College of Nursing, class of '63 celebrated their Golden Jubilee in Miami, Florida. Classmates came from across Canada and U.S., their bond unwavering over all the years. Each and every one of them was an outstanding role model to their families and communities—grounded by faith in God and the class motto "Service Is Our Watchword."

Even though many were grandmothers, they celebrated and danced in elegant evening gowns into the wee hours of the night. Bright and early the next morning, like all resilient people, they went shopping, of course.

Coincidentally, Sammy and Richie were graduating back in Canada, so we didn't stay too long.

The entire family was proud of what decent and mature adults they had become, the wish of every parent. We couldn't ask for more. Personally, it was a special bonus to see Dave and Beth in the presence of their partners, displaying exemplary behaviour to the kids.

Over the next several years, we continued to compete, staying true to the core of our nature. I broke eight Canadian Age records, most with great struggle and uncertainty right up to the last few minutes.

Irene the new crew member for one race.

End of race: tired and happy!

Newspaper articles acknowledged our accomplishments, Association of Canadian Ultrarunners presented me with plaques and the town gave me a Civic Appreciation Award.

And yet, the *most* unexpected was to unfold in front of my very own eyes and ears.

Three Days at the Fair Ultramarathon
Augusta, New Jersey

"I'd like to do a race," said Erlinda, just like that.

"What?" I said trying to grasp this wild notion. "You?"

"Yes. A three day."

"You can't be serious. It's—"

"I want to try, with your help."

"You know as well as I do, this is not like walking the Camino. Think about your blood pressure and parents' medical histories."

"Are you OK with crewing?" She was changing the subject.

"Huh, what? Now I know you're kidding." I grunted. "I mean, how hard can it be?"

She reminded me what CREW stood for: Cranky Runner Exhausted Wife. Ha-ha, but I could barely hear her over the male voice from one side of my head.

Psst, buddy, that means you're not running. She's the one having all the fun. For a moment I thought about it. I really did.

A female voice interrupted from the other side, *You should be ashamed of yourself, after all she's done for you.*

OK, OK. I'm sorry.

To reach the coveted 100 miles, we needed a comprehensive plan designed for her age and experience. Each mile would consist of half walking and half running. The day would be divided into four-hour segments. Each segment allowed 30 minutes for stretch, massage and rest, in that order. Between 1 a.m. and 5 a.m. was sleep time. With the inclusion of bathroom breaks, change of clothes and injury treatment—the daily total on the course should be 17 hours. Sounded easy on paper, but for her this was uncharted territory.

"This is all too much," she said. "I just want to have fun."

Fun? What a strange proposition. "Let's focus on putting up big numbers, Ok?"

"Not OK. Whose race is this anyway?" she said.

I was thinking *mine* but wisely said, "Ours." Compromise always works in our household.

She can have fun and I'll take care of the logistics.

It's a long day's drive to the beautiful fairgrounds in New Jersey, home of the Three Days at the Fair race. After my annoying analysis where to plant the tent and table, we established our site along the one-mile loop.

In keeping with the bosses' wishes, we chatted and joked with the neighbours. You know something, it *was* fun and very worth while psychologically.

For the start, she stood inconspicuously at the back of the pack, arms folded to stay warm, a novice at the wonderful age of 74.

Shortly after they took off, a sobering fact hit me: I couldn't match her multitasking ability. The big challenge was recalling where I had placed something while fussing over her various needs.

The weatherman called for heavy rain, so as an extra precaution I made a quick trip to town for tarp, leaving us (due to credit card problems) with only an Andrew Jackson ($20) bill to get home.

In the meanwhile, she got soaked by the torrential rain, but all our tent's contents remained bone dry.

At one point, purely out of habit, she tried to clean up the inside of the tent.

"Leave that to me. Your job is to move those pretty legs around the course. Go, go, go!" A swat on the butt sent her on the way.

There was no flash, no great speed, just the steady Erlinda I knew. Except, it was one four-hour segment after another—way beyond anything ever before.

In the afternoon heat, the tight T-shirt clung to her breasts, breasts that belonged on Venus de Milo, truly an anomaly for a woman her age. I set aside the lustful urges to settle down by focussing on the task at hand. We were coalescing into a well-functioning team, even though the new roles were often unfamiliar.

Our own food that I prepared was the ideal source of energy, even still, she sneaked an occasional pizza slice or chicken nugget from the race counter. *No point disturbing the humming harmony. Besides, it's called comfort food and she deserves it.*

On the last night with many others asleep, I walked beside her a full mile under the vast, star-filled sky. We chatted suspended in time and space. Ineffable serenity swept through my body and soul. This . . . exquisite ecstasy, I hoped, never to be forgot.

No degree, no career, no empire could ever rival the joy.

I was finally complete, at peace. All my life, I had subliminally assumed it would be about me. But that night I learned my *true* happiness lay in giving myself to her and her desires.

I am because she is.

At 100 miles—her body leaning left, due to one side dominance and pure exhaustion—she rang the milestone bell, smiled and exchanged a few words with the timekeeper.

And still, after all the suffering, she refused to stop. On she continued to endure more neck pain and more leg pain.

When time ran out, she had accumulated 132 miles, setting or breaking eight Canadian Age records.

By the way, we returned home on gas fumes and 50 cents in our pockets.

The following year, Erlinda established eight more Canadian records in the *next* age category, on the simple fact no woman her age had attempted such an endeavour. A pioneer on the senior running frontier. Sometimes, the best years of a life don't have to be before 65.

* * * * *

Without a doubt Doctor Christie was a godsend: approachable, knowledgeable and caring. What more is there to ask for? At the annual checkup, I went directly to my main concern—memory.
I had brought a written list of specific examples of *delayed* recall:

1) Familiar names (like Beth), faces, and words.
2) Where the *r* belonged in *George*.
3) Confused about my exact familial relationship with Dave and the kids.

Also, in my mind's eye I couldn't see anything. The *only* truly disturbing thing about it all—I could not visualize Erlinda's face any more. There was no point in hiding my belief that exposure to sources of electricity or radiation contributed to episodes of memory slowness or loss.

An MRI showed signs of mild cognitive impairment (MCI), a precursor to Alzheimer's. Further investigation was necessary.

For how much longer can I manage our finances? Sooner or later that responsibility will be hers. My errors were costing us—a missed flight (wrong date), and on a trip I left the credit card at home. Twice I forgot to pay the credit card bill.

To bring Erlinda up to speed, I spent an hour explaining just the financial *basics*, and already it overwhelmed her.

"I can't do it. It's too complicated," she said, ending that idea.

I've since simplified the procedures and written explicit instructions for myself; and still it's a painstakingly slow process.

* * * * *

Self-Transcendence 10 Day Race .
Queens, New York City
April 19-29, 2015

For once I didn't mind being on a race's wait list—I had chest pain.

"Don't do any training until we find out what's going on," insisted Dr. Christie. It proved to be three compressed vertebrae (a problem I had been ignoring) and a chronic stomach infection (the antibiotics could wait). For now, back exercises and antacid tablets would get me through. Besides, he felt running was good for me mentally.

An exciting but simple notion popped into my head. Break the 10 Day Canadian Age record, *solely* by walking. The rational behind it? You avoid injuries and therefore spend more time on the course. The difficulty: trusting an unproven strategy, although success at Across the Years was promising; accepting being last for a protracted period; and resisting the natural urge to run with the herd. In one word—patience.

The weather channel warned about the dangerous roads on the morning we were to head out, as I recall. An ice storm during the night had put traffic to a halt. *Do we go? Which route considering our all-season tires?*

Once we got past Buffalo, we eased back in our seats until New York City. My bladder was sending alarming messages but . . . enough about that. The rain had flooded a part of the rutted road in Corona Park, so while Erlinda drove on the narrow shoulder I sought a bush. Finally, "tent village" as many called it.

Everything seemed in place the next morning as I grabbed a few items before going to the Start where Erlinda and everyone waited. The winds had picked up, buffeting our tent. *Will she hold?* Already, one peg dangled in the breeze. *Darn it!* By the time I went around securing all the pegs, my left hand was bleeding from the stray hammer blows. *Calm down George.*

Rain, wind and coolish nights severely tested everyone.

On day five, we were mid-pack and I was starting to press to keep up with a tall Serbian, in a small field of pre-approved athletes from around the globe.

"Let him go," said Erlinda. By easing up and adhering to the walking strategy, I eventually passed him for good.

Around 1 a.m. of the tenth and last night (while Erlinda slept) I —unfocused and incoherent—had wandered off the course (the same course I had circled five hundred times) heading to the shores of a nearby lake.

Where am I?

Luckily, I heard two runners talking, and retraced my steps.

Something had to change, so I looked for the person ahead of me on the leader board, Sergey. The problem was I couldn't find him anywhere.

At one point after crossing the counting line, I heard his name announced.

He was steps behind me all the time, watching me. A cat and mouse game. Guess who was the mouse?

He gave me a thumbs up and I saluted him, smiles stretching on our faces in respect to each other's tactic.

Once I matched the Canadian record, I took a 20-minute nap, the only one of the night. Feeling refreshed and restless, I switched to running the last five hours.

During these races there's so much time to think, all kinds of thoughts. Whipping around the course, I remembered running as a very young boy trying to keep up with Dad's long powerful strides. He had watched me once in the Pittsburgh Marathon. To show that I was worthy of his praise I had over trained and did poorly. If he could only see me now.

I never did pass Sergey, but in our duel we moved up the board considerably.

My final tally: 6th and a *course* age record of 944 km.

In February, Erlinda attended a class reunion (a rare one I missed) in the Philippines while I stayed home hungry and of course lonely. We spoke often. She assured me classmate, Hope, was taking great care of her. Among the fellowship and all the activities, she squeezed in daily workouts.

Sri Chinmoy 6 Day Race
Queens, New York City

Many non-runners can't grasp how physical strain and stress can produce psychological well being, not only after the race, but also throughout the entire ordeal. Even prerace, the body can quiver with excited anticipation. So, admittedly, it is an addiction.

Heartened by the enjoyment of our last race in New York, Erlinda signed up for the 6 Day. A small strong international field lined up, their average age about half hers. She was the oldest.

As a recent convert to the fun principle, *I* now emphasized, "Have fun and let the 'numbers' come naturally." She mixed walking and running. Even though she was quite steady, the middle days were a particular struggle as they were for everyone.

One night, like always, I gave her a massage while she slept on the cot, legs elevated on a suitcase and body covered with several blankets. During the typical examination of the feet, I found a blister. Careful to disinfect it first, I cut it open with sharp scissors (no reaction from her), squeezed fluid out, cleaned with burning alcohol, applied antibiotic cream and sealed with a bandage. Before going to sleep at the back of the car, I kissed her forehead and whispered, "*Mahal kita*, I love you."

In the morning, she was no wiser as to what had happened.

The final result: 8th out of 14, with the equivalent of ten marathons and a World Age Best performance.

"How do you feel?" a reporter asked her immediately after.

"It's nice to be enjoying life and good health."

We laid low for a couple weeks to give the body a chance to recuperate, before flying to Spain for another Camino.

Four days after returning to Canada, still jet lagged, we drove to Ottawa's Terry Fox Track for a race. Let it be known, I questioned the wisdom of competing so soon.

For the better part of 24 hours—by sheer force of will and confidence and metronome steadiness—she covered 106 km, generously smiling the entire time. *Incredible!* There was no need for me to say, "Have fun." With that she established two more World Age Best performances.

At the awards ceremony competitors and their crews voted her, "The Most Inspiring Runner."

Among the cheering audience, I took a picture of her at the podium, holding a giant trophy—her face beaming like the sun.

Pure bliss.

Credit: Susie Kockerscheidt, yorkregion.com

* * * * *

Many a time over the years, I dreamt Mom and Dad were still alive, only to wake up wistfully to the cold, naked truth.

One night Erlinda heard me saying, "I'm in a rush. Got to go."

It was part of a dream. I was in someone's mansion painting a room bright white. During cleanup I spilled a pail of water. *Shoot*! To soak up the mess, I used a discarded piece of carpet and hid it in a plastic bag. In an adjoining room a party was in progress, so I worried someone might have seen me. As I left down the stairs, the owner asked what was in the bag. I opened it wide and showed: nothing of consequence.

"No, no, no. We trust you," said the owner. "You're hard working and do an exceptional job."

From nearby, the spirit of Dad appeared visible only to me. His gaze, steady and observant.

"I'm like my father," I said. "And I'm proud of it."

A bittersweet smile formed on his face; a single tear rolled down the cheek and hung on the chin.

Our eyes locked in a fleeting moment of understanding.

Not able to linger any longer I said to the owner, "I'm in a rush. Got to go."

It's a curious thing that happened one afternoon.

In the process of transferring our home movies to DVD format, I noticed an unopened CD bought long ago in Tokyo, a reminder of the Japanese culture and people.

The tracks ranged from upbeat to mournful. One haunting but comforting melody gave me reason to pause and listen. The woman sang in Japanese, and yet, some words were eerily similar to Croatian; what's more unbelievable—she sounded like Mom.

"Shine my dear…believe in salvation…tell people…let's sing."

Lest you conclude I'm certifiable, I immediately acknowledge this to be an act of my imagination, hoping to reconnect with her on some level, and nothing more.

And so, in the absence of flying at the speed of light to reverse time (like Superman), I finally accepted my reality: no wishful thinking would bring her back. She was safe in heaven and I inhabited this world as I should be. Where for so long persisted pain of loss, now lay solace.

In autumn on the anniversary of my parents' passing, I've walked the Toronto Marathon unregistered, a 'bandit' at the very back of all the paid participants. Then, as I have every year with unwavering loyalty, my pilgrimage takes me to Mount Pleasant Cemetery. With the sun flickering first through the leaves of the old oak and then the Norway maple, I clean up the covered gravestones using a bag of tools provided by Erlinda.

* * * * *

In a tiny room at the Baycrest Memory Clinic, a nurse asked me a few preliminary questions to which I responded without hesitation. Then the main event—an extensive five-hour test by the neuropsychologist.

On the way out I asked the receptionist for the nurse's name.

"That's Jane. You were introduced last time."

I had no recollection of the nurse's face. None.

A few weeks later, I met the psychologist for the results of the big test and the brain SPECT scan.

Apparently, I'm "highly intelligent, with an extensive knowledge of the English vocabulary and a strong ability to appreciate patterns, concepts and relationships." I could have told them that, and saved all the trouble. Also, I'm "thorough and consider all alternatives." They forgot to mention charismatic and really good looking, but I was willing to let that slide.

Now to my concern. A minor problem with thinking speed and memory, compared to people my age. The main finding dealt with attention: "focus can vary and can become distracted if there's too much happening at one time." I work best if I focus on one task at a time.

His conclusion: I'm experiencing anxiety.

"Doesn't the low blood flow in one area, as shown by the MRI and SPECT, suggest mild cognitive impairment," I asked.

"Yes, but the clinical test disputes that."

A follow up test was scheduled in two years. For now, he recommended cognitive behaviour therapy (CBT).

On the topics of electromagnetic hypersensitivity (EH)—the bane of my existence—and my inability to visualise, he declined to comment as it was outside his area of expertise.

Based on limited research on the internet here's what I found out.

Some people make the claim to have EH affecting memory, concentration, mood, anxiety, depression and sleep. Supposedly, they are sensitive to electricity and radiation emitting devices such as electric wires, cellphones and Wi-Fi devices.

A large study in the U.S. found: kids who spend two hours a day on electronics have significantly lower memory and attention span.

Studies show social media screen time is a probable contributor to increasing depression and suicide among young people, as reported by CBS evening news.

Although health organizations accept EH as a syndrome, the cause is unknown.

According to World Health Organization, the connection between symptoms and EH—is unclear.

There was nothing reliable on the inability to visualise.

With an electricity and radiation meter used by professionals, I found unsafe readings in our condo. To mitigate the effects, I make a concerted effort to control exposure time and distance to specific devices. Very beneficial.

Email from Beth:

Hi there beloveds,

Thanks for the email, although this was the first we heard of George undergoing tests and wish him the very best. Let's go with the mild anxiety option!... I remember reading several very interesting and promising articles on the connection between coconut oil and the brain (and Alzheimer's in particular) and how it has helped reverse symptoms. Go with organic, not refined... Ryan and I have often said we wanted George to write a book of memoirs—you both have experienced a great deal in your lives and he has such a great way of writing with humour!...

We love you both and will try to get in touch by phone over the Christmas holidays!!!

Lots of love, Beth

The Cognitive Behavioural Therapy course was helpful. Also, daily meditation, mindfulness and physical activity has reduced the anxiety without a need for medication. As much as possible, I handle one thing at a time and avoid excessive stress. I try to tone down my habit of discussing things ad nauseam, the source of considerable friction. If I sulk, which is rare, it's only for a few minutes and I let Erlinda know what I'm feeling. One look at her beautiful face and smile, and my spirits lift skyward.

And now, to the question raised at the very beginning of the book: Am I deluded? Deranged? *You*, the reader, be the judge.

I have made every effort to present *all* the facts honestly and fairly. By now you know everything—including idiosyncrasies and affliction—about me.

If there are no further questions, I rest my case at the foot of your wisdom.

Usually, the day is planned out on paper the night before. It starts with meditation, so when she wakes up, I'm ready to join her in exercises and stretches, something I would overlook if not for her.

By 6 a.m., on the odd days of the week we're on the indoor track at the recreation complex in preparation for her spring race.

Every weekday afternoon she plays word or card games at the Seniors Centre or in the condo's members lounge. Periodically, there's volunteer assignments.

Socializing is not my cup of tea. In the hallways and streets the neighbors are friendly, but often I can't remember much about them. So I fake it without apparent detection.

As long as I'm pleasant, it should be enough.

Visitors aren't invited to our place nowadays. My choosing. About five hours a day, almost every day, I plod along oscillating between frustration and delight with writing this autobiography. I'm not the sharpest pencil on the table, nevertheless I am on the table and don't plan on rolling off soon. While there's lead, I'll keep writing.

Got cataract surgery booked.

In preparation for this project, I read a few *How To* books and memoirs. Then, I spent an inordinate amount of time dithering over what to write about. Finally, after gathering and piling up in the study all the stored away source material—historical books, diaries, letters, calendars, photo albums, videos and interview notes—I was ready.

Well past a year into this massive undertaking, all I had was an outline and several charts, *trying* to imitate J. K. Rowling way of working.

The first chapter seemed acceptable until a friend read it, totally confused as to what was going on. "Keep it simple," she said even after the rewrite. The second person didn't care for my writing style. Not deterred, I accepted the criticism gratefully and pushed on.

Another maxim, "After I die, I'll have all of eternity to rest" goes by the wayside post lunch, when I (actively?) power nap. *Power* suggests strength as in *power lifter*, so I figure it must be good for me.

As an endurance athlete I should be able to build up slowly from 20 minutes to an hour soon enough.

However, time flies faster than flies, and I have very little to show when the front door opens.

"Anybody home?"

Thanks to Superwife, an elaborate supper—from salad to wine—awaits in less than an hour. After stuffing my face like there's no tomorrow, I look forward to *Dancing with the Stars* or *Amazing Race.*

"Are you watching this?" she used to ask. But now, she wakes me up when it's time to crawl to bed. The open window allows cold air in, reason to snuggle under warm blankets and to sleep, to dream about details of the book.

In the middle of the night, I grab the bedside flashlight and write while I remember.

EPILOGUE

If you tell the truth you don't have to remember anything.
                                        MARK TWAIN

2017

S unday means sleep in day and yet, being a morning person, I'm itching to get up almost as much as I want to talk. I close the window, open the blinds to let the sun stream in and turn up the heat. Taking a moment to enjoy her face, I hear baritone Ed Ames singing the waltz rhythm, "Mary in the Morning." I'm shivering. By the time I'm back in bed, she turns over to snuggle, her skin soft and warm. We whisper like we're revealing deep secrets. To seal the moment, I smother her face with loud, exuberant kisses.

In the bathroom mirror my face shows more lines than the map of New York City. I notice several new streets, more like 8-lane highways? I wander out to the hall.

"I don't know why I went in there," I say.

"Welcome to the club,"

"How's the membership?"

"Expanding every day." We both chuckle.

In search of something to wear I walk into the closet. Most of it is hers: beautiful dresses that still fit after all these decades. Lingering there, I recall preparing for formal night on the cruise ship: her slipping into the strapless, floral gown; showing me the beautiful, bare back; and saying "Zip me up." Stunning!

In the restaurant, heads turned.

The smell of heated blueberry muffins brings me back to here and now. She sings one of our favourites, "Around the world I've searched for you . . ." and whistles the rest of the forgotten lyrics. I melt like butter.

A poor example of a husband I have been too often, but always a faithful one; Her love and loyalty I have never doubted for a minute.

After breakfast, I'm passing by the study and I'm drawn to the two old studio photos on the mahogany bureau—a young girl displaying her dress and a boy wearing his Sunday best.

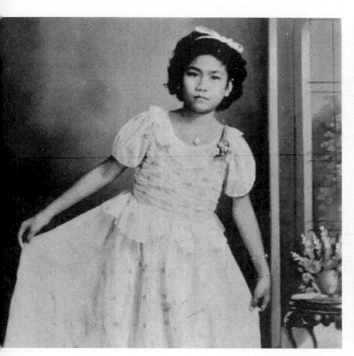

Who could have predicted that two kids from the opposite ends of the globe would meet one day as adults and forge, despite differences, a life together?

I suppose God has it figured out what my ultimate destination is, however, if given a choice, I rather it be right here on Earth. This is home. All I've known. All I want to know.

"Are you ready?" She's all dressed and I'm still in shorts and a T-shirt. Officially it's spring but we need to bundle up for the cold.

Ice patches make her uneasy, so we lock arms like young lovers. Passersby are amused. But we're focussed on the event of the year—Rich's wedding to May Sue.

Since everyone is coming, Erlinda is reviewing for me the main points about each person. The soon to be newlywed's met in Japan where Rich taught English. Sam got a job as entertainment co-co-ordinator on a cruise ship. Twice a year Dave, now manager at a GoodLife Fitness club, and Barbara join her for a cruise.

Although Dave's busy—sounds like the story of my life—he calls me time to time, ever positive. I follow suit. One thing I *do* know: the 'kids' can call Dave anytime and he'll be there as sure as the sun will rise the next day.

Beth and Ryan retired early and found bliss wintering in Mexico.

Lastly, my dear Irene, the link to my past. This I remember better than the rest. She lives comfortably in a "big" (she emphasizes), one-bedroom apartment of a geared-to-income building. The Disability Pension is adequate, enough to make ends meet and put her mind at ease. A small inheritance from a friend is growing steadily. It's for "a rainy day." Neighbours know her as the lady who walks with her dog, miles and miles. For a long while now, her weight has been good thanks to Douglas, the lively and loveable Lhasa Apso. She visits a friend upstairs in the building to the watch TV— *Survivor* is still on the air.

A gust of north wind brings Erlinda and me closer, but I'm confident halcyon days are just around the corner.

"Looks like Wiarton Willy was right about six more weeks of winter," she says.

"I'm not so sure. See that on the horizon?" I point, just as a robin swoops down beside us, chirping for crumbs.

"Not really. What is it?"

"That's winter waving good-bye."

"What about the wind and snow this afternoon?

"She's just blowing us a farewell kiss."

Floating in the air—George Harrison's "Here comes the Sun."

The wind sighs softly.

BIBLIOGRAPHY

Richard West—Rise and Fall of Yugoslavia

Christian L. Glossner—The Making of the Postwar German Economy

George W. Schuyler—Saint John: Two Hundred Years Proud

Wikipedia—Colonization of the Philippines by America - Post World War II economies

AFTERWORD

Anxiety and depression, to one degree or another, have plagued humans from time immemorial. A whispered subject 'til prominent people like Olympian Clara Hughes opened up. Based on statistics, this illness is on the rise with the advent of the digitally dependent lifestyle. No point in hiding and suffering. If that's you, recognize it and take steps to deal with it. Reach out for help. You'll find hope and life will change for the better!

ACKNOWLEDGEMENT

My profound gratitude for Judy Dickens' tireless and patient "beta editing"; Joan Brownlow's fact checking, Canadian spelling corrections, final editing and encouragement. Without them, this book would still be a rough manuscript.

◆◆◆

My appreciation goes to Nori Vogt for helping with Erlinda's nursing education years.

◆◆◆

Librarians are rarely given the credit they deserve, so I need to mention those in Aurora, Newmarket and Toronto

◆◆◆

It was a relatively long phone call that left a significant impression on me. I had contacted KDP (publishing branch of Amazon) customer support.

Sirija Devi, from India I suspected, spoke quickly and professionally.

Sitting in front of the laptop for hours had worn me out, frustrated.

"I don't understand. I'm older and you have a strong accent." *Could be misconstrued,* so I quickly added, "But I respect you. Would you help me out?"

Her speaking turned smooth and patient.

Unmistakable kindness.

When she resolved my issue, I asked, "What time is it there?"

"1 a.m."

With that said, my residual resentment towards the people of the subcontinent disappeared.

◆◆◆

Advance thanks to the reader: who risked time, effort and perhaps even money on my memoir.

George Biondic lives with his wife of forty years in Ontario.

He began this project in late 2017 thinking it would take about two years. So far four have passed with scarcely a day's rest. Nevertheless, there will be errors and all sit squarely on his shoulders.

If you enjoyed the book and feel so inclined, take a moment to do a quick review on Amazon or Goodreads.

Manufactured by Amazon.ca
Bolton, ON

25165093R00208